THE BLACK AGENDA

THE BLACK AGENDA

GLEN FORD

OR Books

New York · London

Published by OR Books, New York and London
Visit our website at www.orbooks.com

All rights information: rights@orbooks.com

First printing 2022

Cataloging-in-Publication data is available from the Library of Congress.
A catalog record for this book is available from the British Library.

Typeset by Lapiz Digital Services.

paperback ISBN 978-1-68219-290-0 • ebook ISBN 978-1-68219-293-1

CONTENTS

GLEN FORD'S IRREPLACEABLE JOURNALISM

MARGARET KIMBERLEY

In the best sense of the word a journalist is someone who brings to the public sphere accurate, well sourced information, and rigorous analysis. Those individuals speak for the marginalized, who can't speak for themselves, and they expose the privileged, who are always given opportunities for expression. They point out the faults of those deemed too authoritative to be questioned. If an outlet claims to write all the news that is fit to print or declares that democracy dies in darkness, their work should be given more scrutiny than credibility. The journalist should be truly independent and skeptical of official narratives. Glen Ford was such a person. His decades of work provide a blueprint for anyone who wants that word to have real meaning and integrity.

I began working with Glen Ford in 2003 when he was co-publisher of *Black Commentator*. At his urging I began writing there weekly, and we later co-founded *Black Agenda Report* with the late Bruce Dixon in 2006. In all of those years Glen was a mentor and a teacher. I saw him open up new worlds of information for thousands of people searching for what is often called alternative news. They are just searching for information that ought to be easily discovered, but is instead disappeared by media outlets and personalities who collude with corporate interests and with the state.

Ford came to his career through an interesting set of life circumstances. He told me that his parents attended the concert where Paul Robeson, Pete Seeger, and other performers were attacked by a right-wing mob in Peekskill, New York in September 1949. Glen was born two months later, prepared to carry on the work of the left from birth.

He was also a Black man who spent part of his childhood and youth in Georgia during the days of segregation, America's apartheid. His father was a local radio station host, and Glen was on the air while still in childhood. His upbringing as a Black leftist growing up in the south in broadcast news gave him a unique perspective and made his work as a journalist irreplaceable.

I think of the retro term "race man" when I think of Glen Ford. It is a term from years gone by, a relic of the days of segregation. A race man was one who was dedicated to meeting the needs of Black people, who constantly thought of their benefit, and struggled alongside the masses to overcome the oppression they were subjected to.

Glen Ford was the consummate race man. In the 18 years that I was privileged to know him, I found that his abiding concern was for the welfare of Black people. He didn't succumb to the nostrums which declared that Black people were to blame for their own problems or that boot straps and respectability politics were the path to liberation. He was uncompromising in his analysis of the United States and its history of anti-Black racism that was practiced domestically and internationally. The *Black Agenda Report* team and its readers were very fortunate to have an Executive Editor who so clearly defined what we call "the Black left perspective."

While the corporate media reported the story of Detroit's bankruptcy with non-subtle narratives that the majority-Black city was badly governed, Glen was among the few who reported that banks pushed the city to financial ruin. He blamed the Black politicians who went along with derivative schemes which drove Detroit over the edge to complete insolvency. Michiganders had approved a referendum opposing the use of emergency financial managers who took control of cities and subjected them to brutal austerity measures such as cutting workers' pensions. But a Republican governor ignored the will of the voters, and in the pages of *Black Agenda Report,* Glen Ford exposed the heist carried out by banks who pushed the city into bankruptcy and then were first in line to be paid.

GLEN FORD'S IRREPLACEABLE JOURNALISM

Glen Ford was the first person to call attention to Cory Booker's astonishing rise to prominence. In Booker's first campaign for mayor of Newark, New Jersey it was Ford who revealed his ties to right-wing organizations such as the Manhattan Institute and the Bradley Foundation. His reporting was so good that Booker's opponent distributed the *Black Commentator* articles which exposed the effort to groom a Black politician willing to carry out austerity, school privatization, and other right-wing initiatives that would ordinarily be anathema to Black voters.

Booker was not the only member of what *Black Agenda Report* referred to as the "Black misleadership class." The politicians and others thought of as leaders are not independent actors, instead they are given money, positions, and some degree of access to the world of the elites in order to influence Black people and get buy-in for the neo-liberal consensus. Glen Ford had a keen eye for their activities, and as a result *Black Agenda Report* did not succumb to the imperative to elevate and protect the Black face in a high place.

Nowhere was that more obvious than in his coverage of Barack Obama's campaign and his presidential administration. While other Black leftists changed their political religion in the wake of Obama's 2008 success, Glen Ford consistently maintained an independent political stance. He called Obama and Hillary Clinton "political twins" who would offer up the same policies which had so badly failed Black people. Ford saw what was coming when he described Obama's ascendancy as the favorite of the 1 percent and marketing which made him appear to be progressive, as "Goldman Sachs and the anti-war movement being on the same page."

Ford regularly exposed the corrupting influence that Obama's presidency had on Black Americans and their long history of radical politics. Once the most left-leaning cohort in the country, the determination to protect Obama pushed a group that always showed the least support for wars and foreign interventions into cheerleaders for whatever their idol cooked up domestically or internationally.

Ford pointed out that in 2002, only four members of the Congressional Black Caucus (CBC) voted in favor of giving George W. Bush authorization to invade Iraq, while in 2011, more than half of that group, twenty-four CBC members, voted to support the U.S. and NATO bombing of Libya. The final success in destroying that nation was a war crime, but the people who once would have called it such were largely silent.

Ford often said that Obama and the Democrats were not the lesser evil, they were just the more effective evil; effective at carrying out the will of the wealthy and the corporations and the military industrial complex while giving the appearance of opposing the people they in fact catered to.

Foreign policy was of great interest to Glen Ford and to readers of *Black Commentator* and *Black Agenda Report*. They were given detailed accounts of the U.S.'s hand in the coup and kidnapping of Haiti's president Jean-Bertrand Aristide. While most of the media ignored Africa or only reported on coups and warfare, *Black Agenda Report* explained the role of U.S. allies Uganda and Rwanda as they pillaged and murdered in the Democratic Republic of Congo. The existence of the United States Africa Command, AFRICOM, is largely unknown, but not to anyone who follows *Black Agenda Report*. Our readers are well aware of the drone bases and other facilities that are now spread throughout the African continent. The standard foreign policy narratives have no place at *Black Agenda Report*. In fact, our readers become experts themselves, and know that most of what they might read and hear elsewhere from supposedly reliable sources is often untrue.

Glen Ford is irreplaceable not just because his writing was so sharp and so clear, but also because his politics were so clearly of the left. He was not a liberal, or a Democrat, or a progressive. He was a Marxist, and he brought that ideology to all that he did. In so doing he revealed important information that is regularly disregarded or disappeared. He also had a talent for making every issue understandable and making connections with the reality of people's lives. When he spoke of the political duopoly, the Republicans and Democrats who provide political theater as they do the work of the ruling classes, no one was confused about what they were witnessing as large numbers lost their homes in the financial crash of 2008 or were forced to take low wage work or even "gig" work, the culmination of capitalist intent for everyone else in the world.

Members of Glen Ford's generation are now among the elders, and others are also passing away. Every year there are fewer and fewer people who share his life experience as a Vietnam War-era veteran and a member of the Black Panther Party. But the passing away of a generation is not new and we can never rely solely upon the living in order to analyze the past.

We rely on documented history passed on by the relentless truth tellers. That is what Glen Ford did. He told the truth about the history of the Thanksgiving holiday, segregation, imperialism, and billionaire rule. We rely on real journalists to help us understand the world. No one did that better than Glen Ford.

August 2021

INTRODUCTION

By way of an introduction to this anthology of my writings on politics and race, it seems appropriate to set out a brief account of my life. I'll keep it short; just sufficient to give a bit of context to the pieces that follow. I hope, at some point in the future, to write a full autobiography.

I was born Glen Rutherford in Jersey City, New Jersey, in 1949. I was a "red diaper baby." My mother Shirley was a consummate political organizer and, in 1958, my father Rudy became the first Black man to host a non-gospel television program in the Deep South. By the age of eleven I was reading newswire copy on my father's radio show in Columbus, Georgia. My professional career began in 1970 at James Brown's radio station in Augusta, Georgia, WRDW-AM, where the "Godfather of Soul" shortened my surname to "Ford." Determined to put radio at the service of the people, WRDW helped empower grassroots activists to challenge the local white power structure, culminating in a Black rebellion that left six dead but pulled the city out of the political backwaters.

After a stint as a reporter at the Communist Party USA's *Daily World* newspaper in New York City, and a close collaboration with the Jersey City chapter of the Black Panther Party—which was then in full retreat from a nationwide police and FBI "final offensive"—I returned to the airwaves in Columbus as a newsman at WOKS-AM radio. There, I tried to replicate the organizing strategy we had deployed in Augusta the previous year, filling the station's hourly newscasts with sound clips from local grassroots activists. Key among them was the newly-organized local chapter of the Chicago-based African American Patrolmen's League, comprised largely of Vietnam veterans whose top priority was fighting police brutality. The Black cops became the point-persons of the local movement when they publicly removed the American flag patches from their uniforms to protest the department's racist intransigence.

Regional and national human rights and labor leaders journeyed to Columbus in solidarity. By summer, the city was under curfew and burning, with multiple arsons nightly for more than two months—fires rumored to have been set by on-duty Black police officers with accelerants provided by Black soldiers at Fort Benning, the neighboring Army base. Columbus was wrenched into a new era by the nation's longest sustained urban rebellion on record.

My next stop was WEBB-AM, Baltimore, another of James Brown's radio stations where, in addition to local reporting, I created my first radio syndication. *Black World Report*, aired on Sunday afternoons, was a half-hour weekly program of national and global news from a Black liberationist perspective. It was a poor man's syndication—the roster of stations broadcasting the program was limited by the availability of used recording tape from WEBB's studios—but the project provided me with experience in national, long-form program production.

In June of 1972 I got my first union job with a living wage at WOL-AM, Washington, D.C.'s top-rated, Black-oriented station. I brought along *Black World Report* and immersed myself in the city's local and national Black political networks. I worked most closely with the African Liberation Support Committee, in solidarity with guerilla movements fighting colonialism and white minority rule on the continent, and with tenants' organizations that, even in the early '70s, were struggling against creeping gentrification of Black neighborhoods. I organized my own speaking circuit under the theme "Merging the Masses, the Media and the Movement," sustained mainly by relatively small honorariums from Black student unions.

It was the Golden Age of Black radio news, a profession that was called into existence by, first, the explosion in the number of Black-oriented radio stations in the '60s and, second, Black people's demand that these stations provide information relevant to their lives and struggles. Black radio news was birthed by the "movement."

Two Black radio news networks were founded in the early '70s. After almost three years at WOL-AM, I was hired by the Mutual Black Network (with eighty-eight affiliated stations), headquartered in downtown D.C., where I soon became Washington Bureau chief, effectively shaping the network's hourly broadcast content. I brought much the same approach to national reporting as I had employed in local news, methodically reworking the list of Black "leaders" that the network's news gatherers would call for reaction to world and national events. Movement activists and other leftists were put on the A-list.

At this time, I reluctantly discontinued production of *Black World Report*, the little syndication I had created in Baltimore three years earlier. I became a founding member of the Washington Association of Black Journalists in my first year at the Mutual Black Network. The WABJ was soon dominated by Blacks from the general corporate media who felt no obligation to the Black political movement that had gotten them jobs. Rather, these corporate climbers saw themselves as performing a "role model" service to Black America simply by holding down prestigious positions. I quit the WABJ shortly before it became part of the newly-formed National Association of Black Journalists (NABJ), which quickly devolved into a kind of guild that counts Black faces in corporate newsrooms but fights for nothing worthwhile to the masses.

On top of my bureau chief duties, during my four years at the network (1973–77) I also served, variously, as Capitol Hill, State Department, and White House correspondent and delivered a daily political commentary, plus three or four hourly newscasts per shift. But a gaping "hole" in the national Black broadcast journalism array cried out to be filled; there was no African American counterpart to the Sunday morning news interview programs *Face the Nation* (CBS), *Issues and Answers* (ABC), and *Meet the Press* (NBC). The three network television institutions generated the newsmaker quotes that made the headlines on Monday morning and shaped much of the national political conversation for the rest of the week. Black America needed its own newsmaking mechanism.

I spent the next three years developing *America's Black Forum* (ABF), which finally debuted with about thirty affiliated stations on January 16, 1977, the same week as *Roots*. *ABF* was the first nationally syndicated Black news interview program on commercial television, produced at ABC affiliate WJLA-TV. The program made Black broadcast history. Over the next four years, *ABF* generated national and international headlines nearly every week. Never before—and never since—had a Black news entity commanded the weekly attention of the news services (AP, UPI, Reuters, Agence France-Presse, and even Tass—the Soviet news agency) and the broadcast networks. *ABF* consistently beat ABC's *Issues and Answers* in the ratings at the network's own Washington affiliate.

Although a considerable journalistic success, *America's Black Forum* began its broadcast life without a sponsor. As the bills piled up, my co-producer Peter Gamble and I searched desperately for an advertiser to fill the commercial slots, or an investor to ward off creditors. To keep *ABF* on the air, we felt compelled to sell a majority interest in the program to a Black investors group in return for assumption and payment of the debt. The program earned its first advertising dollars four months after its debut and was soon operating in the black, allowing *ABF* to pay off its creditors—no thanks to the crooked investors, who never paid a cent of the debt. Peter and I continued to produce *ABF* for the next four years, fighting with the crooks all the while, but knowing that a legal showdown would destroy the syndication. In 1981, rather than risk killing the program that had served Black journalism so well, we sold our remaining shares to the crooks for cash and left the syndication. *ABF* continued on the air for another twenty-five years, but very seldom made news again.

In 1979, while still host, producer, and co-owner of *ABF*, I set up *Black Agenda Reports*—the first project I would give that name—which provided five short-form programs each day on Black women, history, business, sports, and entertainment to sixty-six radio stations. The syndication produced more short-form programming than the two existing Black radio networks combined, but folded when the Reagan administration drastically slashed the budget of *BAR*'s sponsor, Amtrak. I revived the name *Black Agenda Report* when Margaret Kimberley, Bruce Dixon, and I launched our Black weekly internet political periodical in 2006.

Black radio news was in deep decline by the early '80s, a casualty of corporate consolidation and asset inflation in which radio station prices skyrocketed under competing bids from big chains. Small, "stand-alone" owners of one or two stations, many of whom took pride in providing local and national news to their communities, were replaced by chain managers who reported to corporate headquarters thousands of miles away. The Federal Communications Commission (FCC), a creature of presidential appointments, now defined the "public interest" so narrowly that local and national news became optional—and ever more stations were opting out. Increasingly, there was no one at local stations authorized to put syndicated programming on the air; all such decisions were made at corporate headquarters. Black radio news was decimated as hourly local and/or national newscasts became relics of the past. The same thing was happening in white-oriented radio.

True to their class, the Black political establishment was concerned only that minority entrepreneurs be allowed to participate in the corporatization of media. What I would later call the "Black misleadership class" did nothing to safeguard the informational needs of their constituents. And the grassroots movement that had brought Black radio news into existence to serve a previous generation was now dormant.

Amidst this spreading corporate wasteland, I produced the McDonald's-sponsored radio series *Black History Through Music*, aired on fifty stations nationwide. (The sponsor bought the airtime). For two years I was national political columnist for *Encore American & Worldwide News* magazine, founded by the crusading and fearless Black publisher Ida E. Lewis, who was still hanging on in the Age of Reagan. I earned a modest living voicing commercials for radio and television. During this period I also got a kick out of verbally thrashing corporate executives who paid a hefty fee to a Madison Avenue outfit that specialized in preparing executives for encounters with the press. I justified taking on these assignments in the belief that the clients were wasting their money, since corporate journalists would never be as hard on the top brass of big companies as I was. (But if I did do some political harm, I apologize.)

The advent of the first generation of low-cost computers allowed me to publish several issues of the print political journal *The Black Commentator*—a title I would use again twenty years later—and *Africana Policies* magazine. However, I found that distribution of hard-copy publications was prohibitively expensive, and both projects were short-lived.

As an executive board member of the National Alliance of Third World Journalists (NATWJ), I traveled to Cuba, Nicaragua when the Sandinista government was under siege by U.S.-backed terrorists, and Grenada two months before the U.S. military attacked and occupied the island nation. I authored *The Big Lie: An Analysis of U.S. Press Coverage of the Grenada Invasion* (IOJ, 1985).

In 1987 I partnered with Patrice Johnson and Anthony Devon to launch *Rap It Up*, the first nationally syndicated hip-hop music show, broadcast on sixty-five radio stations. During its six years of operations, *Rap It Up* allowed me to play a key role in the maturation of a new African American musical genre that, in its early years, "sampled" snippets of Malcolm X speeches and for a time revived the Black Power political ethos of the '60s.

By the early '90s, however, the corporate recording industry giants were in the process of swallowing up the last of the small, independent labels that had midwifed the genre. "Gangsta rap" was born, not from a racist conspiracy to poison the minds of Black youth, as some believe, but as the result of a corporate label study that found hip-hop's core audience to be the youngest of any genre in commercial music history: eleven-to-thirteen-year-olds. As every observer of childhood development knows, "tweens" of both sexes, but especially males, find almost sensuous pleasure in profanity. Misogynist tirades are tween-aged boys' reflexive way of coping with their own insecurities about how to deal with girls. The recording industry interpreted the study's results to mean that the tween market would be most profitably served by flooding it with profane, misogynist song lyrics.

INTRODUCTION

Gangsta rap was the undoing of *Rap It Up*. Although our team was hyper-vigilant in splicing out bad language, affiliate stations feared their broadcast licenses would be in peril if they continued to air the show. Rev. Jesse Jackson denounced gangsta rap and demanded station programmers purge it from their playlists. *Rap It Up* ceased production in 1993.

The Telecommunications Act of 1996 set off a new round of corporate consolidation, but a new medium was emerging that could be useful to purveyors of "information for liberation." By the year 2000 over half of American households owned a computer and Black internet users were carving out their own cyber spaces. I was working at a Black weekly newspaper that I helped found in northern New Jersey when longtime colleague Peter Gamble phoned to suggest that I consider finding an internet audience for my political commentary. We had not collaborated for almost twenty years, but by conversation's end plans were begun for a full-blown magazine to be called *The Black Commentator*—predecessor of the extant *Black Agenda Report*. Articles from both publications appear in this anthology.

PART I

THANKSGIVING

NO MORE AMERICAN THANKSGIVINGS

Thanksgiving is reserved by history and the intent of "the founders" as the supremely white American holiday, the most ghoulish event on the national calendar. No Halloween of the imagination can rival the exterminationist reality that was the genesis, and remains the legacy, of the American Thanksgiving. It is the most loathsome, humanity-insulting day of the year—a pure glorification of racist barbarity.

We at *The Black Commentator* are thankful that the day grows nearer when the almost four centuries-old abomination will be deprived of its reason for being: white supremacy. Then we may all eat and drink in peace and gratitude for the blessings of humanity's deliverance from the rule of evil men.

Thanksgiving is much more than a lie—if it were that simple, an historical correction of the record of events in 1600s Massachusetts would suffice to purge the "flaw" in the national mythology. But Thanksgiving is not just a twisted fable, and the mythology it nurtures is itself inherently evil. The real-life events—subsequently revised—were perfectly understood at the time as the first, definitive triumphs of the genocidal European project in New England. The near-erasure of Native Americans in Massachusetts and, soon thereafter, from most of the remainder of the northern colonial seaboard, was the true mission of the Pilgrim enterprise—Act One of the American Dream. African Slavery commenced contemporaneously—an overlapping and ultimately inseparable Act Two.

The last act in the American drama must be the "root and branch" eradication of all vestiges of Acts One and Two—America's seminal crimes and formative projects. Thanksgiving as presently celebrated—that is, as a *national political* event—is an affront to civilization.

Celebrating the Unspeakable

White America embraced Thanksgiving because a majority of that population glories in the fruits, if not the unpleasant details, of genocide and slavery and feels, on the whole, good about their heritage: a cornucopia of privilege and national power. Children are taught to identify with the good fortune of the Pilgrims. It does not much matter that the Native American and African holocausts that flowed from the feast at Plymouth are hidden from the children's version of the story—kids learn soon enough that Indians were made scarce and Africans became enslaved. But they will also never forget the core message of the holiday: that the Pilgrims were good people, who could not have purposely set such evil in motion. Just as the first Thanksgivings marked the consolidation of the English toehold in what became the United States, the core ideological content of the holiday serves to validate all that has since occurred on these shores—a national consecration of the unspeakable, a balm and benediction for the victors, a blessing of the fruits of murder and kidnapping, and an implicit obligation to continue the seamless historical project in the present day.

The Thanksgiving story is an absolution of the Pilgrims, whose brutal quest for absolute power in the New World is made to seem both religiously motivated and eminently human. Most importantly, the Pilgrims are depicted as *victims*—of harsh weather and their own naïve yet wholesome visions of a new beginning. In light of this carefully nurtured fable, whatever happened to the Indians—from Plymouth to California and beyond, in the aftermath of the 1621 dinner—must be considered a mistake, the result of misunderstandings, at worst, a series of lamentable tragedies. The story provides the essential first frame of the American saga. It is unalloyed racist propaganda, a tale that endures because it served the purposes of a succession of the Pilgrims' political heirs, in much the same way that the Nazi-enhanced mythology of a glorious Aryan/German past advanced another murderous, expansionist mission.

4

Thanksgiving is quite dangerous—as were the Pilgrims.

Rejoicing In a Cemetery

The English settlers, their ostensibly religious venture backed by a trading company, were glad to discover that they had landed in a virtual cemetery in 1620. Corn still sprouted in the abandoned fields of the Wampanoags, but only a remnant of the local population remained around the fabled Rock. In a letter to England, Massachusetts Bay colony founder John Winthrop wrote, "But for the natives in these parts, God hath so pursued them, as for 300 miles space the greatest part of them are swept away by smallpox which still continues among them. So as God hath thereby cleared our title to this place, those who remain in these parts, being in all not 50, have put themselves under our protection."

Ever diligent to claim their own advantages as God's will, the Pilgrims thanked their deity for having "pursued" the Indians to mass death. However, it was not divine intervention that wiped out most of the natives around the village of Patuxet but, most likely, smallpox-embedded blankets planted during an English visit or slave raid. Six years before the Pilgrim landing, a ship sailed into Patuxet's harbor, captained by none other than the famous seaman and mercenary soldier John Smith, former leader of the first successful English colony in the New World at Jamestown, Virginia. Epidemic and slavery followed in his wake, as Debra Glidden described at IMDiversity.com:

> In 1614 the Plymouth Company of England, a joint stock company, hired Captain John Smith to explore land in its behalf. Along what is now the coast of Massachusetts in the territory of the Wampanoag, Smith visited the town of Patuxet according to *The Colonial Horizon*, a 1969 book edited by William Goetzinan. Smith renamed the town Plymouth in honor of his employers, but the Wampanoag who inhabited the town continued to call it Patuxet.
>
> The following year Captain Hunt, an English slave trader, arrived at Patuxet. It was common practice for explorers to capture Indians, take them to Europe and sell them into slavery for

220 shillings apiece. That practice was described in a 1622 account of happenings entitled *A Declaration of the State of the Colony and Affairs in Virginia*, written by Edward Waterhouse. True to the explorer tradition, Hunt kidnapped a number of Wampanoags to sell into slavery.

Another common practice among European explorers was to give "smallpox blankets" to the Indians. Since smallpox was unknown on this continent prior to the arrival of the Europeans, Native Americans did not have any natural immunity to the disease so smallpox would effectively wipe out entire villages with very little effort required by the Europeans. William Fenton describes how Europeans decimated Native American villages in his 1957 work *American Indian and White relations to 1830*. From 1615 to 1619, smallpox ran rampant among the Wampanoags and their neighbors to the north. The Wampanoag lost 70 percent of their population to the epidemic and the Massachusetts lost 90 percent.

Most of the Wampanoag had died from the smallpox epidemic, so when the Pilgrims arrived they found well-cleared fields, which they claimed for their own. A Puritan colonist, quoted by Harvard University's Perry Miller, praised the plague that had wiped out the Indians for it was "the wonderful preparation of the Lord Jesus Christ, by his providence for his people's abode in the Western world.

Historians have since speculated endlessly on why the woods in the region resembled a park to the disembarking Pilgrims in 1620. The reason should have been obvious: hundreds, if not thousands, of people had lived there just five years before.

In less than three generations the settlers would turn all of New England into a charnel house for Native Americans, and fire the economic engines of slavery throughout English-speaking America. Plymouth Rock is the place where the nightmare truly began.

The Uninvited?

It is not at all clear what happened at the first—and only—"integrated" Thanksgiving feast. Only two written accounts of the three-day event exist, and one of them, by Governor William Bradford, was written twenty years after the fact. Was Chief Massasoit invited to bring ninety Indians with him to dine with fifty-two colonists, most of them women and children? This seems unlikely. A good harvest had provided the settlers with plenty of food, according to their accounts, so the whites didn't really need the Wampanoag's offering of five deer. What we do know is that there had been lots of tension between the two groups that fall. John Two-Hawks, who runs the Native Circle website, gives a sketch of the facts:

> "Thanksgiving" did not begin as a great loving relationship between the pilgrims and the Wampanoag, Pequot and Narragansett people. In fact, in October of 1621 when the pilgrim survivors of their first winter in Turtle Island sat down to share the first unofficial "Thanksgiving" meal, the Indians who were there were not even invited! There was no turkey, squash, cranberry sauce or pumpkin pie. A few days before this alleged feast took place, a company of "pilgrims" led by Miles Standish actively sought the head of a local Indian chief, and an 11 foot high wall was erected around the entire Plymouth settlement for the very purpose of keeping Indians out!

It is much more likely that Chief Massasoit either crashed the party, or brought enough men to ensure that he was not kidnapped or harmed by the Pilgrims. Dr. Tingba Apidta, in his *Black Folks' Guide to Understanding Thanksgiving*, surmises that the settlers "brandished their weaponry" early and got drunk soon thereafter. He notes that "each Pilgrim drank at least a half gallon of beer a day, which they preferred even to water. This daily inebriation led their governor, William Bradford, to comment on his people's 'notorious sin,' which included their 'drunkenness and uncleanliness' and rampant 'sodomy.'"

7

Soon after the feast the brutish Miles Standish "got his bloody prize," Dr. Apidta writes:

> He went to the Indians, pretended to be a trader, then beheaded an Indian man named Wituwamat. He brought the head to Plymouth, where it was displayed on a wooden spike for many years, according to Gary B. Nash, "as a symbol of white power." Standish had the Indian man's young brother hanged from the rafters for good measure. From that time on, the whites were known to the Indians of Massachusetts by the name "Wotowquenange," which in their tongue meant cutthroats and stabbers.

What is certain is that the first feast was not called a "Thanksgiving" at the time. No further integrated dining occasions were scheduled, and the first, official all-Pilgrim "Thanksgiving" had to wait until 1637, when the whites of New England celebrated the massacre of the Wampanoag's southern neighbors, the Pequots.

The Real Thanksgiving Day Massacre

The Pequots today own the Foxwood Casino and Hotel in Ledyard, Connecticut, with gross gaming revenues of over $9 billion in 2000. This is truly a (very belated) miracle, since the real first Pilgrim Thanksgiving was intended as the Pequot's epitaph. Sixteen years after the problematical Plymouth feast, the English tried mightily to erase the Pequots from the face of the Earth, and thanked God for the blessing.

Having subdued, intimidated, or made mercenaries of most of the tribes of Massachusetts, the English turned their growing force southward, toward the rich Connecticut valley, the Pequot's sphere of influence. At the point where the Mystic River meets the sea, the combined force of English and allied Indians bypassed the Pequot fort to attack and set ablaze a town full of women, children, and old people.

William Bradford, the former Governor of Plymouth and one of the chroniclers of the 1621 feast, was also on hand for the great massacre of 1637:

Those that escaped the fire were slain with the sword; some hewed to pieces, others run through with their rapiers, so that they were quickly dispatched and very few escaped. It was conceived they thus destroyed about 400 at this time. It was a fearful sight to see them thus frying in the fire . . . horrible was the stink and scent thereof, but the victory seemed a sweet sacrifice, and they gave the prayers thereof to God, who had wrought so wonderfully for them, thus to enclose their enemies in their hands, and give them so speedy a victory over so proud and insulting an enemy.

The rest of the white folks thought so, too. "This day forth shall be a day of celebration and thanksgiving for subduing the Pequots," read Governor John Winthrop's proclamation. The authentic Thanksgiving Day was born.

Most historians believe about seven hundred Pequots were slaughtered at Mystic. Many prisoners were executed, and surviving women and children sold into slavery in the West Indies. Pequot prisoners that escaped execution were parceled out to Indian tribes allied with the English. The Pequot were thought to have been extinguished as a people. According to IndyMedia, "The Pequot tribe numbered 8,000 when the Pilgrims arrived, but disease had brought their numbers down to 1,500 by 1637. The Pequot 'War' killed all but a handful of remaining members of the tribe."

But there were still too many Indians around to suit the whites of New England, who bided their time while their own numbers increased to critical, murderous mass.

Guest's Head on a Pole

By the 1670s the colonists, with eight thousand men under arms, felt strong enough to demand that the Pilgrims' former dinner guests, the Wampanoags, disarm and submit to the authority of the Crown. After a series of settler provocations in 1675, the Wampanoag struck back under the leadership of Chief Metacomet, son of Massasoit and called King Philip by the English. Metacomet/Philip, whose wife and son were captured and sold into West Indian slavery, wiped out thirteen settlements and killed six hundred adult white men before the tide of battle turned. A 1996 issue of the *Revolutionary Worker* provides an excellent narrative.

In their victory, the settlers launched an all-out genocide against the remaining Native people. The Massachusetts government offered a twenty shillings bounty for every Indian scalp, and forty shillings for every prisoner who could be sold into slavery. Soldiers could enslave any Indian woman or child under fourteen they could capture. The "Praying Indians" who had converted to Christianity and fought on the side of the European troops were accused of shooting into the treetops during battles with "hostiles." They were enslaved or killed. Other "peaceful" Indians of Dartmouth and Dover were invited to negotiate or seek refuge at trading posts—and were sold onto slave ships.

It is not known how many Indians were sold into slavery, but in this campaign, five hundred enslaved Indians were shipped from Plymouth alone. Of the 12,000 Indians in the surrounding tribes, probably about half died from battle, massacre and starvation.

After King Philip's War, there were almost no Indians left free in the northern British colonies. A colonist wrote from Manhattan's New York colony: "There is now but few Indians upon the island and those few no ways hurtful. It is to be admired how strangely they have decreased by the hand of God, since the English first settled in these parts." In Massachusetts, the colonists declared a "day of public thanksgiving" in 1676, saying, "there now scarce remains a name or family of them [the Indians] but are either slain, captivated or fled."

Fifty-five years after the original Thanksgiving Day, the Puritans had destroyed the generous Wampanoag and all other neighboring tribes. The Wampanoag chief King Philip was beheaded. His head was stuck on a pole in Plymouth, where the skull still hung on display twenty-four years later.

This is not thought to be a fit Thanksgiving tale for the children of today, but it's the real story, well-known to the settler children of New England at the time. The white kids who saw the Wampanoag head on the pole year after year knew for certain that God loved them best of all, and that every atrocity they might ever commit against a heathen non-white was blessed.

There's a good term for the process thus set in motion: nation-building.

Roots of the Slave Trade

The British North American colonists' practice of enslaving Indians for labor or direct sale to the West Indies preceded the appearance of the first chained Africans at the dock in Jamestown, Virginia in 1619. The Jamestown colonists' human transaction with the Dutch vessel was an unscheduled occurrence. However, once the African slave trade became commercially established, the fates of Indians and Africans in the colonies became inextricably entwined. New England, born of up-close-and-personal, burn-them-in-the-fires-of-hell genocide, led the political and commercial development of the English colonies. The region also led the nascent nation's descent into a slavery-based society and economy.

Ironically, an apologist for Virginian slavery made one of the best, early cases for the indictment of New England as the engine of the American slave trade. Unreconstructed secessionist Lewis Dabney's 1867 book *A Defense of Virginia* traced the slave trade's origins all the way back to Plymouth Rock:

> The planting of the commercial States of North America began with the colony of Puritan Independents at Plymouth, in 1620, which was subsequently enlarged into the State of Massachusetts. The other trading colonies, Rhode Island and Connecticut, as well as New Hampshire (which never had an extensive shipping interest), were offshoots of Massachusetts. They partook of the same characteristics and pursuits; and hence, the example of the parent colony is taken here as a fair representation of them.
>
> The first ship from America, which embarked in the African slave trade, was the *Desire*, Captain Pierce, of Salem; and this was among the first vessels ever built in the colony. The promptitude with which the "Puritan Fathers" embarked in this business may be comprehended, when it is stated that the *Desire* sailed upon her

voyage in June 1637. *[Note: the year they massacred the Pequots.]* The first feeble and dubious foothold was gained by the white man at Plymouth less than seventeen years before; and as is well known, many years were expended by the struggle of the handful of settlers for existence. So that it may be correctly said, that the commerce of New England was born of the slave trade; as its subsequent prosperity was largely founded upon it. The *Desire*, proceeding to the Bahamas, with a cargo of "dry fish and strong liquors, the only commodities for those parts," obtained the negroes from two British men-of-war, which had captured them from a Spanish slaver.

Thus, the trade of which the good ship *Desire*, of Salem, was the harbinger, grew into grand proportions; and for nearly two centuries poured a flood of wealth into New England, as well as no inconsiderable number of slaves. Meanwhile, the other maritime colonies of Rhode Island and Providence Plantations, and Connecticut, followed the example of their elder sister emulously; and their commercial history is but a repetition of that of Massachusetts. The towns of Providence, Newport, and New Haven became famous slave trading ports. The magnificent harbor of the second, especially, was the favorite starting-place of the slave ships; and its commerce rivaled, or even exceeded, that of the present commercial metropolis, New York. All the four original States, of course, became slaveholding.

The Revolution that exploded in 1770s New England was undertaken by men thoroughly imbued with the worldview of the Indian-killer and slaveholder. How could they not be? The "country" they claimed as their own was fathered by genocide and mothered by slavery—its true distinction among the commercial nations of the world. And these men were not ashamed, but proud, with vast ambition to spread their exceptional characteristics West and South and wherever their so-far successful project in nation-building might take them—and by the same bloody, savage methods that had served them so well in the past.

At the moment of deepest national crisis following the battle of Gettysburg in 1863, President Abraham Lincoln invoked the national fable that is far more central to the white American personality than Lincoln's battlefield "address." Lincoln seized upon the 1621 feast as the historic "Thanksgiving"—bypassing the official and authentic 1637 precedent— and assigned the dateless, murky event the fourth Thursday in November.

Lincoln surveyed a broken nation, and attempted nation rebuilding, based on the purest white myth. The same year that he issued the Emancipation Proclamation, he renewed the national commitment to a white manifest destiny that began at Plymouth Rock. Lincoln sought to rekindle a shared national mission that former Confederates and Unionists and white immigrants from Europe could collectively embrace. It was and remains a barbaric and racist national unifier, by definition. Only the most fantastic lies can sanitize the history of the Plymouth Colony of Massachusetts.

"Like a Rock"

The Thanksgiving holiday fable is at once a window on the way that many, if not most, white Americans view the world and their place in it, and a pollutant that leaches barbarism into the modern era. The fable attempts to glorify the indefensible, to enshrine an era and mission that represent the nation's *lowest moral denominators*. Thanksgiving as framed in the mythology is, consequently, a drag on that which is potentially civilizing in the national character, a crippling, atavistic deformity. Defenders of the holiday will claim that the politically corrected children's version pro-motes brotherhood, but that is an impossibility—a bald excuse to prolong the worship of colonial "forefathers" and to erase the crimes they commit-ted. Those bastards burned the Pequot women and children, and ushered in the multinational business of slavery. These are facts. The myth is an insidious diversion—and worse.

Humanity cannot tolerate a twenty-first century superpower, much of whose population perceives the world through the eyes of seventeenth century land and flesh bandits. Yet that is the trick that fate has played on the globe. The English arrived with criminal intent—and brought wives and children to form new societies predicated on successful plunder. To justify the murderous enterprise, Indians who had initially cooperated with the squatters were transmogrified into "savages" deserving displacement and death. The relentlessly refreshed lie of Indian savagery became a truth in the minds of white Americans, a *fact to be acted upon* by every succeeding generation of whites. The settlers became a singular people confronting the great "frontier"—a euphemism for centuries of genocidal campaigns against a darker, "savage" people marked for extinction.

The necessity of genocide was the operative, working assumption of the expanding American nation. "Manifest Destiny" was born at Plymouth Rock and Jamestown, later to fall (to paraphrase Malcolm) like a rock on Mexico, the Philippines, Haiti, Nicaragua, etc. Little children were taught that the American project was inherently good, Godly, and that those who got in the way were "evil-doers" or just plain subhuman, to be gloriously eliminated. The lie is central to white American identity, embraced by waves of European settlers who never saw a red person.

Only a century ago, American soldiers caused the deaths of possibly a million Filipinos whom they had been sent to "liberate" from Spanish rule. They didn't even know who they were killing, and so rationalized their behavior by substituting the usual American victims.

Colonel Funston of the Twentieth Kansas Volunteers explained what got him motivated in the Philippines: "Our fighting blood was up and we all wanted to kill 'niggers.' This shooting human beings is a 'hot game,' and beats rabbit hunting all to pieces." Another wrote that "the boys go for the enemy as if they were chasing jack-rabbits. . . . I, for one, hope that Uncle Sam will apply the chastening rod, good, hard, and plenty, and lay it on until they come into the reservation and promise to be good 'Injuns.'"

Last week in northern Iraq another American colonel, Joe Anderson of the 101st Airborne (Assault) Division, revealed that he is incapable of perceiving Arabs as human beings. Colonel Anderson, who doubles as a commander and host of a radio call-in program and a TV show designed to win the hearts and minds of the people of Mosul, had learned that someone was out to assassinate him. In a wild mood swing common to racists, Anderson decided that Iraqis are all alike—and of a different breed. He said as much to the *Los Angeles Times*.

"They don't understand being nice," said Anderson, who helps oversee the military zone that includes Mosul and environs. He doesn't hide his irritation after months dedicated to restoring the city: "We spent so long here working with kid gloves, but the average Iraqi guy will tell you, 'The only thing people respect here is violence . . . They only understand being shot at, being killed. That's the culture.' . . . Nice guys do finish last here."

Colonel Anderson personifies the unfitness of Americans to play a major role in the world, much less rule it. "We poured a lot of our heart and soul into trying to help the people," he bitched, as if Americans were God's gift to the planet. "But it can be frustrating when you hear stupid people still saying, 'You're occupiers. You want our oil. You're turning our country over to Israel.'" He cannot fathom that other people—non-whites—aspire to run their own affairs, and will kill and die to achieve that basic right.

What does this have to do with the Mayflower? Everything. Although possibly against their wishes, the Pilgrims hosted the Wampanoag for three no doubt anxious days. The same men killed and enslaved Wampanoags immediately before and after the feast. They, their newly arrived English comrades, and their children roasted hundreds of neighboring Indians alive just sixteen years later, and two generations afterwards cleared nearly the whole of New England of its indigenous "savages," while enthu-siastically enriching themselves through the invention of transoceanic, sophisticated means of enslaving millions. The Mayflower's cultural heirs are programmed to find glory in their own depravity, and savagery in their most helpless victims, who can only redeem themselves by accepting the inherent goodness of white Americans.

Thanksgiving encourages these cognitive cripples in their madness, just as it is designed to do.

November 27, 2003

PART II

BUSH AND KATRINA

THEY HAVE REACHED TOO FAR: BUSH'S ROAD LEADS TO RUIN FOR HIMSELF AND HIS PIRATES

We are all assembled, the world's people, awaiting the Pirates' lunge at history. The Bush men have made sure we pay rapt attention to their Big Bang, their epochal Event, after which the nature of things will have changed unalterably to their advantage—they think. The Bush men are certain of our collective response, convinced that once we have witnessed The Mother of All War Shows, humanity will react according to plan, and submit.

Bush was already savoring the New American Century just days ago, when he summoned his underlings from Britain and Spain to the Azores to make yet another final pronouncement. "We concluded that tomorrow is a moment of truth for the world," Bush said.

Spoken like a King. Or The Man Who Would Be King.

Rudyard Kipling's tale of an English colonial soldier drunk on his imagined power over the natives is eerily appropriate. The projected fruits of Shock and Awe—the power to pillage the world with impunity—utterly bedazzled and blinded the perpetrators of the staged holocaust, even before the Event itself had unfolded. In the days between the final U.S. ultimatum and the invasion, American political and corporate media players were visibly shaken by the clear and unanimous world revulsion at U.S. imperiousness.

"Are we going back to The White Man's Burden?" Arab League U.N. Ambassador Yahya Mahmassani shot at CNN's startled Wolf Blitzer. "Is this the twenty-first century?"

Yes, it is, and George Bush and his armies cannot wrench away the provenance of Time to lift again the Burden that even Kipling knew the White Man was not fit to bear.

No one can predict the specific ways in which nations and movements will resist Bush's aggression against civilization. What is certain is that the Pirates have succeeded in arraying important sectors of every other nation on the planet in opposition to Washington's hegemony. Bush has made the name that is our patrimony—"America"—a curse on the lips of much of the world.

If Shock and Awe is essentially a horrific psychological warfare exercise—and it is—the assault on humanity's collective sensibilities has already had disastrous, unintended effects.

Although they are incapable of realizing it, the Bush men have revealed themselves to the world— the audience for Shock and Awe—as grotesquely ugly, brutish, irredeemably repugnant human beings whose touch must be avoided under all circumstances. Every plan and project of individuals and nations will be shaped by having witnessed a racist America raining fire on a weaker people—and reveling in the crime.

Bush's plan for world domination was doomed before the burning, blasting, thundering, screaming display. The Pirates have accelerated the processes of their own ruin.

As we wrote in the March 6 issue of *The Black Commentator*:

The impending war against Iraq is an oil currency war, a preemptive strike against the euro's potential to challenge the U.S. dollar as the sole denominator of petroleum purchases. By seizing the Iraqi oil fields and positioning itself to do the same in Saudi Arabia, Iran and throughout the Persian Gulf, the Caspian Sea and South Asia, the U.S. can stop the euro cold and rule as its own OPEC, awesomely armed and dreadfully dangerous. The dollar will remain supreme, backed by the oil reserves of the globe.

THEY HAVE REACHED TOO FAR: BUSH'S ROAD LEADS TO RUIN FOR HIMSELF AND HIS PIRATES

That was the plan. However, as the world watched the U.S. morph into its predatory essence month by month, a collective, global withdrawal from America became apparent. Clyde V. Prestowitz Jr., president of the Economic Strategy Institute and author of the forthcoming book *Rogue Nation*, describes the phenomenon:

> Over the past year, private foreign investment in the United States has fallen dramatically. It has been partially offset by increased buying of U.S. Treasury notes by Asian governments. But, at the same time, some governments like Russia have also begun to shift some of their reserve currency holdings from dollars to euros. As a result, we have seen the dollar fall in value against the euro by about 25 percent. That kind of a decline occurs when foreigners decide to put their money someplace other than the United States.

War is the great and terrible engine of history. Bush and his Pirates hope to employ that engine to harness Time and cheat the laws of political economy, to leapfrog over the contradictions of their parasitical existence into a new epoch of their own imagining.

Instead, they have lunged into the abyss, from which no one will extricate them, for they will be hated much more than feared.

In attempting to break humanity's will to resist, the Bush pirates have reached too far.

March 20, 2003

NO BLACK PLAN FOR THE CITIES, DESPITE THE LESSON OF KATRINA

"Katrina is a metaphor for abandoned urban America," said Rev. Jesse Jackson as he prepared to lead a "Reclaiming Our Land" march in New Orleans late last month. "There is no urban policy, and there must be."

Rev. Jackson is wrong. An urban policy does exist, hatched in corporate boardrooms and proceeding at various stages of implementation in cities across the nation. Urban America is not being "abandoned." Rather, the corporate plan calls for existing populations to be removed and replaced, incrementally, a process that is well underway. And the land is being "reclaimed"—by Big Capital, with the enthusiastic support of urban politicians of all races from coast to coast.

The problem is not the lack of an urban policy, but the failure to formulate progressive Black urban policies and plans. Corporate America and finance capital have both general and detailed visions of what the cities should look like and which populations and enterprises will be nurtured and served by these new and improved municipalities—"renaissance" cities of the (near and, in some places, very near) future.

Corporate planners and developers believed they had been blessed by nature when Katrina drowned New Orleans, washing away in days the problem-people and neighborhoods that would ordinarily require years to remove in order to clear the way for "renaissance."

Greed led to unseemly speed, revealing in a flash the outlines of the urban vision that would be imposed on the wreckage of New Orleans. As in a film on fast-forward, the "plot" (in both meanings of the word) unfolded in a rush before our eyes: Once the Black and poor were removed, an urban environment would be created implacably hostile to their return. The public sector—except that which serves business, directly or indirectly—would under no circumstances be resurrected, so as to leave little "space" for the re-implantation of unwanted populations (schools, utility infrastructure, public and affordable private housing, public safety, health care).

The bargaining power of labor would be reduced to zero by the systematic introduction of itinerant and often undocumented workers to replace the exiled African Americans—who are the most union-friendly workers ("joiners") of all, a documented fact well-known in corporate America. Much of the land previously inhabited by the now-superfluous exiles would be put to other uses (parks and golf courses, etc.) or designated for no use at all under flood safety or environmental rationales. As a result, the value of the remainder of land in New Orleans would in time increase dramatically, making some people richer than before and rendering low-cost housing prohibitive in the future.[*]

Most importantly, the "new" New Orleans would no longer accommodate a Black majority (previously 67 percent), thus ensuring that the "renaissance" could proceed politically unencumbered in what corporate folks call a "stable" and "positive" business environment.

Black New Orleans and its diaspora have heroically—desperately!—resisted the schemes of national, state, and local capital and governments. They have won some tentative victories (among them, retaining a Black, although thoroughly corporate, mayor) and been joined by many ardent allies. Some reduced semblance of the old Black city will rise from the muck and ruin, thanks to sheer force of will on the part of residents and the solidarity of scores of progressive organizations and thousands of individual volunteers. Corporate plans for the "new" New Orleans, which began surfacing in the most grotesquely "ugly American" fashion

[*]   https://www.blackagendareport.com/node/images/stories/029/ NOLAnewNOLAmap.jpg.

just weeks after the Great Flood while hundreds of bloated bodies were still unidentified and unclaimed (some still are), laid out in some detail schemes to reinvent the city by allocating land to its "optimum" uses (for business) and attracting and retaining the most "desirable" population (for corporate purposes). None of these grand plans projected a Black population numbering more than 30 percent—apparently, the maximum proportion tolerable in the "ideal" urban environment.

Against huge odds, Black New Orleans—including activists who commute to do battle from as far away as Houston—has struggled against the privatization and charterization of what remains of the educational system. They have fought to preserve the largely intact public housing stock, despite the Bush regime's determination to wipe the projects off the face of the city map. They attempt to rebuild their homes in places where government at all levels erects every conceivable obstacle. Of necessity, these are largely defensive actions of a people under siege on all fronts, their ranks and resources drastically depleted. But Black New Orleans has not failed; they continue to struggle to overcome the greatest single calamity ever to befall a U.S. city, exponentially compounded by racist barbarians in government and business acting in concert.

It is African American leadership institutions that have failed Black New Orleans, and left inner city populations across the land defenseless in the face of Big Capital's schemes to remake urban America in whiteface. The exodus from New Orleans, and the effective lockout that followed, were like a giant wave crashing down on the city. Elsewhere in Black America, these same corporate Black-removal forces propel a rising tide of gentrification that does not ebb. Big Capital's urban offensive threatens to irrevocably disperse the population base of Black political power, rendering forever moot all dreams of meaningful African American self-determination. If Black America fails to come to grips with the profound change in corporate investment and development strategies that has occurred over the past several decades, other "chocolate cities" will soon share the same fate as New Orleans—only on a slower schedule.

Of the top twelve cities in Black population, seven saw a loss in African Americans as a percentage of total residents between 1990 and 2000:

New York City (1)
Chicago (2)
Houston (5)
Los Angeles (7)
Washington (9)
Dallas (11)
Atlanta (12)

Katrina events, of course, would push New Orleans (previously Black city Number 10) into the African American population percentage loss column, in the most horrific fashion imaginable.

Four cities among the top twelve became Blacker in the 1990–2000 decade:

Detroit (3)
Philadelphia (4)
Baltimore (6)
Memphis (8)

There is no question that some of the slippage in the Black proportion of population in seven top cities is due to immigration, mainly Latino. However, the U.S. Census Bureau drastically changed the way it counts Hispanics between the 1990 and 2000 censuses, making it impossible to reliably measure the impact. What is immediately apparent is that the seven cities that became less Black in the '90s are all concentrated corporate headquarters locations or, in the case of Washington, D.C., the headquarters of the federal government. These are places that corporate and finance capital are most keen to "make over" to provide the urban "ambience" believed most amenable to their employees, management, and clients, and for the general sake of corporate prestige.

Let there be no doubt, however, that the general "back to the cities" corporate imperative—resulting in gentrification—will soon begin tilting other heavily Black municipalities in the same direction. Newark, New Jersey, once considered among the quintessential "chocolate cities," went from 58.5 percent Black in 1990 to 53.5 percent in 2000. Since then, the center city "renaissance" project has gone into high gear, attracting thousands of prized white professionals. By 2010, Newark is likely to no longer have a Black majority. Atlanta will be significantly less Black.

New York's de-Blackening has been the most dramatic. For the first time since the so-called Draft Riots of 1863 (actually, a monstrous anti-Black pogrom that slaughtered hundreds) forced tens of thousands of African Americans to flee the city permanently, the 2005 U.S. Census update showed a net loss of Black population for the city as a whole. Also for the first time, Latinos suffered a net loss in population in Manhattan, ground zero for the nation in both gentrification and corporate headquarters. Black numbers in Manhattan have been dropping for some time. Political impacts inevitably follow.

Others will maintain that the decline in Black proportions in central cities is a sign of progress, because African Americans are rapidly suburbanizing. However, as anyone who knows the environs of Washington, D.C., understands, a great chunk of the Black exodus across jurisdictional lines is "push-out"—the direct result of gentrification of the inner city. In many cases, the ghetto has simply moved across the city line. Upscale Blacks— and the term is quite relative, especially when considering wealth, or net worth—are also priced out of the most attractive city neighborhoods. They encamp on the periphery, occupying homes formerly owned by whites who have fled the poorer Blacks who were forced out of the city.

The result is a scattering of African Americans and dilution of Black political power in a growing number of central cities. There can be no comparison between the political, cultural, and social impact of Black majorities in suburban jurisdictions such as Prince George's County, Maryland and DeKalb County, Georgia, and Black political control of great cities like Washington and Atlanta. And the frenzy of gentrifying in Chicago may preclude that city from ever again electing a Black mayor.

The flow of Big Capital to the cities signifies the end of a cycle that began after World War II. Fearing a return of Great Depression-like conditions with the end of defense industry hyper-production, and the political turmoil that would follow among the millions of returning soldiers and sailors, the federal government and corporate America launched the biggest public works and private investment project in human history: the suburbanization of a continent-wide nation. The grand design flipped the script on patterns of habitation that had prevailed since the dawn of civilization. The rich had always lived in the centers of cities, where the amenities are, while the poor were relegated to the periphery. That pattern still holds everywhere else on the globe—except in the United States.

Blacks were left out of the Great Makeover but inherited the cities—many of which lost half or more of their white populations to the suburbs, over time—by default. After many decades of suburbanization the inevitable happened, a phenomenon closely resembling a classic capitalist crisis of overproduction. The suburbs had stretched too far, commutes were too long, the infrastructure was strained by the artificial and historically unnatural sprawl and the impossibility of providing city-style amenities to far-flung suburbs. The over-stretched rubber band began to snap back.

In the interval between the post-war urban white exodus—which was well underway long before the Black rebellions of the '60s, and was much more a "pull" than a "push"—and today's encroaching gentrification, African Americans won nominal political power in many cities. Now the *fin de cycle* is upon us. African Americans in general, and Black politicians in particular, seem to have never considered that the era of "chocolate cities" might end, or the consequences to Black welfare and political power. On the contrary, most Black politicians, having had no plan of their own for their cities, made careers of bending over frontward—deeply—to attract corporate investment on *any* terms (as do most of their white counterparts). At the current stage of the cycle, for many heavily Black cities, there is no need to bend over—the corporations are coming for their own reasons, with briefcases full of plans for another Great American Makeover. Large-scale Black removal is integral to the project.

Katrina showed everyone with eyes and ears the full scope of the corporate plan, whose outlines had long been evident in New York, Chicago, Washington, Atlanta, and elsewhere. Gentrification is actually the result of methodical corporate penetration, a planned process requiring intimate collaboration with local government. In the absence of *Black* plans for urban makeovers, corporate plans will prevail, and a slow and tortuous African American exodus will result. The conclusion is obvious: Blacks that aspire to leadership must dive into urban planning with a vengeance. As I wrote on July 29, 2004 :

> We must disrupt and supersede corporate development schemes, by becoming city planners in the service of the people. We must take the initiative away from the corporations, who are currently in possession of all the data that make up the life of a city, and who use it selectively to present their self-serving brand of "development" as the only option available. We must redefine the term "development," to mean change that benefits the people impacted by the project. Development that does not meet that definition is unacceptable.

Had the post-1970 crop of urban Black leadership used the intervening decades to formulate urban plans and policies that transformed the cities in ways that served the needs of the new Black majorities and pluralities, they would now be capable of bargaining with onrushing capital—and would have had something to offer to the people of New Orleans as corporations presented plans for the *coup de grace* on the Black majority. But the misleadership class spent their terms in office wasting the historical opportunity, and the window is rapidly closing.

Only an urban movement for *democratic development,* rooted in mass mobilization of city residents around comprehensive plans for the betterment of the existing population within the city's borders, can tame the corporate juggernaut and preserve urban Black political power. When the window shuts—after Black populations are scattered—the game will be over.

May 9, 2007

THE AGE OF KATRINA—NOT OBAMA

Barack Obama supporters would have you believe that their candidate's presidential nomination is the glorious, straight-line culmination of the Black Freedom Struggle whose previous high-water mark, they believe, was the 1963 March on Washington, the forty-fifth anniversary of which coincides with this week's Democratic National Convention. Obama's public relations agents attempt to bracket the history of modern U.S. race relations within a marketable forty-five-year period that begins with a snippet from Dr. Martin Luther King's "I Have a Dream" speech and ends—for the time being—with the grand peroration of Obama's acceptance speech before the cheering multitudes in Denver. These dates are presented as the bookends of Black struggle, to be amended and extended when President Obama delivers his State of the Union Address in January.

To the most hopelessly besotted Obamites, their candidate's speech on Thursday will herald a crack in time, after which posterity will speak of Before-Obama (BO) and After-Obama (AO) eras, and the transcendental Age of Obama.

Having conjured up a nonexistent "mass movement" to describe what is actually a corporate financed and directed electoral campaign that *has not championed a single issue worthy of historical note* (don't dare cite partial Iraq withdrawal and for-profit health care schemes), the Democrats now patch Dr. King's speech into the prologue to the Book of Obama for the purpose of consigning real mass agitation strategies to the past, for all time.

Yet, the unedited version of history—the real deal—commemorates another imminent anniversary, one that starkly illuminates the true political character of the age: Katrina. The events that followed the hurricane's arrival in New Orleans on August 29, 2005 would reveal the diabolical intentions of U.S. rulers towards African Americans: to methodically remove Blacks from the central cities of the nation. The ongoing, orchestrated catastrophe also demonstrated beyond doubt the moral bankruptcy and political impotence of Black national "leadership." As I wrote in October 2005: "If Black America fails to configure its human, organizational, and material resources to effectively resist the theft and ultimate disfigurement of New Orleans, then we will be forced to confront the existence of fundamental, crippling flaws in the African American polity."

The "man-made disaster in the Gulf" provided what may have been "the last chance to build a real Movement, encompassing the broadest sectors of Black America." Certainly, a critical mass of "the people" were eager to intervene. Hardly a Black church was without some Katrina-aid project, thousands of students journeyed to New Orleans as soon as logistics were made available, and popular awareness of the raw injustice of government policy was universal. But pure rot pervaded national Black political circles—as was clear within six months.

"The Congressional Black Caucus, which claims to be the 'conscience of the Congress,' has shown itself to be an appendage of the White House leadership," I wrote in February 2006. "They slavishly followed Minority Leader Nancy Pelosi's command to make the Democratic Party look good—as opposed to the Republicans—rather than directly address the crisis that was affecting their own people. Forty-one of the forty-two Black members of Congress obeyed Pelosi's edict that the House Committee on Katrina be boycotted. They accepted the order that Democratic legislators would not attend the meetings of the Katrina committee, because it was stacked against the Democratic Party."

Only Cynthia McKinney, who was soon to lose her House seat from suburban Atlanta, bucked Pelosi's edict to boycott the Katrina hearings. Pelosi's unspoken but transparent motive was to distance the Democratic

Party from issues considered too "Black" in the run-up to congressional elections in November 2006. The CBC, as a body, weighed compliance with their party leader versus rescue of Black New Orleans, and chose Pelosi—who would continue to smother the Katrina issue after Democrats gained control of the House.

Katrina, that horrific assault on Black humanity, dignity, and civilizational rights—the Right to Return and participate in the reconstruction of their city—was (and remains) the greatest test of Black leadership since the days of generalized White Terror in the South following the collapse of Reconstruction. As the world watched, hundreds of thousands of African Americans were effectively evicted from their city and have since been prevented by every foul and evil means possible from returning.

There was method to this madness. The hurricane had simply provided "disaster capitalism" with an instant route to gentrification, a goal that takes years to accomplish by the usual methods of public and private urban coercion. Human rights lawyer Bill Quigley, who has documented the river of crimes perpetrated against the people of New Orleans since August 29, 2005, has compiled a "Katrina Pain Index—New Orleans Three Years Later." It shows a city in which even the size of population is in dispute. The City Council claims 321,000 residents, the U.S. Census Bureau says only 239,000 remain—a loss of 132,000 or 214,000 from a pre-Katrina population of 453,000, 67 percent Black. No one can agree on the current racial breakdown.

Local, state, and national forces, public and private, have conspired relentlessly to keep New Orleans unlivable to the unwanted classes. Public transportation is down 80 percent. A majority of Black residents were renters, yet no renters have gotten anything from the $10 billion Road Home Community Block Grant. Rents are up 46 percent, most public housing demolished or marked for destruction, while 71,657 "vacant, ruined unoccupied houses" anchor metropolitan New Orleans in social death. The city is number one in physical death by murder, while psychiatric hospital beds are down 56 percent. Three hundred Louisiana National Guardsmen patrol the streets, in lieu of cops.

Is it any wonder that only 11 percent of families have returned to the Lower Ninth Ward? The Katrina crisis continues because Power is determined that the Black and poor will not be permitted reentry.

Barack Obama denies that racism plays any role in this. "There's been much attention in the press about the fact that those who were left behind in New Orleans were disproportionately poor and African American. I've said publicly that I do not subscribe to the notion that the painfully slow response of FEMA and the Department of Homeland Security was racially based. The ineptitude was colorblind," said Obama on his website on September 6, 2005. He still says so.

For three years, Power has ensured that the New Orleans Black Diaspora remains scattered. For the forces of organized racism, it is a success story; there's nothing inept about it. Barack Obama will do nothing to facilitate the return of Black New Orleans, since no "malice" was intended. "I see no evidence of active malice, but I see a continuation of passive indifference on the part of our government towards the least of these." But Obama is worse than "passively indifferent." By denying the reality of racism, he transforms the monumental injustices of Katrina into motiveless mistakes that somehow continue to replicate themselves to the disadvantage of the same group of people.

There is no reason for the Black New Orleans diaspora to expect any relief from an Obama presidency. In fact, there is no reason to expect anything historically unusual or unique from a President Obama other than his physical Blackness. Katrina, on the other hand, is the most dramatic manifestation of an implacable racism coiled deeply in the ruling structures of American society, primed to remove concentrations of Blacks from places of value. This overarching imperative to "Negro removal" can become aggressively active in an instant—as we learned in the days following August 29, 2005—or proceed about its work block by block over years, until the offending population is eliminated. Fast or slow, the end results are the same: seven of the top twelve cities in Black population saw a loss in African Americans as a percentage of total residents between 1990 and 2000.

THE AGE OF KATRINA—NOT OBAMA

Slow-acting Katrinas in the form of gentrification are what Black folks can expect—and must find ways to resist and defeat—from the ruling Lords of Capital for the foreseeable future, Obama or no Obama. There will be no "age" named after the handsome, articulate, and oh-so-slick but otherwise ordinary corporate candidate for president who used to call himself Barry. This is the Age of Katrina, and Barry is part of the problem.

August 26, 2008

PART III

THE DLC AND BLACK MISLEADERSHIP

KATRINA, WAR, IMPEACHMENT, AND THE BLACK GULAG

It is way past time that long-held assumptions of how African Americans will forge a path to social justice and political self-determination be re-examined. Two-plus generations of reflexive fealty to the Democratic Party have resulted in Democrats behaving more like Republicans. Uncritical applause for Black faces in high places has brought us betrayal on an unprecedented scale. At this juncture in history, African Americans face the political crises of Katrina, escalating imperial war as national policy, failure to impeach flagrant criminals in public office, and the ongoing horror of mass Black incarceration. Past "allies" and current misleaders must be discarded, and a new movement begun.

We are witnessing the final dissolution of both the Democratic Party and established Black leadership formations as effective agents of domestic social change and world peace. Corporate power has swallowed the Party whole, and is smothering or absorbing the residue of what was once a powerful Black people's movement. The devastation is all but complete, as is evident when one examines the response to the crises of Katrina, the Iraq War, the necessity to impeach, and the hellish and inexorable growth of a Black American Gulag through mass incarceration.

The Black Gulag—the product of a people-savaging national public policy that began as a mass white societal response to the '60s Freedom Movement and metastasizes each year regardless of crime rates—isn't even an issue for Democratic leadership. No wonder, since both Democrats and Republicans have conspired over two generations to place a million African Americans behind bars at any given moment, creating a toxic prison *culture* that poisons every arena of Black life. During the watch of Democratic front-runner Hillary Clinton's husband Bill, more Blacks were thrown in prison than under any other president in history.

Mass Black incarceration is not a priority among Black elite formations, either. A deep historical current in Black political culture avoids even a discussion of horrendous imprisonment rates that tear at the very fibers of Black society. Preachers would rather internalize and moralize the ongoing state assault on Black life, while the Black *mis*leadership class, as I have written, is "more embarrassed than outraged" at the volcanic emergence of a million-man-and-woman Black Prison Nation, through which doors multiple millions of the next generation will pass.

The battle against Black mass incarceration cannot be said to have been lost, because it never began. These are the rotten fruits of the impotence of—no, betrayal by—the class that demanded the Freedom Movement be shut down after Dr. Martin Luther King's death, so that they would have the space and quiet to pursue newly available business and public office opportunities. Vote for me, or support my economic upward mobility, and it will set you free, said the New Class. They lied, and the masses of Black Americans are less politically focused than at any time since Emancipation. More have lost their basic freedoms than at any time since slavery.

Katrina—the monstrous boil on the national political body that burst with the levees, two years ago—should have been a watershed moment for Black America, a grotesque but clarifying historical window into the real nature of U.S. society and its rulers. For the masses of Blacks, it was. Young people who never knew Jim Crow in the raw were forced to recognize basic truths, as when Kanye West uttered what to him seemed a revelation: "George Bush doesn't care about Black people."

House Speaker Nancy Pelosi, having left Katrina out of her "first hundred hours" agenda in January, this month toured New Orleans with a fifteen-member Democratic delegation, making the proper noises of solidarity with the fraction of the Black population that remains. She was also careful not to offend the white Democrats who are as culpable as Republicans in preventing the city's far-flung diaspora from achieving their "right to return," "right of citizenship in the city," "right to partici-pate in the rebuilding" of New Orleans and the other rights outlined in the twelve-point Citizens Bill of Rights promulgated by the African American Leadership Project on September 22, 2005, less than a month after the deluge.

Pelosi's response to the pleas of Black New Orleans was to muzzle House Democrats, including the Congressional Black Caucus, barring them from participating in Republican-led hearings on Katrina and its after-math. The rationale was that the GOP, then in control of all committees, would dominate the conversation. But of course, the same logic would have precluded Democratic participation in any hearings on any subject while Republicans remained in the majority—yet the injunction was only imposed on Katrina. Pelosi's real concern was that the Katrina issue was, in Chuck D's immortal words, "Too Black, Too Strong," and might cause white voters to identify the Democratic Party too closely with African Americans, endangering prospects of capturing the House in 2006. As a body, the Congressional Black Caucus swallowed Pelosi's Kool-Aid, with the notable exception of Rep. Cynthia McKinney, who participated in the hearings in defiance of leadership.

The same "don't get too close to the Blacks" rationale dictated that Pelosi leave Katrina out of her "first one hundred hours" pitch in the 2006 mid-term campaign. Then, this spring, Pelosi unleashed Black lawmakers and others to hold hearings on a variety of Katrina-related subjects, a gesture that looked more like loosening a safety valve on Black discontent than a prelude to restoration of New Orleans' original population. Black Democratic Whip James Clyburn (SC) announced the belated offensive, but eighteen months after the catastrophe. The historical moment had passed, skillfully circumvented by the congresswoman from San Francisco, and acquiesced to by a meek and compliant Black Caucus. There can be no doubt that, as the 2008 elections near, Pelosi will again quash all substan-tive proposals to make Black New Orleans whole, once again aggressively shedding excessive Democratic Party identification with Black interests.

The August Democratic tour of the Gulf was a pitiful gesture, a harmless and farcical "Black Summer of Discontent" that will pass unnoticed by history.

Black *mis*leadership, as presently constituted, is also fated for the dustbin, having utterly failed the historical test of Katrina. As I wrote in October 2005, "Cruel history presents the catastrophe as an unwanted opportunity, a test of Black people's capacity for the *operational* unity craved by the vast bulk of African Americans. The pain and anger in Black America is all but universal, and demands *collective* action, the outcome of which will largely define the true State of Black America as it has evolved over the last two generations."

If Katrina could not galvanize Black institutional structures to decisive action, resulting in the mobilization of millions, then those structures are moribund and flaccid. The lost opportunity for mass Black action can never be regained. Contrast this with the response of mainly Hispanic immigrants, their sons and daughters, to the threat of repressive legislation. Millions of Latinos staged coordinated demonstrations in scores of cities, with the active assistance of Spanish-language media. Yet, on the Black side of the divide, as we wrote in the inaugural issue of *Black Agenda Report*:

> If the national Black political infrastructure, such as it is, could not set masses in motion after Katrina, when African Americans were as one in their concentrated anger and collective will to do something, then what currently passes for leadership will never effectively mobilize Black folks for anything. They have lost the tools and desire to fight, and cannot function as leaders even when the people cry out for common action.
>
> Had Black people been called out en masse, they would have come—but the historical moment has slipped away, wasted. In a few years, a new generation of Black activists will deploy themselves in structures of radical resistance, their world views shaped by the multiple crimes of Katrina. But in the near term, it must be recognized that not only have African Americans been

numerically overtaken by Hispanics, we have been eclipsed in mass organizing as well.

War—by now one of the few pistons running the engine of the U.S. economy, while also guaranteeing its eventual collapse—is the enemy of every agenda item of the Historical Black Consensus. George Bush's policy of endless warfare condemns Black America to permanent deferral of urban transformation, in all its aspects. There can be no revitalization of the cities—except under corporate terms under which Black removal is a prerequisite—while the public treasury is poured into the black hole of the War Industry.

In the aftermath of 9/11, decades of struggle against racial profiling were erased in an instant; now, every non-Aryan-looking person is fair game for profiling, and Black complaints are deemed petty, as if removed from history. Vast income and wealth disparities must take a back seat—*all* the way to the back—to the spending imperatives of war, most of which ultimately winds up in the hands of what I dubbed the "Pirate Class," epitomized by Halliburton, Bechtel, and other pillars of the ruling order—which also happen to be the behemoth "reconstructors" of the Katrina-ravaged Gulf region. Wars have always accelerated the rate of structural change in societies. Corporate wars, the only kind the U.S. wages, these days, direct all restructuring to the most non-productive corporate coffers.

The forces that animate George Bush intend to keep the restructuring process on full throttle. As I wrote in December 2002, three months *before* the U.S. invasion of Iraq: "The predator-scavenger class must . . . reproduce itself to meet the demands of permanent war, changing fundamentally the relationship of forces within American business as a whole. The Cheney-Bush pirates are about to birth a new brood of billionaire pillagers and parasites *with no direct connection to the well-being of the domestic economy* and those of us who depend on it."

Black folks used to complain about the abandonment of the cities, and our resultant disproportionate suffering. Permanent War, an integral component of the latest stage of U.S. imperialism, marginalizes everyone but the super-privileged, and Black folks most of all. Yet much of Black leadership and the African American public reflexively support Barack Obama, whose imperial bent is not even closeted. Obama wants to add one hundred thousand additional soldiers and Marines to the U.S. Armed Forces—more manpower for the imperial mission that feeds the coffers of War Industry and starves out any hope of domestic social transformation. No "new" New Orleans that embraces the aspirations of the original population, no revitalized cities in which the current needs of residents are served. No wonder Obama has no plan for urban America or to ameliorate rampaging inequalities; militarism will ensure there will be no money, no matter who is president.

Hillary Clinton, who garners most of the other fraction of Black support, is the wife of the man who crushed majority Democratic opposition to NAFTA "free trade" legislation, in an alliance with Republicans. This version of "free trade" and war are pieces of the same cloth, as are the unequal rules of the dollar-based oil business, and international bankers' "debt" practices in the developing world. All must be backed up by the ultimate threat of military enforcement of the prevailing order. Thus, Obama's call for one hundred thousand new troops as the U.S. continues its unique "mission" in the world.

African Americans have historically opposed U.S. military adventures abroad. "White Man's Wars," we used to call them—and still do, as all the data show. But a bankrupt Black *mis*leadership, many of whom mollify their constituents with occasional anti-war rhetoric, at the end of the day gives a pass to the militarism that will be the death of every Black dream of a just society. Genuine anti-war lawmakers like California congresspersons Maxine Waters and Barbara Lee are among the exceptions in the Congressional Black Caucus; many other CBC members have signed on to the Out of Iraq Caucus that Waters and Lee lead, but nevertheless vote for continued funding of the war. In the Congress, Black leadership becomes a charade, and "progressive" white Democratic leadership, the mask Nancy Pelosi continues to wear, is most often mislabeled.

Impeachment—the only way to stop the criminals in power from committing executive mayhem, and to prevent succeeding presidents of either party from using the tools of oppression inherited from Bush—is a no-brainer in Black America. As *BAR*'s Bruce Dixon wrote last week, "No constituency is as heavily in favor of impeachment as Black America." The entire roster of the Congressional Black Caucus should be on record as favoring impeachment of Bush and Cheney, by popular acclamation of their constituents—but only a fraction is. African Americans and genuine progressives look to my old friend, Rep. John Conyers, chairman of the Judiciary Committee where impeachment proceedings must begin, as a leader on this issue. But Conyers' leader is Nancy Pelosi, the Speaker of the House. Although many of us anticipated more of him in this crisis, he cannot possibly be expected to act as a Black "leader." He is embedded in a white-dominated Democratic Party machinery that long ago decided Blacks were an albatross around their necks—even though many of them cannot win dogcatcher offices without us.

If there is a fool out there that thinks we are advocating some kind of accommodation with Republicans, he should check into the nearest psych ward. We must go back to basics, to the ingredients that brought us so far in such a short time in the brief period of the Freedom Movement. Moribund *mis*leadership must be replaced by mass mobilizers, organizers responsive to the essentially progressive instincts of the Black public at-large—a people whom noted political scientist Michael Dawson describes as politically akin to "Swedish Social Democrats," far to the left of what passes for "liberal" in white American terms.

Our enemy is corporate capital, which has polluted every nook and cranny of electoral and traditional Black politics. The Congressional Black Caucus has been broken like an egg. Black institutions contort themselves and their agendas to seek corporate funding. The corporate media voice is a monotone, celebrating the rise of a "new" generation of "Black leaders" that rejects confrontation with the powers-that-be and, like Barack Obama, questions the relevance of race-based grievances. That's money talking. But we are a loud people, and our voices will be heard.

August 22, 2007

THE "OBSCENE FOURTEEN" HOUSE NSA NEGROES

Last week, fourteen Black members of the U.S. House indelibly marked themselves as tools of the Surveillance State, wholly unfit to represent any African American constituency. The "Obscene Fourteen" aligned with Democratic and Republican leadership to narrowly defeat (217-205) a bill that would have defunded the National Security Agency's program to spy on the telephones of every American household. Had only half of these U.S. House Negroes acted in accordance with the overwhelming sentiments of their constituents—and with the historical Black Consensus on peace and social justice—the Bush-Obama surveillance regime would have been dealt its first serious setback in more than a decade of fascism-in-the-making. All fourteen should be excised, like a malignancy, from the African American polity.

The Black people of Texas are especially ill-served. All four Black congressional representatives—Al Green, Sheila Jackson-Lee, Eddie Bernice Johnson, and newcomer Marc Veasey—voted with the NSA spies and their current boss in the White House, as did three of the four Georgia Black lawmakers: Sanford Bishop, Hank Johnson, and David Scott. Two of Florida's three Black congresspersons pledged allegiance to universal surveillance: Corrine Brown and Frederica Wilson. Here is a complete list of the Obscene Fourteen:

Terri Sewell (AL)
Corrine Brown (FL)
Frederica Wilson (FL)

Sanford Bishop (GA)

Hank Johnson (GA)

David Scott (GA)

Robin Kelly (IL)

Donald Payne Jr. (NJ)

Gregory Meeks (NY)

G.K. Butterfield (NC)

Al Green (TX)

Sheila Jackson Lee (TX)

Eddie Bernice Johnson (TX)

Marc Veasey (TX)

Five of the shameless lawmakers openly advertise themselves as "progressives." Florida's Frederica Wilson and Corrine Brown, Texas' Eddie Bernice Johnson and Sheila Jackson-Lee, and Georgia's Hank Johnson are members of the Progressive Congressional Caucus, where Jackson-Lee serves as a vice chair. But then, House Democratic Leader Nancy Pelosi, who bullied a minority of her party into line with the president and House Republican leadership, was once upon a time a co-chair of the PCC. (Steven Horsford, the Nevada Black Congressman, is also a PCC member. He failed to vote on the NSA bill.)

Nearly two-thirds of the Congressional Black Caucus were in their right minds last week. Among the twenty-five "yes" votes for defunding the NSA program were, commendably, Rep. James Clyburn, the South Carolina lawmaker who serves as House Assistant Democratic Leader, but balked at towing Pelosi's and Obama's line, and North Carolina's Mel Watt, who awaits confirmation as the new head of Federal Housing Finance Agency, for which he will need a full court press from the White House.

The Cardinal Sin

In making common cause with the Surveillance State, the Obscene Fourteen have thrown in their lot with the same forces that have, for the past two generations, placed Black America under hyper-surveillance—the foundation of both mass Black incarceration and the social environment that allows the stalking and murder of hundreds of innocent Black people every year in the United States. African Americans, more than any other U.S. constituency, have an *existential* interest in ending the Surveillance State. In that struggle, the Obscene Fourteen and their ilk are more than useless; they have chosen the side of the enemy and will inevitably commit more treachery.

Back in October of 2002, only four members of the Black Caucus voted for George Bush's War Powers Act, Congress' consent to the invasion of Iraq. Of the four, only Georgia's Sanford Bishop—who voted, predictably, for continued NSA bulk telephonic spying—remains in the House. William Jefferson (LA), Harold Ford Jr. (TN), and Albert Wynn (MD) are thankfully gone. Yet 2002's "Four Eunuchs of War" have been replaced and reinforced in infamy by today's Obscene Fourteen—a full third of the CBC. In the intervening decade, the historical Black Consensus on peace and social justice has been assaulted as never before by the massive entrance of corporate money into Black politics, and the ascent of a corporatist Black militarist to the White House—which are two aspects of the same phenomenon. The Obscene Fourteen have chosen their side in the U.S. War Against All. The last place such persons belong is in leadership positions among the people who suffer most from racial and political surveillance.

July 13, 2013

DETROIT IS THE NEXUS OF NEW AMERICAN APARTHEID

On October 5 and 6 in Detroit, the International People's Assembly will hold a conference Against Banks and Against Austerity. By that time, many of the ten thousand partygoers expected at this week's Congressional Black Caucus annual gala will just be getting over their hangovers, having spent thousands of dollars apiece strutting around DC hotel lobbies celebrating their personal upward mobility amidst Black America's greatest economic and political crisis in modern times. The conference in Detroit is about the real world, where Wall Street is devouring the public sphere and driving actual living standards inexorably downward for the vast bulk of Americans, especially people of color.

Detroit is the epicenter of the African American economic and political crisis, an 85 percent Black metropolis whose citizens have been stripped of their fundamental democratic rights so that their public assets and private pensions can be confiscated by the finance capitalist class. Wall Street now runs the city outright, through an emergency financial manager. A similar regime prevails in all of Michigan's largely Black cities, resulting in the disenfranchisement of more than half the state's Black population. What is emerging in the second decade of the twenty-first century is a new version of American Apartheid, in which the inhabitants of largely Black urban centers are denied a meaningful vote or the legal capacity to safeguard their collective and individual property from the grasping hands of the rich. In the language of declining capitalism, this is called austerity, but in America it takes the form of a racialized order in which concentrated populations of Blacks have no rights that the bankers are bound to respect. While the partygoers clink their glasses at the Black Caucus gala in Washington, a great political and economic implosion is unfolding in urban America, with Detroit as ground zero.

The International People's Assembly conference demands that the so-called debt to the banks be canceled, not just for Detroit—which supposedly owes Wall Street $22 billion—but for cities, school systems, states, and countries around the world that have been purposely made into debt slaves for the rich. Workers' pensions and jobs, and the vital services they provide to the community, must be guaranteed. This is a critical demand, since the emergency management regime in Pontiac, Michigan, has stripped the municipal workforce down to twenty in a city of sixty thousand. The unemployed must be put back to work repairing the damage inflicted on Detroit by the bankers' foreclosure and disinvestment policies. Public education, which is rapidly being privatized, must be restored to the public sphere and fully funded.

There are many more demands, but the solution begins with real popular democracy and the disempowerment of the banks. The struggle also requires the rejection of what has passed for Black leadership in Detroit and the rest of America: a chattering, swaggering, class of self-servers who have been selling the people down the river ever since they got a taste of power on the backs of the Black Freedom Movement of the '60s. These are the folks who will be toasting President Obama this week, in Washington, a servant of the banks who cares no more for the people of Detroit than for the people of Damascus, or Baghdad, or Mogadishu.

September 18, 2013

THE SIEGE OF DETROIT: A WAR OF BLACK URBAN REMOVAL

Like the rapist who insists his victim "wanted it," Detroit emergency manager Kevyn Orr claims city retirees were expressing "strong support for the city's plan to adjust its debts" when they voted to accept a 4.5 percent cut in their meager pensions. Corporate media echoed the state appointee's interpretation of the court-ordered ballot, in which about half the thirty-two thousand eligible workers and retirees participated. In reality, Detroit's pensioners were violated in broad daylight, stripped of retirement protections and forced to choose whether to die in poverty or an even more extreme destitution.

Earlier this year, as part of the Shock and Awe of state-imposed bankruptcy, Orr threatened to cut pensions by 26 percent, in defiance of Michigan state constitutional protections. He was backed by federal bankruptcy court judge Steven Rhodes, who has brushed aside every objection from lesser, non-corporate beings. Rather than risk the loss of one-quarter of an already meager $20,000 a year pension, 73 percent of retirees and workers accepted the lesser cut, plus an end to cost-of-living increases. This was not an election, but the cruelest coercion—a rape of the elderly, who were forced not only to acquiesce to their own further impoverishment, but also to give up the right to challenge the process in court.

Corporate media routinely ascribe such obscene assaults to "the city," as in "the city's plan to adjust its debts." But the City of Detroit has no such plans; it has no power, and its citizens have no meaningful vote, except of course when given an ultimatum to endorse cuts to their own pensions. Detroit's elected officials cannot pass laws, and collect a salary at the pleasure of dictator Kevyn Orr, who is answerable only to the ruling class, as directly represented by the Fortune 500 clients of the law firm that spawned him, Jones Day. (Orr's nominal boss, Gov. Rick Snyder, answers to the same people.) The state-imposed emergency manager is authorized to *usurp* the powers of the city—to act as a dictator—but he is not the city in any but the most technical, legalistic sense. For Orr to refer to himself as "the city" is a sick hubris—a hustler lawyer invoking the royal "We". However, when the media describe Orr's decrees as actions by "the city"— knowing full well how Orr is despised in Detroit government and the city at large—they are liars, pure and simple; co-conspirators in the corporate crime.

The people of Detroit have no rights that corporations and their servants in government are bound to respect. Indeed, the emergency manager laws have been used to disenfranchise the residents of every largely Black city and school district in the state, encompassing more than half the Black population of Michigan. (The people of Michigan rejected the legislation in a referendum, but Republican lawmakers simply passed a near-identical measure, as if nothing had happened.)

The 82 percent Black metropolis is under siege, in the medieval sense of the term. Just as ancient armies deprived towns under siege of food and water, to starve and thirst them into submission, so Kevyn Orr has caused the Detroit Water and Sewage Department to cut off tens of thousands of residents, in an escalating trajectory of systematically inflicted mass punishment and pain designed to make life in the city unbearable for a huge proportion of the population.

This is a war against a Black city, and a blueprint for future aggressions aimed at shrinking "chocolate cities" across the nation. What Katrina accomplished through the sudden advent of flood, the corporate strategists in Michigan intend to achieve by emergency dictatorship, privatization, and blatantly racist official barbarism.

Orr announced a fifteen-day "pause" in water shutoffs—similar to a temporary truce in siege warfare—as much to give cover to bankruptcy judge Rhodes who, while no less bestial than the managing dictator, seems more sensitive to public perceptions. United Nations experts condemned the shutoffs as constituting "a violation of the human right to water and other international human rights." Thousands demonstrated in downtown Detroit, and others carried out direct actions, blocking the vehicles of disconnect crews. Two lawsuits have been filed to halt the water torture. One by the Michigan Welfare Rights Organization, the People's Water Board, the Michigan chapter of the National Action Network, Moratorium Now, and a host of individuals challenges Orr's actions as a violation of residents' constitutional and contractual rights. A class action suit, launched by the NAACP Legal Defense Fund, says the cutoffs are racially motivated. The private companies that have been empowered to act for Detroit's Water and Sewage Department "are basically Caucasian companies," said attorney Alice Jennings. "The folks who are being cut off are almost 100 percent African-American."

And that is, of course, the whole point. The finance capitalists that run this country would like to disenfranchise the entire population so that money could exercise its exclusive "freedom of political speech" and action, unimpeded. In order to generate the least resistance, the model for urban corporate rule must be created in Black America, just as privatization of public education was modeled in the inner cities. White folks won't care, and Black folks don't matter. Certainly, it doesn't matter to President Obama, who has signed off on every element of the siege of Detroit (and has been far more effective than George Bush in privatizing the public schools as well).

Most importantly, finance capital—Wall Street, the people who employ Kevyn Orr and his Jones Day law firm—demands the shrinkage of Black urban populations as a prerequisite for full-scale investment in the cities. Urban assets are devalued by the mere presence of large numbers of Black people, for the simple reason that most white people continue to refuse to share space with African Americans. Therefore, the "chocolate cities" must go, as a condition for urban "renaissance."*

This is a fight against urban Black expulsion and deportation. If there is more than a whiff of the Third Reich in the connotation, it is absolutely appropriate.

July 23, 2014

---

* See "Banksters Demand Black Removal as a Condition of Investment," *Black Agenda Radio*, July 21, 2014.

THE DEMOCRATIC ROAD TO BLACK RUIN

Without overwhelming Black support, especially in the South, Hillary Clinton could not have achieved her insurmountable lead over the Democratic challenger from her left, Bernie Sanders. Although Blacks are the most left-leaning ethnic bloc in the United States—the most pro-peace constituency and the group that most closely resembles Sanders' beloved "Scandinavian Social Democrats" on economic issues—the bulk of Black voters have aligned themselves with the right wing of the Democratic Party, leading corporate pundits and pollsters to categorize Blacks as a "moderate" constituency within the Democratic sector of the duopoly electoral structure. Based on national voting behavior, the "left" side of the Democratic Party spectrum is now dominated by younger whites, who are locked in a struggle with their elders, Blacks and, to a lesser degree, Hispanics for the "soul" of the Party.

Of course, the Democratic Party has no soul; it is a rich man's machinery controlled by Hillary Clinton's patrons on Wall Street—a fact that most Black voters understand quite well. They are fully aware that Clinton is deeply connected to the "fat cats" with the resources to mount a billion-dollar-plus campaign against the Republican/White Man's Party in November. The likelihood that the GOP candidate will be the unapologetically racist Donald Trump lends urgency to their allegiance with Clinton, the cackling war criminal and former "Goldwater girl" who co-championed all of her husband's mass Black incarceration and poor Black family-crushing initiatives the last time they were in the White House.

Black voters knew of these facts when half of them favored Hillary over Barack Obama in 2008, until Obama won the Iowa caucuses and proved that white folks would actually support a Black candidate. The bulk of Black voters clearly do not hold the Clintons' shameless corruption against them in 2016. On the contrary, the Clintons' ties to super-rich *Democrats* are seen as assets in what Black voters perceive as an eternal war with the Republican/White Man's Party and *its* billionaires—one of whom is the GOP's scariest candidate for president.

Members of the Black misleadership class—who are virtually all Democrats, and whose allegiances are to the party structure that enriches them personally, not their Black constituents—insist that Blacks are engaged in "strategic voting." Nothing could be further from the truth. In behaving as the national bulwark of the worst elements of the Democratic Party, Black voters ensure their perpetual marginalization and powerlessness. Such a "strategy" serves only to lock Black people in a quadrennial vortex of fear, in which only two outcomes are possible: either the triumph of the White Man's Party/Republicans or electoral victory for Black people's worst enemies among the Democrats. It wins nothing for Blacks, and amounts to a kind of self-mutilation that strips African Americans of their own politics and makes them electoral fodder for Wall Street and accomplices in U.S. Empire.

Black self-determination—Black people's independent ability to shape their own collective destiny—fits nowhere in the Black misleadership class' political designs. All they seek is "representation" in the Democratic Party and its sponsoring corporations—meaning, appointments and contracts for themselves. Since questions of policy, that is, the future of Black folks, and of the world, are irrelevant to their personal "strategic" positioning within the corridors of power, these misleaders reduce Black politics to a discussion of how African Americans can maximize their usefulness to the Democratic Party through their votes. It really goes no further than that, which is why this self-serving class has never produced a "Black agenda" worthy of the name. Their only concern is to be part of whatever policies are formulated by the real rulers: the Lords of Capital.

Black independent political action, both on the streets and in alternative electoral formations, is anathema to these "representationists," for whom, to paraphrase Frederick Douglass, the Democratic Party "is the ship; all else is the sea." The misleaders have left Black people shipwrecked.

They have acquiesced to the Democratic Party's doctrine that Blacks should be divided among voting districts, so as to spread their dependably Democratic votes to the strategic advantage of the Party, an issue that is right now before the U.S. Supreme Court. They dilute the voting power of their own constituencies, to reduce Blacks to an adjunct of white Democrats, unable to wield local power as a bloc, and insufficient to carry on a meaningful intra-Black debate on the future of their communities. For the Black Democratic operative, discussions of Black Power are anathema. Their organizing principle is: All Power to the Democratic Party.

On the national level, it means all power to the deepest pockets in the Party, the most corporate-connected politicians—like Hillary Clinton. Locally, this "strategy" results in the election of the most conservative, corporate- and white folks-friendly Black politicians. We see the results in city halls across the country, and in the composition of the Congressional Black Caucus. The Democratic Party's policy of diluting the Black vote has produced a bumper crop of Black politicians that enthusiastically collaborate in the gentrification of their cities, replicating the Party's electoral logic through systematic dispersal of African Americans.

The crisis of Black politics is that self-determination has been purged from the discussion, leaving African Americans directionless, confused, and at the mercy of corporate mercenaries in the service of a Democratic Party that is hegemonic in the Black community. In the absence of an independent Black politics, no progress is possible—only defeat, irrelevance, and dispersal at the hands of Democrats or Republicans.

March 23, 2016

THE VALIDITY AND USEFULNESS OF THE TERM "BLACK MISLEADERSHIP CLASS"

In what he called "an afterthought" to his December 21 article on "The Black Political Class and Network Neutrality," *BAR* Managing Editor Bruce Dixon dropped an unexpected bomb. He now has "deep reservations" about use of the term "Black misleadership class" because "it implies that there is or ought to be a class of good and righteous black leaders." The term is "sloppy and imprecise," Dixon writes, adding (I hope) sarcastically: "Maybe the good ones are supposed to be the 'real' blacks and the bad ones unreal. Maybe the difference [is] having or lacking character, table manners, home training or 'real' blackness, or even some kind of black magic."

This is all quite cute but bears no connection to the way the term "Black misleadership class" has been deployed by every one of *BAR*'s editors, including Dixon, since the publication's inaugural issue in October 2006—and by Dixon, Margaret Kimberley, and myself in our previous duties at *The Black Commentator*. It is as if Bruce imagines that he has been in the company of narrow Black cultural nationalists all these years and has finally broken loose from such mysticism. He appears to believe that his colleagues—and, apparently, his former self—have been guided by perceptions of Black leaders' "authentic or inauthentic blackness," rather than their "class allegiance."

It's a broad brush, and inflicted on the wrong people. The language of Black "authenticity" seldom appears in *Black Agenda Report*, and virtually never from the pens of its editors. During Barack Obama's first presidential campaign, his boosters, mainly in the corporate media, claimed that Obama's Black detractors were obsessed with the idea that he lacks "authentic" Blackness. However, *BAR*'s problem with Obama has always been that he is a corporate warmonger—an "authentic" toady for the ruling class. Our critique of Obama has consistently focused on the class that he *serves*. But Bruce seems to remember things differently.

I have so deeply embraced the "Black misleadership class" terminology that I thought I coined it myself. But a thorough Google search of both *BAR* and *The Black Commentator* provides no evidence of my authorship. Instead, the first use of "Black misleadership class" by *anyone* appears in the March 17, 2005 issue of *The Black Commentator*, then under my editorship, in an article by James Warren titled "Thirty-Seven Years of Non-Struggle Misleadership." Warren, who described himself as having "been active in the Black and Labor movement for over 35 years," refers variously to a Black "misleadership class" and "Black mis-leadership" as standing in the way of "our most prized possession . . . the ordinary working class men and women waking up as if from a deep sleep."

The next reference to the term appears in the title of Bruce Dixon's February 9, 2006 piece, "Failure of the Black Misleadership Class." However, "misleadership" does not appear in the rest of the body of the work. Instead Dixon uses the term "black leadership" seventeen times. Three months later on May 11, 2006, Dixon refers to the "black misleadership class" and later "the black business leadership class" in an article titled "The Black Stake in the Internet."

In an article titled "The Black Caucus' Fatal FOX News Embrace" that has disappeared from the archives of *Black Agenda Report* but was picked up by *Common Dreams* on June 6, 2007, Leutisha Stills refers to "the groveling mentality of a Black misleadership class that watches African Americans get their asses kicked every day of the year by Rupert Murdoch and the entirety of corporate media."

I don't show up in Google using the BMC term until October 9, 2010, when I condemn "a misleadership class that sells out the people at every turn" in a video of a speech to the Black Is Back Coalition.

BAR editors Marsha Coleman-Adebayo, Ajamu Baraka, and Margaret Kimberley have all used the term, in articles posted on March 12, 2015, September 14, 2017, and January 18, 2017, respectively. Coleman-Adebayo blasted the "Black mis-leadership class" for orchestrating an elaborate kabuki theatre in the city of Selma, Alabama"; Baraka excoriated the "black mis-leadership class" for fully participating in "the process to deliver the people's resources to the ruling elite"; and Kimberley denounced Atlanta Congressman John Lewis for exemplifying "everything that is wrong with the Congressional Black Caucus, the Democratic Party and the black misleadership class."

Nellie Bailey, an editor and co-host of the weekly *Black Agenda Radio* program, is a consistent user of the term. Indeed, until Bruce Dixon's recantation of December 21, all of *BAR*'s editors cited the sins and crimes of the "Black misleadership class"—with Dixon and me blasting the BMC most often.

Brother Dixon now prefers to substitute "political" for "misleader." He writes that the "black political class" (Dixon does not capitalize "Black"—I do) "happens to be a class to which most of us don't belong." But he is the one guilty of "sloppy" and "imprecise" usage. Bruce and I and the rest of the activist/writers/analysts at *BAR do* belong to the broad Black political class. He is restricting membership in the political classes to elected officials and, presumably, lobbyists, corporate media commentators, and business-friendly civic organization "spokespersons" who carry the rulers' political water. Grassroots political activists are written out of Dixon's definition of "politics," even those who dedicate most of their waking hours to "people's" causes. Most Black preachers and academics (except those the media award the title "public intellectual") would be excluded, too. The bourgeoisie certainly prefer the narrowest definition of political class, restricted to those who speak for Power.

For those of us who don't work for the rulers, "political class" winds up being of little use, much like the term "the chattering classes." We all chatter. The question is: Who is chattering to whom, about what, and in whose interests?

"Black misleadership class" is not a "scientific" term. It is weaponized political terminology, with specific meaning based on Black historical and current political realities. Most often, in our usage at *BAR*, the term refers to those Black political forces that emerged at the end of the '60s, eager to join the corporate and duopoly political (mostly Democrat) ranks, and to sell out the interests of the overwhelmingly working-class Black masses in the process. It is both an actual and aspirational class, which ultimately sees its interests as tied to those of U.S. imperialism and its ruling circles. It seeks representation in the halls of corporate power, and dreads social transformation which would upset the class's carefully cultivated relationships with Power.

We know who these people are, based on their political behaviors. Our job, as conscious "political" people, is to expose their treachery so that the Black masses will reject their "misleadership."

The following is excerpted from my article, "Black Folks are Going Nowhere Until We Discard the Black Misleadership Class:"

> The current Black misleadership class voluntarily joined the enemy camp—calling it "progress"—as soon as the constraints of official apartheid were lifted. They exploited the political and business opportunities made possible by a people's mass movement in order to advance their own selfish agendas and, in the process, made a pact with Power to assist in the debasement and incarceration of millions of their brothers and sisters. In the case of Black elected officials, their culpability is direct and hands-on. The professional "interlocutors" between African Americans and Power, from the local butt-kissing preacher to marquee power-brokers like Al Sharpton, serve as the Mass Black Incarceration State's firemen.

Students of Black history will immediately recognize the role played by these Black "firemen." They are the "house Negroes" that Malcolm X inveighed against, the aspiring or professional "type of Negro" who, when the master's house started burning down, "would fight harder to put the master's house out than the master himself would."* Malcolm struggled on behalf of the "field Negro," the working-class masses. "House Negro" and "field Negro" were not scientific terms; they were political weapons that resonated among the Black masses. They had sharp, cutting edges, designed to rebuke and isolate the internal enemy, and to discourage other Black people from collaborating with the ruling class.

Our mission today is no different.

In 2013, in a speech at Howard University marking the first national conference of Students Against Mass Incarceration, I explained why BAR makes "full use" of the term "Black misleadership class:"

> Some folks might think we mainly use it as an insult. And we DO. We believe that denunciation and shaming of those behaviors and politics that are destructive to our people is a good and useful thing to do. When people who claim to be Black leaders aid in the destruction of our people, they deserve to be insulted—"buked and scorned," as we used to say. So, of course we mean to insult these people that we call the Black misleadership class. . . . They wanted to put their own upwardly mobile faces in high government and corporate places. That meant preserving the system— not tearing it down. They wanted to celebrate their own upward mobility, not agitate for social transformation. So, after 1968, they helped shut the Movement down.
>
> In order to consolidate their own political power, and curry corporate favor, the Black misleadership class directed Black people's energies toward the narrowest electoral politics and the crassest materialism. Their modus operandi is to treat the masses of Black people as cheerleaders for the upward strivings of a few. The ultimate expression of that madness is that the Black misleadership class poured all of its energies into protecting a symbol of ultra-upward Black mobility—Barack Obama—while the bottom fell out for the Black masses.

---

* Malcolm X, Wayne State University, January 23, 1963.

This is the same class that has historically been far more ashamed over Mass Black Incarceration than outraged. They resent those Blacks who have been caught up in the criminal justice system, because they mess up the petty bourgeois picture of Black America that they like to paint. They have no use for the rest of us, except as props in their for-profit productions.

So, damn right, we like to insult the Black misleadership class. It's part of our political work. They need to be insulted. We need a Movement, not just to deal with our external enemies, but also our internal ones. Because they are killing us, from the inside out.

Brother Dixon may be willing to give up a perfectly good weapon, but I am not.

Down with the Black misleadership class! Power to the people!

January 4, 2018

PART IV

DUOPOLY

BOTH MAJOR U.S. PARTIES ARE PLAGUES ON HUMANITY

There has never been a dime's worth of difference between the Clintons (Bill and Hillary) and Barack Obama, and less than ten cents separates the worldviews of these Democratic political twins from the Bush wing of the Republican Party.

Each has their individual quirks. Barack destroys international order and the rule of law while dabbling at song; Bill dismantled the U.S. manufacturing base and threw record numbers of Blacks in prison as he toyed with his trumpet; George W. played the fool who would Shock and Awe the world into obedience; and Hillary is the evil crone that curses the dead while screaming "We are Woman!" But they are all the same in their corporate soullessness.

They all lie for a living, and they live to lie. Hillary Clinton commingled official and personal criminality through the medium of email. Knowing that, in a life dedicated to crime, she could never successfully sequester her private and public conspiracies, Hillary privatized all her email correspondence during her tenure as Obama's secretary of state (in the perfect spirit of neoliberalism). The fate of millions of Haitians whose country's earthquake and development "aid" are under the Clinton family thumb were doubtless bundled into the tens of thousands of messages she erased on leaving Foggy Bottom.

Republicans have harassed her ever since, seeking an electronic smoking gun to show Clinton's cowardice or lack of resolve to "stand up for America" and "our troops" or some other nonsense. What the Benghazi affair proves is that the Obama administration was just as intent as the

Republicans to maintain the fiction that the "rebels" put in power by seven months of NATO bombing of Libya were not various flavors of Islamic jihadists—some of whom were already turning on their erstwhile masters. The U.S.-Saudi project to create and nurture the international jihadist network is a bipartisan venture that dates to Jimmy Carter's presidency—and, therefore, nothing for Democrats and Republicans to fight about. However, the GOP's churning of Clinton's emails does provide a glimpse into her quest to run for president in 2016 as the woman who vanquished Muammar Gaddafi ("Qaddafi" or simply "Q" in Clinton's usage).

A number of Clinton's correspondences were with Sidney Blumenthal, a former Clinton family spin-master who wrote nasty things about Barack Obama while working for Hillary's 2008 presidential campaign, which made it impossible for her to hire him at the State Department. Nevertheless, Clinton needed his talents for hype for the campaign ahead. Their emails in the summer of 2011 discussed how Hillary's status as stateswoman could soar when the Libyan leader was finally eliminated. "This is a historic moment and you will be credited for realizing it," wrote Blumenthal, feeding the crone's huge gizzard of ego, according to an article in Monday's *New York Times*. "You must go on camera," wrote Blumenthal. "You must establish yourself in the historical record at this moment." Hillary was anxious to seize the time to establish what Blumenthal described as "the Clinton Doctrine."

The *Times* piece somehow concludes that Obama stole Clinton's thunder with an 1,100-word speech in late August, declaring: "The Gaddafi regime is coming to an end, and the future of Libya is in the hands of its people." But Hillary best expressed the ghoulishness of America's ruling duopoly two months later in October, when Gaddafi was savagely butchered by screaming jihadists. "We came, we saw, he died," cackled the banshee.

In the annals of global diplomacy, no more vulgar words have been spoken by a major power foreign minister or head of state. Yet, Clinton's calculated quip perfectly encapsulates the bloodlust that is the common characteristic of both the governing duopoly of the United States and their suckling children in ISIS and the other proliferating al-Qaida factions.

Thanks to Seymour Hersh, we now have a much more plausible scenario for the May 2, 2011, demise of Osama bin Laden, the "OG" of the U.S.-Saudi-spawned global jihad, whose body will never be located. Virtually the entire U.S. account of his death is a lie, repeatedly contradicted on its own terms—another layer of fictional Americana in the age of empire in decline.

Clinton was hard-pressed to imagine how she might trump the president's bin Laden deathwatch extravaganza. Her opportunity came five months later, when she delivered her gruesome paraphrase of Julius Caesar on the occasion of Col. Gaddafi's murder. In the context of Washington's deeply racist foreign policy, Gaddafi and bin Laden were equally deserving of death, although Gaddafi was among the most fervent and effective fighters against Islamic jihadists: his government was the first in the world to request a global arrest warrant against bin Laden.

The Libyan Islamists were quickly transferred to the new U.S.-NATO-Saudi-Qatari front lines in Syria. The CIA station in Benghazi was at the center of the action and got burned in the wild and unwieldy process of herding jihadists, who find it difficult to take orders from "infidels," even when the "Crusaders" are paying the bills and supplying the weapons.

The U.S. consulate and CIA station in Benghazi were attacked on September 11, 2012. The next day, the Pentagon's intelligence agency issued a report predicting that a "Salafist principality"—another term for an Islamic State—would likely arise in Syria as a result of the war, and that "Western countries, the Gulf States and Turkey are supporting these efforts." Moreover, the establishment of such an Islamic "principality" would create "the ideal atmosphere for AQI [al-Qaida in Iraq, which became ISIS, ISIL, and the Islamic State] to return to its old pockets in Mosul and Ramadi" in Iraq—events that have since transpired.

The Defense Intelligence Agency report didn't say so, but the "Western Powers" included the United States, through its CIA. The document was declassified this year as the result of a suit by a libertarian right-wing legal outfit. The people of the world continue to be fed the fiction that the U.S. is engaged in a long, twilight struggle against al-Qaida Salafists whose international network was created by, and continues to benefit from, "Western countries, the Gulf States and Turkey."

However, the 2012 Pentagon warning about the rise of an Islamic State may have had some effect on U.S. policy in Syria. One year later, in September 2013, President Obama backed off his threat to bomb Syria in "retaliation" for a chemical missile attack against civilians—a crime much more likely committed by western-backed Salafists. The conventional wisdom is that the Russians tricked a hapless Secretary of State John Kerry into agreeing to the peaceful, internationally supervised destruction of Syria's chemical arsenal; or that the refusal of Britain's Parliament to go along with an air assault on Syria made the U.S. position untenable; or that Obama feared losing a vote on the issue in the U.S. Congress. None of this rings true to me. The United States is not easily deterred by the opinions of Europeans, who in the end accept Washington's acts as a *fait accompli*. And, it was not clear that Obama would have lost the vote in Congress—a vote that he requested, while at the same time declaring that he did not need the legislature's permission to "punish" Syria for crossing his "red line."

I think that high Pentagon officials and elements of the Obama administration—probably including the president himself—took the Benghazi disaster and the Defense Intelligence Agency report to heart and decided that it was better to keep bleeding the Syrians and their Russian, Lebanese, and Iranian allies through a prolonged war than to bomb al-Qaida into power. For the U.S., regional chaos is preferable to the triumph of the, ultimately, unmanageable Salafists—unchained.

The thirty-plus year war against Iran would, however, be ratcheted up. The Bush administration was snatched back from the brink of a military assault against Teheran in 2007 when, to the great consternation of Vice President Dick Cheney, all sixteen U.S. intelligence agencies declared, publicly and unanimously, that Iran had abandoned its nuclear weapons program years before.

The spooks reaffirmed their consensus in the 2010 National Intelligence Estimate—again, that there was no evidence Iran has any intention of making a bomb. The Obama administration has since avoided asking the intelligence agencies for their analysis on the issue, knowing they would get the same answer. Instead, they rely on Israeli propaganda, pick and choose various "experts" from inside and outside the arms control "community," or simply put forward unsupported statements on Iran's capabilities and intentions: the Big Lie. While Bush was humiliated by facts supplied by his own intelligence experts, Obama has escalated the confrontation with Iran, applying crippling sanctions and the whole range of low-level warfare, in close collaboration with Israel—proving, once again, that Obama is the "more effective evil."

Obama has nearly completed knocking off victims on the "hit list" of countries that George Bush was working on when General Wesley Clark ran across it in 2002. Iraq, Syria, Libya, and Somalia have been invaded since then, and Sudan was stripped of a third of its territory. Only Iran and Lebanon remain intact and outside the U.S. imperial umbrella.

The Republican-Democratic duopoly plays tag team in promoting the Project for a New American Century, a doctrine promulgated by neoconservatives in 1997 that has served as the guiding light of both the Bush and Obama administrations. The differences between the two teams are merely rhetorical. The Bush regime is described as "unilateralist," although it employed the same "Coalition of the Willing" approach to aggressive war as does the Obama administration. President Obama claims the right to disregard and methodically undermine international law through "humanitarian" military intervention, whereas Bush claimed to be "spreading democracy." Same weapons systems, same mass murder, same objective: U.S. domination of the planet.

There's nothing democratic or humanitarian about the U.S. imperial project. Therefore, its maintenance requires the deployment of 24/7 psychological operations worldwide, but directed primarily against the U.S. public. Republican strategist Karl Rove was far more honest than his Democratic counterparts when he explained to a reporter, back in 2004: "We're an empire now, and when we act, we create our own reality. And while you're studying that reality—judiciously, as you will—we'll act again, creating other new realities, which you can study too, and that's how things will sort out. We're history's actors . . . and you, all of you, will be left to just study what we do."

Election seasons are reality-creation festivals, during which the two corporate parties pretend to put forward different visions of the national and global destiny. When, in fact, they answer to the same master and must pursue the same general strategy.

The continuity of GOP-Democratic rule—the near-identical depravity—is horrifically evident in the Democratic Republic of Congo, where six million people have been slaughtered by U.S. surrogates since 1996: the largest genocide since World War II. Successive U.S. administrations—Bill Clinton, George W. Bush, and Barack Obama, assisted by Secretary of State Hillary Clinton and Susan Rice, the high U.S. official most deeply implicated in the entirety of the genocide—have armed, financed, and covered up the Congolese holocaust. Each administration has collaborated with its predecessor to hide the crime and obscure the question of guilt—and then to continue the killing.

Decent people do not vote for political parties that produce such fiends, who deserve Nuremburg justice of the capital kind. Any talk of "lesser evils" is both stupid and obscene.

July 1, 2015

VECTOR OF FEAR: BLACKS AND THE DEMOCRATIC PARTY

Bernie Sanders has succeeded in stalling the Clinton juggernaut in Iowa and is expecting a resounding victory next week in New Hampshire. However, the euphoria will fade as his supporters confront the likelihood that their quest to transform the Democratic Party "from below" will be derailed in the South by Blacks, who are the decisive bloc, or outright majorities, in the region's Democratic primaries, and who make up about a quarter of the Party's support nationwide. It is a great paradox that the Sanders campaign will almost certainly be rejected by the very voters whose fundamental political leanings are most closely aligned with the "Scandinavian social democratic" model on which Sanders has based his career.

Black voting behavior over the past two generations all but guarantees they will back the national Democratic candidate they perceive as most likely to defeat the Republicans—the "White Man's Party." White supremacy and the rule of capital in the U.S. are buttressed, electorally, by two pillars: 1) the bifurcation of the major party system into a White Man's Party, whose organizing principle is white supremacy, and another party that is somewhat more inclusive of Blacks and other "minorities," and 2) control of both parties by capital. For Blacks, the Democratic Party is a trap within a trap. If the overarching, perceived necessity is to block the Republican/White Man's Party at every electoral juncture, then Blacks see no option but to huddle under the Democratic tent, despite the fact that it is, like the Republicans, a Rich Man's Party.

It is a politics of fear, born of generations of raw terror at the hands of the White Man's Party. The modern Democratic Party, like the post-Civil War Republican Party, is not a haven, but an enclosure, which Blacks fear to exit. At root, Black participation in the Democratic Party is not a matter of free allegiance, but the perception that there is no other effective means to hold back the barbarians of the White Man's Party.

In practice, it is institutionalized group panic, a stampede every four years. Blacks are drawn into the jaws of the Democratic Party, not by ideological affinity, but *in search of protection from the Republicans.* This is an entirely different dynamic than an alignment based on thoughtful examination of political platforms. It's not about picking a candidate or party that sees the world as most Black people do, from the left side of the spectrum on matters of social justice and peace. Rather, the overarching objective is to choose a candidate from the Democratic wing of the Rich Man's duopoly who is best equipped to defeat his or her Republican counterpart. Under these stilted circumstances, the Democratic candidate's actual political positions become *near irrelevant* to the Black primary voter, compared to the candidate's perceived ability to win a national election. The question becomes, is the Democrat strong enough to beat back the latest offensive from the GOP?—which Black people perceive as an *existential* threat. In the grip of that mindset, the contestant that is richer, better connected to the party apparatus, and more acceptable to masses of white voters is the better Black choice.

When the voter is seeking protection from what is seen as the greater, more racist evil, rather than searching for a candidate and party that takes positions more aligned with the Black political world view, independent politics goes out the window. Indeed, independent, leftist electoral campaigns can be viewed as a going AWOL from the fight, or worse, collaborating with the Republican enemy. Fear turns Black politics on its head. Since Black people are the most left-leaning constituency in the United States, the paradoxical nature of their behavior in national elections renders problematical the whole question of independent Left and Black electoral activity.

VECTOR OF FEAR: BLACKS AND THE DEMOCRATIC PARTY

In 2008, Black voters did not support Dennis Kucinich, a more genuine social democrat and peace candidate than Bernie Sanders, or John Edwards, who kicked off his campaign in New Orleans and positioned himself significantly to the left of the ideological twins Hillary Clinton and Barack Obama. About half of Black Democrats did not favor Barack Obama until he won white favor in Iowa, thus proving to Black voters that he could beat the Republicans. Blacks voted for Jesse Jackson in his 1984 and '88 primary campaigns, but he opted out of an independent run for president, preferring to remain in the role of "power broker" within the Democratic enclosure. It's not likely that Black voters would have supported Jackson in an independent race anyway. When Ted Kennedy challenged Jimmy Carter from the left in 1980, his effort collapsed largely from lack of support from Black elected officials, who stuck with the Georgia peanut farmer even after he had shown himself to be a deeply conservative politician (a founding "neoliberal") whose austerity policies opened the door to Ronald Reagan.

The Black Radical Tradition is real and enduring, but it is not expressed through participation in the Democratic Party. Rather, entrapment in the Democratic Party enclosure (within the larger Rich Man's duopoly) grotesquely warps Black political behavior. This distortion profoundly diminishes the prospects for progressive electoral activity in the United States. More directly, the Black electoral imperative to seek *protection* from the Republican/White Man's Party reduces African Americans to an appendage of the Democratic Party apparatus and, thus, of the capitalists that fund and control the Party. It subverts the essentially progressive nature of the Black polity, objectively enfeebling Black America, even as rich white Democrats pander to Black voters as the "soul" of the party.

It is true that the Democrats would collapse were it not for the Black core of the party. It is also probable that that would be a good thing. What is certain is that the Democratic Party oozes out of every orifice of Black civic society like a stinking pus, sapping the self-determinist vitality of the people and transforming every Black social structure and project into a Democratic Party asset.

73

Black people—massed, organized, and fearless—shook this nation to its bones in the 1960s, before the Democratic Party achieved political hegemony in Black America, when there were less than two handfuls of Black congressional representatives and only some hundreds of Black Democratic officeholders to hold us back. Today, Democratic operatives attempt to smother the incipient Black grassroots movement in their lethal embrace—and some elements of that movement have eagerly hugged them back. The task of Black activists and their allies is to ensure that our first and last hope—movement politics—once again becomes central to the struggle, so that we can, as Dr. Cornel West puts it, "break the back of fear." This will require the most intense internal struggle among Black Americans to break the chains that bind us to that vector of fear, the Democratic Party.

February 3, 2016

THROW OFF THE DEAD WEIGHT OF THE DEMOCRATIC PARTY

This is a slightly edited version of remarks I delivered at a "Presidential Elections and the Key Issues of Our Time" debate held at the Unitarian Universalist Church in San Francisco on February 6. The event was sponsored by the Socialist Action Party, the Green Party of Alameda County, the San Francisco Peace and Freedom Party, Bay Area Solidarity, and the San Francisco Progressive Democrats of America.

Power to the People!

The Bernie Sanders people are, naturally, quite excited by polls that say their candidate has drawn virtually even with Hillary Clinton among national Democrats. Some folks might think that we at Black Agenda Report might be upset with those numbers, since our managing editor, Bruce Dixon, has said that Bernie is a "sheep dog" for Hillary.

But the truth is, it's a good thing that Sanders is doing well in the polls. It's a measure of public sentiment against corporations and Wall Street among Democrats. We should all welcome such expressions of public sentiment. The problem is, the Democratic Party is not a vehicle that is capable of actually challenging Wall Street.

It is said that Wall Street is to the Democrats what Big Energy is to the Republicans: their Sugar Daddy. And that is accurate. It's why Barack Obama's 2008 race was the first billion-dollar presidential campaign. That situation will not, and cannot change, even if Sanders continues to rely on

$27 individual donations in the primaries. He will still be sheep-dogging for the Democrats.

I said last night in Oakland that the best result that can occur from the Sanders campaign would be that it leads to a split in the Democratic Party, somewhat like the split that occurred in the old Whig Party, over slavery, in the years before the Civil War. That split led to the birth of a new, anti-slavery Republican Party, the demise of the Whig Party, and ultimately, to Black Emancipation.

I would love to see such a split in the Democratic Party, leading to the end of the rich man's duopoly system and the creation of a new, broadly based, anti-Wall Street and anti-imperialist party—and/or the blossoming of other left-wing parties. This would be an historical continuity of the Occupy Movement that succeeded in popularizing the slogan of the 1 percent versus the 99 percent, which laid the basis for the mass public sentiment that is expressed, to some degree, in Bernie's poll numbers.

There is also a lot of talk about how Bernie has succeeded in "moving Hillary to the Left." That's ridiculous. The Sanders campaign has only succeeded in forcing Hillary to tell the biggest lies of her non-stop lying career. In any case, Clinton and the rest of her ilk will continue to lie about their plans for governance, because they serve the rich people that control the Republican-Democratic duopoly.

Let's go back to Bernie's poll numbers. These polls that show Sanders drawing even with Clinton nationally do not show the racial breakdown. Increasingly, pollsters don't break down the numbers by race, or they lump all "minorities" together—which is almost as bad.

But, from what we do know, Blacks are the least likely ethnic constituency to vote for Bernie. This is historically consistent with Black voting behavior in national Democratic primary elections and presents a great paradox and contradiction that goes to the heart of the Black political crisis. Black people are the most left-leaning group in the United States, on issues of war and peace, and social justice. This fact is affirmed by every poll on peace and economic issues over generations, and most dramatically, it is affirmed by Black grassroots movement behavior—when such movements exist.

In terms of pro-union sentiment, at the top of the list is Black women, followed by Black men, then Hispanic women, followed by Hispanic men, then white women and, at the bottom of the list, white men. This too has been the case for generations. The Black Radical Tradition not only exists, it is measurable in the present day—EXCEPT on national primary election days in the Democratic Party. Which is why the Bernie Sanders campaign is all but certain to be derailed by Black voters Down South, where Blacks are majorities of the Democratic electorate in a number of states and the decisive bloc in many others.

This, despite the fact that Blacks most resemble the Scandinavian Social Democrats that Bernie Sanders sees as his model. The noted Black social demographer Michael Dawson's studies have shown that the biggest bloc of Black voters are most like Swedish Social Democrats, and that a very large number of them are "more radical than that."

However, in national primary elections, these Black Social Democrats— these pro-peace, pro-social justice, pro-union folks,—fail to express their own political sentiments at the polls. That's why the corporate media often list Blacks among the so-called "moderate" voters, as opposed to "liberal," even though most Blacks are to the left of liberal.

My own studies have found that Blacks who describe themselves as "moderate" or even "conservative" are, in fact, to the left of whites who call themselves "liberal" on core issues of war and peace and economic justice. That's because the whole U.S. Black political spectrum is to the left of the white political spectrum. There are, in fact, two separate spectrums, and the self-defining labels do not match.

However, Black national voting behavior is inconsistent with Black ideological characteristics. Indeed, Black voting behavior often betrays Black people's politics. The reason lies in what Blacks perceive as the purpose for voting in national elections, and how they view the Democratic Party.

THE BLACK AGENDA

The nature of the American duopoly system is that one of the parties will always be the White Man's Party, with white supremacy as its organizing principle. In this era, it's the Republicans. In a past era, it was the Democrats. Both parties are of course Rich Man's Parties.

Throughout U.S. history, Blacks have sought protection from the White Man's Party in the bosom of the other party, the one that is more inclusive of minorities. They want the party that opposes the White Man's Party to pick the strongest possible candidate. The question of whether that candidate actually agrees with them, ideologically, becomes secondary or even irrelevant. Blacks will vote against their own politics, in order to pick a winner.

Huge numbers will even vote against their own race, all things being equal, to pick what they believe is the strongest candidate against the Republicans—the White Man's Party. Which is why half of Black voters, and most Black elected officials, refused to support Barack Obama against his ideological twin Hillary Clinton until after the Iowa primary in 2008. Only after Obama won in a white state did Blacks abandon Hillary Clinton, wholesale.

Blacks are deeply anti-war, but they are quite willing to vote for Democratic warmongers. They may ideologically resemble Scandinavian Swedish Social Democrats, but they don't vote that way in national elections. Blacks are the most redistributionist constituency in the country, but they rejected Dennis Kucinich, a genuine social democrat, and John Edwards, who kicked off his campaign in New Orleans and pitched it directly to Blacks in 2008. Instead, they rallied around the two corporatists, Clinton and Obama, as the antidote to the White Man's Party.

Is there something wrong with African Americans? No, there is something wrong with America, its history and its race and class dynamics. There is something wrong about this two-party system, where both parties are Rich Man's Parties, and one of the parties is always the White Man's Party. The duopoly system traps Blacks in the Democratic Party and keeps them there on the premise that only Democrats can beat the White Man's GOP.

The numbers in 2016 show Black voters are operating under the same dynamic. They know Sanders is to the left of Clinton, but their priority is victory for the Democratic Party, and they are willing to sacrifice their own politics in its cause. This is the acute contradiction.

The Democratic Party is hegemonic in Black America. I'm not just talking about the fact that Black elected officials are overwhelmingly Democratic. The mainline Black civic organizations—the NAACP, the Urban League, and the rest—are annexes of the Democratic Party. So are most Black churches. The party's tentacles even reach down to the Black sororities and fraternities. And now, with the emergence of an incipient grassroots movement for the first time in two generations, the Democratic Party has moved quickly to absorb and render it harmless to the Rule of the Rich.

That's to be expected. What is worse, is that elements of the new movement appear eager to embrace the Democrats back. One leader of a faction of what is called the Black Lives Matter movement is running for mayor of Baltimore—as a Democrat, of course.

DeRay Mckesson's Campaign Zero met twice with Hillary Clinton and failed to make anything that could be called a substantial demand. He is also a fanatical proponent of charterization of the public schools. His candidacy is getting more play in the corporate media than all of the other City Hall hopefuls in Baltimore.

Democratic Party politics kills Black politics. The two cannot coexist. If you want a real Black grassroots movement, you have to fight the Democratic Party, tooth and claw.

Bernie Sanders' supporters think they can transform the Democratic Party "from below." They are wrong.

Black people ARE the "below" in America, and we make up a quarter of the Democratic Party. But Blacks haven't transformed the Democratic Party by our overwhelming presence. Instead, the Party has transformed us—and overwhelmed our radical politics.

The solution is to throw off the dead weight of that party.

Bernie Sanders, the Democrat, does not represent some kind of turning point in history, although his supporters seem to think so. The turning point in history comes with masses of people in the streets, fighting BOTH Rich Man's Parties.

Power to the People!

February 11, 2016

HILLARY STUFFS ENTIRE U.S. RULING CLASS INTO HER BIG, NASTY TENT

Hillary Clinton is celebrating in the bloated expanse of the "Big Tent" Democratic Party she and Bill have dreamed of building since their days in the backwaters of Arkansas. Slick Willie and his wife have succeeded in assembling under one party roof nearly the whole of the U.S. ruling class and their hordes of attendants and goons. The scam that undergirded the duopoly system that has served the Lords of Capital so well for so long has come undone. Thanks to a white nationalist billionaire who was too spoiled to play by the corporate rules, the two parties of the ruling class have become one.

It's a funky place to be, especially for the traditional Black, brown, and labor "base" of the party, now squished into a remote and malodorous corner of the tent, near the latrine, clutching the pages of a party platform that was never meant to bind anyone. These Democratic stalwarts appear intoxicated, high on the idea that they are part of a united front against the "fascist" Donald Trump and his imaginary storm troopers. The brass sound of martial music is heard, far off in the catered center of the tent. The generals have arrived, barking strategies to make Syria safe for "our" jihadists, re-bomb Libya, re-re-re-bomb Afghanistan, Pakistan, and Somalia, and teach Russia and China the full meaning of geopolitical strangulation. Hillary's cackle rings out above the bombast. She is pleased with her uniformed recruits.

Wall Street is also in the house, too big to jail and definitely too fat for this tent. Michael Bloomberg, the seventh-richest man in the country; Warren Buffet, who could buy and sell Bloomberg; and lesser plutocrats Meg Whitman and Mark Cuban are part of Clinton's "bipartisan cadre of billionaires." Billionaires are by nature bipartisan since they have no loyalties to country or party—only to their class. They are in Hillary's Big Tent to trash one of their own, Trump, who has betrayed his class by raging against the free flow of money and jobs across borders, a heresy of the first order that is at the heart of Capital's flight from the GOP this year. Clinton claims she opposes the Trans-Pacific Partnership corporate trade deal, but only the fools squeezed into the corner near the latrine feel compelled to believe her. The Democratic Party platform they clutch so tightly says the opposite.

Spooks and goons infest the tent, like lice. Many "national security" operatives like to describe themselves as "non-partisan," claiming they cause mass death and chaos for God and country, not party. Such a spook is Michael Morell, a former acting CIA director who gained entrance to Hillary's Big Tent after penning a *New York Times* article charging Donald Trump with "endorsing Russian espionage against the United States, supporting Russia's annexation of Crimea and giving a green light to a possible Russian invasion of the Baltic States." Trump, said Morell, is "an unwitting agent of the Russian Federation." This is Morell's first outing as a Democrat, but he fits right in with the weird, new ambiance in Hillary's Big Tent, a place where the supposedly center-left party goes McCarthyite on the *Republican* candidate—a historical role reversal.

The Big Tent nearly burst at its seams when fifty self-described senior Republican national security officials flashed their invitations and surged into the Queen of Chaos's VIP section. "None of us will vote for Donald Trump," said a letter brandished by the assorted assassins, mass murderers, and imperial predators, including former CIA and NSA director Michael Hayden, regime-change specialist John Negroponte, former deputy secretary of state and World Bank president Robert Zoellick, former secretaries of Homeland Security Tom Ridge and Michael Chertoff, and Eric Edelman, former national security advisor to Vice President Dick Cheney.

Robert Blackwell, a former aide to Henry Kissinger, endorsed Clinton, encouraging speculation that the Master of Destruction himself—the (onetime) Most-Wanted War Criminal in the World—would drag his evil carcass into Hillary's tent. Kissinger is a dear friend of Bill and Hill, if we can believe that real friendships exist among such creatures. According to *Politico*, "a person close to Clinton" has sent out feelers to GOP foreign policy big shots Condoleezza Rice, James Baker, and George Shultz as well, which would make Hillary's tent a true place of Resident Evil.

Those fat cats that want to avoid the crush of the crowd at Hillary's tent can simply send her the money they usually give to the GOP, which is apparently what donors to this year's non-Trump Republican presidential candidates are doing. Contributors to the Jeb Bush, John Kasich, Lindsey Graham, and Chris Christie campaigns are more likely to send another check to Hillary Clinton than to Donald Trump.

Lesson: Clinton has inherited the Republican money base, which means she is the candidate of the "bipartisan" moneyed classes, period.

She is the candidate of the imperial war machine, whose operatives have flocked to her corner in dread of Trump's willingness to make "deals" with the Russians and Chinese. She is the candidate of multinational corporations, which are perfectly confident she is lying about her stance on TPP and other trade deals. And she is the candidate of the CIA and its fellow global outlaws, who will thrive as never before with a president in the White House who laughs while saying "We came, we saw, he died" when the leader of an African country is murdered by Islamic jihadists supported by the United States.

The pestilence raging in Hillary's Big Tent will inevitably lead to the death of millions, especially in Africa, and possibly of life on Earth. The demons swarming in her entourage are real, proven evils—as is she. On foreign policy, Trump's stated positions are far less aggressive, yet, the "doomsday" scenario is successfully spun around his candidacy, not hers. This is partly because Trump's raging and racist white American nationalism makes him seem like the "type" that would nuke on impulse, despite his rather consistent calls for less confrontation in the world— and even as Clinton promises to engage in new heights of provocation. However, the main reason the smell of Armageddon clings to Trump's candidacy is that the corporate news media, as a sector, has coalesced behind Clinton (whose husband multiplied corporate media wealth with the Telecommunications Act of 1996). They, too, have squeezed into the Big Tent.

The whole damn ruling class is now ensconced in the Democratic Party, the most dramatic effect of the breakdown of the duopoly system set off by Donald Trump's white nationalist, anti-"free" trade revolt in the Republican ranks. I predict the Clinton ticket will outspend Trump by five to one, by far the widest margin in modern U.S. election history—that is, since the dawn of the television age. However, Trump's historic defeat will not demobilize the 30 percent or so of the white population that makes up his core support: the angry white nationalists. They will find political expression, either through continued dominance of the Republican Party, or in alternative venues.

It is the Left that has yet to find its footing.

It will take time, and a great deal of work, for the other shoe to fall— for a viable social democratic electoral alternative to arise to pull Blacks, browns, and white progressives out of Hillary's Big Tent, and for an independent Black politics to reassert itself. Getting the Greens a secure place on the ballot, with 5 percent of the vote in November, is just a start. The real work of the next four years is in the streets, with social movements that sharpen the issues and illuminate the contradictions of capitalist rule in a white supremacist, imperial America. This struggle must incorporate a fierce discussion on the meaning of "fascism," possibly the most misused term in the U.S. political vocabulary.

Fascists fly drones over other people's countries. At home, they wear blue. The most dangerous ones are hanging out in Hillary's Big Tent.

August 10, 2016

CLINTON'S BASKET OF "DEPLORABLES"

Speaking to a room full of rich contributors, Hillary Clinton dumped half of Donald Trump's supporters into a "basket of deplorables . . . racist, sexist, homophobic, xenophobic, Islamaphobic—you name it." Actually, considerably *more* than half of Trump's legions match up with most or all of those terms, which is why the Republicans have been the White Man's Party since the '60s, replacing the Demo-Dixiecrats. With white supremacy as their organizing principle, Republicans have won white majorities in every national election since 1968. Clinton's husband Slick Willie teamed with Al Gore and other white southern Democrats to form the Democratic Leadership Council in the 1980s to stem the attrition of whites to the Republicans by mimicking the GOP on racially coded issues like welfare and crime. The former Arkansas governor reckoned he could win the White House in 1992 at the expense of Black people, who are trapped by the very nature of the duopoly system in the Democratic Party.

Bill Clinton appealed to the racist and sexist elements of his constituency and rewarded his corporate backers by ejecting millions of disproportionately Black women and children from the social safety net, unleashing the greatest surge of mass Black incarceration in modern history. His wife and fellow lawyer, acting as co-president, raged against young Black "super-predators" that needed to be "brought to heel"—words she has recently been forced to regret, but not "deplore." The Clinton's destruction of Aid to Families with Dependent Children caused welfare rights advocate Peter Edelman to resign his subcabinet post and prompted his wife, Marian Wright Edelman, founder of the Children's Defense Fund, to describe the Clintons as "not friends in politics." Yet, Hillary Clinton continues to feature her youthful stint as a lawyer for the Children's Defense Fund as proof of her compassion for poor Black children, while the Black misleadership class pretends to have no memory of the '90s and their own complicity in the Clintons' "deplorable" racism and sexism.

Hillary Clinton spares half of Trump's supporters the shame of reduction to deplorabledom in recognition that some "basket people" feel left out by government and the economy and are "just desperate for change." However, as the candidate of the corporate status quo, Clinton offers nothing but more of the same and must therefore—just like Trump—run a campaign of name-calling and demonization not witnessed since the McCarthy era. Having definitively turned their party to the right a generation ago, the Clintons now see an opportunity to use Donald Trump's destruction of the Republican Party as we knew it to forge a unitary corporate super-party encompassing all the Democrats' base constituencies, Democrat-friendly Wall Street and Silicon Valley plutocrats, plus those oligarchs and "national security" and "defense" circles that have traditionally been linked to the GOP. Only the rump of Trump "deplorables" would be left outside the "Big Tent," along with a small and disorganized Left. That's the plan.

The lines that Hillary draws around her Big Tent are rhetorical, not substantive, since she has nothing of substance to offer to any mass constituency. The duopoly system is in terminal crisis because capitalism is no longer capable of "reform": All is crisis and chaos under the reign of hegemonic finance capital, whose captains create nothing while monetizing everything. These are the Lords of Capital that have sustained the once-and-future First Couple with $153 million in speaking fees to keep the mansion lights burning in the interim between their tours in the White House. The Clinton Foundation is a creature of Slick Willie & Wife's ongoing contract with the international ruling class.

Hillary's global mission, like Barack Obama's, is to crush the old order of sovereign nation states regulated by international law, and impose a U.S.-enforced corporate dominion over the planet. In that sense, the

Trans-Pacific Partnership and its trans-Atlantic counterpart flow from the same source as drone warfare, "humanitarian" regime-change warfare, and jihadist proxy warfare, and are inseparable from economic sanctions warfare and the emerging battlefield of cyberwar.

In terms of deplorability, nothing else comes close. Hillary's mission, as the public agent of multinational capital, is the triumph of capitalist Manifest Destiny—a global nightmare that is antithetical to any vision of democracy held by any of the world's peoples. Therefore, the mission is relentlessly pursued, but never articulated. Instead, defamation becomes the language of U.S. foreign policy. Russian President Vladimir Putin becomes "Hitler" in Hillary's mouth—an effective declaration of war or intent to assassinate. When Muammar Gaddafi was murdered by U.S.-backed jihadists in Libya, Hillary cackled, "We came, we saw, he died"—an execration beyond deplorable by any diplomatic or civilized standard.

Last week, she met with a "bipartisan" group of "national security leaders"—translation: imperial warmongers that serve both parties—to call attention to the fact that most of the spooks, warmongers, and global destabilizers are in her Big Tent. She immediately read Trump, who (sometimes, but not always) opposes "regime change," out of the foreign policy consensus: "National security experts on both sides of the aisle are chilled by what they're hearing from the Republican nominee," she said.

Among the "leaders" in the room was David Petraeus, the retired general who advocates the U.S. openly arm the jihadists of al-Nusra, the al-Qaida affiliate in Syria (until they changed their name, with al-Qaida's blessing), supposedly to fight ISIS. Clinton does not find this one bit "deplorable." She deserves a "basket" all her own, labeled "unspeakable" toxic entity.

September 14, 2016

FASCISM WITH A DEMOCRATIC PARTY FACE

If anyone thought that *BAR* was being shrill when we said that a late-stage capitalist variety of fascism was brewing in Hillary Clinton's Big Tent, the "fake news" offensive proves our point. On the heels of President Obama's outburst on his farewell tour of Germany, where he twice whined about the dangers of well-packaged "misinformation" on the internet, the Democrat-friendly *Washington Post* conveyed legitimacy to the propagators of a list of two hundred web sites designated as "Russian propaganda outlets and sympathizers"—including *Black Agenda Report*, the only Black outlet to make the cut.

Although totally devoid of substance, the *Post* article was no overnight wonder, but a methodically crafted facsimile of investigative reporting that was no doubt produced on orders from the paper's top management, if not its owner, Amazon mogul Jeff Bezos. Bylined reporter Craig Timberg refused to name the people behind his principal "source," the website *Is It Propaganda or Not*, in order to avoid their "being targeted by Russia's legions of skilled hackers"—a new twist on journalistic ethics that no real editor would abide. This piece was boss sanctioned.

PropOrNot seems to have arrived out of nowhere a few months ago. Its anonymous spokesperson, when contacted by *The Intercept*'s Glenn Greenwald and Ben Norton, claimed to oversee "over 30 people, organized into teams," but said, "We cannot confirm or deny anyone's involvement."

The other "team of experts" cited by the *Post* operate out of the Foreign Policy Research Institute. The FPRI was founded in the 1950s by a now-deceased Austrian-born right-winger named Robert Strausz-Hupé and has been searching for Russians in every dark corner ever since. FPRI Fellow Clint Watts could offer nothing juicy for the *Post* article except that the Russians "want to essentially erode faith in the U.S. government or U.S. government interests." Watts co-authored an article on a site called *War on the Rocks* titled "Trolling for Trump: How Russia is Trying to Destroy Our Democracy." He writes:

> Russia is helping Trump's campaign, yes, but it is not doing so solely or even necessarily with the goal of placing him in the Oval Office. Rather, these efforts seek to produce a divided electorate and a president with no clear mandate to govern. The ultimate objective is to diminish and tarnish American democracy. Unfortunately, that effort is going very well indeed.

From the FPRI's standpoint, it is immaterial whether Russia was trying to affect the outcome of the election (something the U.S. routinely does in countries around the world, including this month in Germany, where Obama said he'd vote for President Merkel if he could). Anything that tends to "diminish and tarnish American democracy" serves the Russians, or so the reasoning goes. Facts that reflect badly on the U.S. political and economic system are, therefore, subversive. The very word "imperialism" is a crime of some kind.

The amateurs at *PropOrNot* are even cruder. The sites on its list were put there for "behavioral" reasons, says their anonymous Führer. Thus,

> In an important sense it does not matter whether they are being knowingly directed and paid by Russian intelligence officers (although some of them undoubtedly are), or whether they even knew they were echoing Russian propaganda before being called out: If they continue to do so, for whatever reasons, their willingness to uncritically echo Russian propaganda makes them a tool of the Russian state. The term "useful idiot" often applies, and calling them out is justified, appropriate, and valuable.

The object, however, is not just to "call out" the listed sites, but to prosecute and suppress them, since they may "have violated the Espionage Act, the Foreign Agent Registration Act, and other related laws."

Clearly, there *is* a conspiracy afoot, involving the outgoing president, the woman he hoped would succeed him, the Democratic Party apparatus they lead, and the corporate media and national security establishment that came together in Hillary Clinton's Big Tent after Donald Trump wrecked the Republican side of the corporate electoral duopoly. Trump's campaign positions against the free outward flow of capital and jobs, via NAFTA and TPP-type corporate rights deals, and his stated reluctance to pursue "regime change" against states that "kill ISIS" caused panic among his brethren in the ruling class. They had lost control of the political narrative, and feared that a heretic might take over the State.

Had Clinton won the election, she would have begun a campaign of repression against the Left along the same national security lines as the *Washington Post* article, with that paper probably leading the propaganda charge. The Obama administration and *Post* owner Bezos are quite tight, politically. Back in 2013, when Obama was still trying to reach a "grand bargain" with the Republicans in Congress, he proposed lower corporate tax rates as a way to spur economic growth and showcased the Amazon distribution center in Chattanooga, Tennessee as a model—despite the deplorable working conditions, low pay (less than $12 an hour, to start), and heavy use of part-time and contract workers at the plant. His White House economist Gene Sperling told the press, "We should be looking for other avenues of progress, other 'grand bargains' that can be for middle class job growth." Bezos closed the deal on *the Washington Post* the same year. His paper is clearly the go-to media for the Democrats' brand of fascism, which is crazily cloaked as an *anti*-fascist crusade.

The term "fascist" is bandied about today more than at any time since 1969, but there is little discussion of what fascism actually looks like in the twenty-first century. The truth is, it looks like Democrats *and* Republicans; it operates through the duopoly, the political apparatus of the ruling class. Donald Trump's fascism is largely the residue of the fascism of apartheid

America, under Jim Crow, which had many of the characteristics of—and in some ways presaged—the "classic" fascism of pre-World War II Europe. The establishment corporate Democratic and Republican brand of fascism is far more racially, sexually, and culturally inclusive, but just as ruthless. And, at this moment in history, the corporate Democratic fascists are the more aggressively warlike brand.

These fascists also fight each other, sometimes viciously—as we are now witnessing. But they mesh and overlap more than they differ. Donald Trump rants about taking away people's citizenship for burning the flag, but Hillary Clinton introduced her own flag-burning measure when she was a senator. And Trump could become a regime-change fanatic in an instant. It's all part of the menu in the late-stage capitalist duopoly.

As *BAR* editor and senior columnist Margaret Kimberley wrote in her article, "Who's the Fascist?":

> In just the last 40 years American presidents or their allied partners in crime have killed people in Iraq, Iran, Afghanistan, Pakistan, Congo, Somalia, Haiti, Grenada, Gaza, Kosovo, Serbia, Sudan, Syria, Libya and Yemen. What do they have to do to be called fascists? Showing bad manners seems to be the only thing that sets off expressions of outrage among Americans.

The Democrat-Fascists are most concerned with maintaining their endless wars for global domination. Therefore, their hit list is heavy with anti-war folks, mostly right-wingers who dance to Trump's "America First" tune. The leftist sites on the Democrats' hit list are:

opednews.com
paulcraigroberts.org
consortiumnews.com
counterpunch.org
globalresearch.ca
truth-out.org
greanvillepost.com
truthdig.com

informationclearinghouse.info
voltairenet.org/en
moonofalabama.org
nakedcapitalism.com
zerohedge.com

November 30, 2016

FACEBOOK IS NOT YOUR FRIEND

Facebook has declared war on political dissent. In a rash of purges last week, the behemoth corporation banned thirty pages, with a total of twenty-two million fans, on the grounds that the accounts were "created to stir up political debate in the US, the Middle East, Russia and the UK." At the top of the list were the anti-police lawlessness pages *Cop Block*, *Filming Cops*, *The Free Thought Project* and *Police the Police*, with a combined audience of 8.1 million. The other banned pages range across the non-establishment spectrum, from the reactionary *Right Wing News*, to *Punk Rock Libertarians,* and the pro-marijuana page, *Hemp*.

These pages are "inauthentic," Facebook claims, because they "use sensational political content" to "drive traffic to their websites." Of course, the *New York Times,* the *Washington Post,* and virtually every other organ of corporate media also maintain Facebook pages that are designed to "drive traffic to their websites." The daily content of these imperial propagandists is filled with "sensational" stories that are designed to inflame the public, laying the groundwork for endless wars—most often on evidence that turns out to be fictitious. Yet Facebook has enlisted as "fact-checkers" the same corporate media that vouched for the presence of weapons of mass destruction in Iraq, spread lies about Viagra-fueled mass rape by Muammar Gaddafi's soldiers in Libya, and continue to mask the U.S. alliance with al-Qaida fighters in Syria. These same corporate "news" organs have treated allegations of Russian collusion with Trump during the 2016 elections as fact—without a shred of evidence—in order to whip up a new Cold War.

Polls have long showed that the U.S. public—of all racial and political shades—no longer believes the corporate media version of reality, which almost routinely turns out to be false, and which Black people have always known to be false. This crisis of legitimacy for the ruling class and its media organs became acute in 2016, when the wildly unpredictable Donald Trump seemed to threaten the gentlemen's agreement between the two corporate parties on regime change warfare and so-called free trade. Barely a week after Trump's surprise victory at the polls, outgoing President Barack Obama, on a visit with German Chancellor Angela Merkel, called for the imposition of a standardized version of truth.

"Because in an age where there's so much active misinformation and it's packaged very well and it looks the same when you see it on a Facebook page or you turn on your television," said Obama. "If everything seems to be the same and no distinctions are made, then we won't know what to protect." Or, as he put it later in an interview with David Letterman: "One of the biggest challenges that we have to our democracy is the degree to which we do not share a common baseline of facts."

Obama was calling for censorship of the internet, and for corporate media to reassert its ideological supremacy in defense of the ruling order. The "danger" was not to democracy, but to the legitimacy of the corporate rule.

A week after Obama's remarks in Germany, the *Washington Post* published the first salvo in the censorship offensive, with an article titled, "Russian propaganda effort helped spread 'fake news' during election, experts say." The "experts" were anonymous members of the shadowy organization *PropOrNot*, whose identities the *Post* insisted on concealing. The *PropOrNot* list slandered two hundred websites, including many of the best left-wing addresses on the web, as "witting or unwitting" dupes of Russia. *Black Agenda Report* had the distinction of being the only Black-owned site on the list.

Facebook was dragooned into the censorship frenzy under relentless pressure from Democrats in Congress, who dutifully embraced the role of chief warmongers when Trump started making noises about improving relations with the Russians. Fully two-thirds of Americans are active monthly Facebook users who assumed that the service's constant invitations to share what's on their minds included political thought. Not anymore. Mark Zuckerberg's behemoth, that began as a student social networking service at Harvard fourteen years ago, is now valued conservatively at $140 billion and claims to reach 2.23 billion monthly active worldwide users, 214 million in the United States. Facebook is indispensable to maintaining the global corporate monopoly on truth—as is Google, another mega-monopoly of the internet. Both have joined the censorship project in defense of empire in decline.

An internal Google document assessed that: "In response to public outcries about the accessibility of unsavory and harmful content, tech firms have been adjusting their software to make it harder to stumble upon it." The firm was talking about itself, and the "public" it is responding to is actually the capitalist ruling class, seeking to regain legitimacy through censorship. Google has rigged its algorithms to hide blacklisted sites during web searches, resulting in decreased visitation of up to 75 percent. They are strangling the Left, including *Black Agenda Report*.

Facebook has signed on to the new Cold War, under the ruse of protecting U.S. elections from Russian interference. "We're excited to launch a new partnership with the Atlantic Council, which has a stellar reputation looking at innovative solutions to hard problems." In the real world, the Council is the global public relations and think tank resource for NATO, the U.S.-led military alliance, funded by the whole constellation of war industries. Facebook has outsourced its censorship project to the Deep State.

Clearly, the Revolution will not be "friended" by such people. Some Black folks may celebrate Facebook's purges, glad that white supremacist Trump boosters and other overt racists are among the targets. But majorities of white people in the U.S. supported Trump, and there is no possibility that Facebook or any other corporation could effectively police—or even recognize—the racism of most of their users. But they do silence the cop-watchers. What Facebook is attempting to enforce is the absolute authority of the corporate media as the arbiter of Truth—a dictatorship of the white moneyed classes. And that can never be in Black folks' interest.

October 17, 2018

PART V

OBAMA

THE GREAT BLACK HAJJ OF 2009

They were pilgrims, one million African Americans bent on fulfilling a solemn, silly, tearful, giddy, deep-felt, mindless, gottabethere obligation. They were the faithful, the heretics, the high priests and lowlifes, the innocent and the guilty-as-sin. All were committed to a once (or, at least, first) in a lifetime trek to Washington to bear witness to The Biggest Black Event in History, as so it must have been, based on the numbers. And oh yes, there were white folks there too, about an additional million. Let it be recorded that all ethnicities were welcomed at the great Black Hajj of 2009.

Obama, the one-word incantation—Oh-Bah-Mah!—would not be denied. The sea of humanity lapped at his feet, as the mountain had come to Muhammad.

The Black multitudes waited to be told who they were, and why they were there. They learned that "Our economy is badly weakened, a consequence of greed and irresponsibility on the part of some, but also our collective failure to make hard choices and prepare the nation for a new age." They cheered in acknowledgement of their shared culpability in the "collective failure" that had destroyed the global financial system, the workings of which were beyond their capacity to comprehend, much less influence. Yet, they must be guilty of something. Obama said so.

He informed his followers that "Homes have been lost, jobs shed, businesses shuttered." This they already knew, many through painful, personal experience. What is to be done? Well, "in the words of Scripture," Obama proclaimed, "the time has come to set aside childish things." Things like boorishly interrupting the nation's business (now Obama's business) with complaints about particular African American grievances such as chronically high jobless rates, neglected schools, gross criminal injustice, housing segregation. Citing the litany is bad form—damn near un-American, Obama seemed to indicate.

He pressed the point. "On this day, we come to proclaim an end to the petty grievances and false promises, the recriminations and worn-out dogmas that for far too long have strangled our politics." Who was Obama talking about? In hindsight, possibly Obama was referring to those whom he knew would in less than a week be complaining that he had delayed congressional action on "universal" health care, dashed the hopes of besieged homeowners in need of a law that would allow judges to adjust their mortgages, abandoned the Gulf Coast Civic Action bill to create one hundred thousand jobs and affordable housing for Katrina-ravaged Americans, and put organized labor's Employee Free Choice Act on the back burner. Yes, that would be cause for "recriminations" and deployment of "worn-out dogmas" regarding the people's rights to health care, housing, jobs, and dignity.

Obama, object of the Great Hajj, personification of Black Mecca, continued: "Our capacity remains undiminished. But our time of standing pat, of protecting narrow interests and putting off unpleasant decisions— that time has surely passed." Even far out near the Washington Monument, pilgrims understood that Obama was preparing to lower the boom on some undeserving, "narrow interests" that had malingered on the public dole for too long. What they may not have noticed in preparing to join the Hajj—at considerable sacrifice, for some—was that two weeks before, Obama had revealed the "unpleasant decisions" he was contemplating. Social Security and Medicare were "a central part" of his planned overhaul of federal spending.

Those who thought the battle of Social Security had been fought, and won, back in George W. Bush's first term, were mistaken. This time, Obama the Democrat is putting "entitlements" on the chopping block, on his own initiative. Few on the Mall understood his meaning. No

THE GREAT BLACK HAJJ OF 2009

surprise—Obamites characteristically invest their own meanings to his speeches, while remaining oblivious to his actual political positions.

In seventeen minutes, it was over, and the pilgrims began to disperse. Obama had spoken of "a nagging fear that America's decline is inevitable, that the next generation must lower its sights." In fact, Black people haven't lowered their expectations, but instead, imagine that their wildest dreams have come true in the form of Obama. It is an unsustainable delusion, which Obama himself will dispel over time. But you couldn't tell the 2009 hajjis that. As with the Jewish farewell, "Next year in Jerusalem," they left Washington making plans for January 20, 2013.

January 27, 2009

OBAMA'S EMERGING LEGACY: WARS, BANKERS, AND FOR-PROFIT HEALTHCARE

As of this writing, the Progressives for Obama website still exists, a relic of Left delusion that should have died of embarrassment months ago. Barack Obama has, indeed, grown in the presidency—but not into the FDR-like figure of his leftish supporters' imaginations. Nor has his presence in the Oval Office served to spur Blacks and progressives to dramatic action, creating the "push" that Left Obamites had predicted would allow their champion to act on his more "liberal" instincts. Quite the contrary. The "Obama Effect" has led to the near-total collapse of the Left—both its white and Black wings—and made the nation safe for rule by finance capital and militarists.

The military, finance capital, and health care corporations (insurers are a branch of finance capital) are winning every important battle because, on fundamental issues, President Obama is on their side. It is he who crushed the anti-war bloc in the U.S. House; who silenced and marginalized single-payer advocates, while fawning over health profiteers; who engineered the greatest transfer of wealth in human history to bankers, leaving them free to once again ruin themselves and the rest of us.

So let us give President Obama his due. He not only smashed the Left opposition, he humiliated them. There is no longer an anti-war bloc in the U.S. Congress. It began to evaporate when Obama took office. The Out of Iraq Caucus has dissolved. The Progressive Congressional Caucus cannot find a mission. And the Congressional Black Caucus can claim only eight members worthy of the label "progressive." The list of CBC members among the thirty-two Democrats that voted "No" to Obama's $106 billion Iraq and Afghanistan war request is so short, it can be taken in at a glance. Here are the few, the brave:

> Barbara Lee (CA), Maxine Waters (CA), Diane Watson (CA), John Lewis (GA), Donna Edwards (MD), John Conyers (MI), Keith Ellison (MN), Donald Payne (NJ)

Less than seven years ago, only four members of the CBC supported George Bush's Iraq War Powers: Harold Ford, Jr. (TN), William Jefferson (LA), Albert Wynn (MD), and Sanford Bishop (GA). In the pages of *The Black Commentator,* I called them the "Four Eunuchs of War" and felt confident in writing:

> The rest of the 36 voting members of the Congressional Black Caucus defended Black America's political legacy, voting No. Rep. Barbara Lee (CA) led half of her CBC colleagues in support of her "alternative to war" resolution, demonstrating once again that African Americans are the core of the forces of peace and justice in the U.S.

It's been all downhill for the CBC since 2002, a steady slide into corporatism and irrelevance. With the Black progressive "core" definitively demobilized since January 20, the Left is largely adrift. Obama has accomplished what George Bush could not: virtually silence progressive voices in Congress, so that he can stoke the fires of war on two fronts without significant challenge from the legislative branch. It is a great victory, so why not congratulate the president, and give him the elemental respect of recognizing that he is—or is trying his best to be—a Man of War?

A Murdered Dream

Kudos, again, to the president, for such adroitness in killing a dream whose time appeared to have come: single-payer health care. Obama made non-persons of health care reform's best friends in the Democratic Party, barring them from White House-sponsored health care events. The president erected a big tent that included everyone except single-payer advocates who, from Obama's perspective, are the enemy. Instead, he wheels and deals and even invents nonexistent agreements with Big Pharma, Big Hospitals, and Big Insurance, all the while vowing to slice huge chunks out of Medicare and Medicaid.

Obama apologists offer their usual excuse: The president must huddle and compromise with the profiteers if he is to get any kind of health care passed. The single payers are well-meaning spoilers. Obama had to muzzle them, so he could get down to business on a practical plan.

What should be clear as day to any lucid, rational observer of the last 150-plus days, is that Obama has not compromised with anybody. Certainly, he never even thought to compromise with single-payer advocates—he simply shut them out of the discussion. And he was never able to effectively compromise with the health care profiteers and their political servants, since Obama never submitted a plan of his own or endorsed anyone else's. Instead, he encouraged everybody and their momma except single-payer advocates to fashion their own plans—creating a cacophony of what Rep. Conyers aptly calls "crap." In the end, he will throw his weight behind one or another pile of health care crap.

Is Obama incompetent? Only if you believe he sincerely wants a health care plan that is as close to the ideal of health-as-a-right as possible, in which case, yes, he has been amazingly incompetent. But why disrespect our president? Give the man credit for knowing what he is doing. Assess his efforts according to the clear logic of his actions, for he has worked wonders.

Obama has succeeded in shutting out of the debate proponents of an idea supported by an overwhelming majority of Americans and an even larger segment of his own party. According to a June 12–16 New York Times/CBS News poll:

> Seventy-two percent of those questioned supported a government-administered insurance plan—something like Medicare for those under 65—that would compete for customers with private

insurers. . . . Sixty-four percent said they thought the federal government should guarantee coverage, a figure that has stayed steady all decade.

Only 20 percent of respondents oppose a Medicare-for-all-type plan. It would require the awesome power of a still very popular president to hold back a mob that is composed of damn near everybody, but Obama is up to the task. At the end of the process—this crap storm—that he has so skillfully set in motion, Obama will settle on a legislative contraption that will not even cover all the forty-five million-plus currently uninsured. For-profit health care will be safe for the remainder of his term, and possibly much, much longer.

Give Obama his props. He has turned the tide against real reform at a time of generalized crisis, when the chances for creating a civilized health care system were most propitious. He is a wonderment!

The Bankers' Man

Even a man of Obama's vast talents cannot easily hide the fact that the federal government (including the Federal Reserve) has "spent, lent or committed $12.8 trillion . . . to stem the longest recession since the 1930s," as reported by the Bloomberg financial news service on March 31. The vast bulk of the money has gone to finance capitalists, most of it on President Obama's watch. It is easily the largest transfer of national treasure in planetary history, accomplished in the relative wink of an eye, mostly outside the legislative process. By comparison, the 2008 Gross Domestic Product (GDP) of the United States—that is, the value of every good and service produced by every man, woman, child, and enterprise of any kind in the nation—was $14.2 trillion. By the end of March, the feds had "spent, lent or committed" a sum equal to 90 percent of last year's total economic activity in the United States—and still counting.

The Obama administration's façade is cracking on the macroeconomic issue. Despite his hollow protestations, it is now generally perceived that Obama's team is allowing "the banks" to get away with murder, theft, and mayhem. In reality, the finance capitalist class is virtually inseparable from Obama's economic apparatus; one is an extension of the other. Larry Summers, Tim Geithner, Robert Rubin, Paul Volker, and the rest of Obama's economic Rasputins will no more "rein in" finance capitalists than they would put shackles on themselves.

Once again, I must ask that you respect President Obama. Allow him to surround himself with people of like mind, men and women with whom he shares a core worldview. Do not belittle our president by grumbling that he is being "manipulated" by "the bankers." Accept that he is a strong leader, who knows what he wants to accomplish and is wise enough to choose a team that reflects his vision. The Obama administration serves the bankers' interests because Obama wishes to do so.

This will be his undoing—not his expanding wars, not the health care fiasco—and much sooner than most think. Obama's sham banking regulations were unveiled to great fanfare—and bombed, colossally, on the front page of the *New York Times*. In language that an economics columnist for the "gray lady" of corporate media seldom deploys against sitting presidents, Joe Nocera wrote:

> Everywhere you look in the plan, you see the same thing: additional regulation on the margin, but nothing that amounts to a true overhaul. . . . Firms will have to put up a little more capital, and deal with a little more oversight, but once the financial crisis is over, it will, in all likelihood, be back to business as usual.

Nocera's headline read, "Only a Hint of Roosevelt in Financial Overhaul." William Greider, writing in *The Nation*, a bastion of "Progressives for Obama," concluded that "most of Obama's reforms are insubstantial gestures, not actual remedies."

Kevin Baker's devastating piece in the July issue of *Harper's* stripped the emperor naked. Obama was not, as his progressive followers imagined, the second coming of Franklin Delano Roosevelt. Rather, he is the political soul mate of FDR's predecessor, Herbert Hoover:

> Much like Herbert Hoover, Barack Obama is a man attempting to realize a stirring new vision of his society without cutting himself free from the dogmas of the past—without accepting the inevitable conflict. . . . The common thread running through all of Obama's major proposals right now, is that they are labyrinthian solutions designed mainly to avoid conflict. The bank bailout, cap-and-trade on carbon emissions, health-care pools—all of these ideas are, like Hillary Clinton's ill-fated 1993 health plan, simultaneously too complicated to draw a constituency and too threatening for Congress to shape and pass as Obama would like. They bear the seeds of their own destruction.

Baker is too kind. He persists in assigning Obama the most progressive of motives, when the content and consistency of his actions point to a profoundly corporate frame of mind and outlook. The president "avoids conflict" with the banks because he has no basic problem with them occupying the commanding heights of power in U.S. society.

It is better, and ultimately more respectful, to judge a politician or any person by the accumulated body of his work. Based on his record as candidate and president to date, it is plain that Obama sees the world as the bankers see it. He accepts their advice because he agrees with it. He shares their core ethic, and is therefore always forgiving of their "excesses." The fate of his presidency is entwined with theirs.

At some point in the near future Barack Obama will become inextricably associated in the public mind with Big Capital—and deservedly so. No one can predict when this perceptual critical mass will be reached, but once it has occurred, it sticks.

The aftershocks of the recent meltdown and the before-shocks of the next onrushing crisis of capitalism will bring a cascade of calamities to the doorstep of the White House. With each crisis, Obama will do what we now know comes natural to him: protect capital at all costs to society as a whole. With their champion saddled with such baggage, it will be interesting to see when "Progressives for Obama" become extinct.

June 24, 2009

WHAT PART OF "WE NEED JOBS" DOES OBAMA NOT GET?

It is as if Americans have lost the very language of social justice. The Congressional Black Caucus, finally in a mood to confront the White House on the jobs issue, find themselves having to explain that legislators have a "moral obligation" to fight for their constituents' interests.

There is no greater testimony to the vast amount of ground Black America has lost over the past three decades than the Congressional Black Caucus's recent press conference on the need for jobs and elementary fairness in the current economic crisis. Caucus chairperson Barbara Lee began with a brief outline of the long-standing—and, in some cases, worsening—economic disparities that afflict African Americans, facts that are well known to the White House and congressional leadership, to whom the Caucus' appeal was directed. The Black lawmakers found it necessary to point out that they are "morally obligated to address these systemic inequalities"—obligations that President Obama has categorically rejected on numerous occasions, invoking the rich man's slogan, "A rising tide lifts all boats."

A generation ago, such reactionary nonsense would have been met with wholesale denunciation in Black political circles. But as we begin the second decade of the twenty-first century, a Black Democrat in the White House can get away with speaking like Ronald Reagan, while Black members of Congress are compelled to present moral justification for seeking redress of economic injustices.

Forty years ago, a Republican president, Richard Nixon, would have felt quite comfortable agreeing with the Black Caucus' concerns about economic fairness. Yet today, the nation's first Black president bristles at every suggestion that gross racial inequalities call for executive and legislative action.

So great is the weight of decades of right-wing assaults on the very idea of economic parity among the races, Black congresspeople feel the need to repeatedly emphasize that they are not proposing racial formulas for job creation, but programs based on need—on the principle that those who have been harmed the most should be targeted for greater assistance.

"We're not talking about race," said chairperson Barbara Lee. "We're talking about the hardest hit." And in fact, the United States Congress has never funded a program to create "Black" jobs, but rather, they have created jobs in urban America and jobs for residents of areas with high levels of poverty.

President Obama treats every appeal for attention to Black unemployment as if it is an unreasonable, or even illegal, demand. To be blunt, he sounds just like those professional white racists that make their livings claiming Blacks seek new and special privileges, when nothing could be further from the truth. The Black Caucus proposes to bring back jobs programs from the '70s. Detroit's Carolyn Kirkpatrick would like to see the rebirth of the Comprehensive Employment and Training Act (CETA) and Representative John Conyers would reinvigorate the Humphrey-Hawkins Full Employment Act, which has been on the books, but unfunded, for over thirty years. No one is talking about reinventing the wheel in jobs creation. For two generations, during every election cycle, Blacks have demanded a Marshall Plan to combat unemployment in the cities, where it just so happens that most Black people live. Every election cycle, that is, until the last one, when Black politicians made no demands whatsoever on candidate Barack Obama. Black America is now paying the cost of giving Obama a free pass.

December 22, 2009

FIRST BLACK PRESIDENCY HAS DRIVEN MANY AFRICAN AMERICANS INSANE

A section of Black America has lost their minds—literally—unable to make contact with reality since November 2008. Despite the horrific and disproportionate damage suffered by Blacks in the Great Recession, a psychologically impaired group of African Americans believes they are better off than before the recession began, and that the future is bright. When Obama entered, their powers of reason exited.

When debating Black supporters of President Obama, there often comes a point where even the most fervent Obamites can find no coherent defense for the president's pro-Wall Street and militaristic policies, when his refusal to even consider race-targeted solutions to race-based problems becomes simply indefensible. Typically, at that point, the Obama supporter will play the psychological card. The advent of the First Black President, they say, has been of incalculable psychological benefit to Black people, especially to Black children, who can now project themselves into an infinity of possibilities because a Black family is in the White House. Hallelujah!

This psychological argument is the Obamites' last bastion of defense, especially the "What about the children?" trump card. Yet there is mounting and disturbing evidence that the psychological harm done to Black people by Obama's presidency may be even greater than the economic and political damage. Barack Obama's presidency is driving millions of African Americans insane—stone-cold out of their minds.

FIRST BLACK PRESIDENCY HAS DRIVEN MANY AFRICAN AMERICANS INSANE

The insanity is documented in the Pew Research Center's recent report, "How the Great Recession Has Changed Life in America," which shows that Black America, the group that has been the most damaged, by far, in the Great Recession, is also the most enthusiastic about the state of the economy. Twenty-five percent of Blacks tell pollsters that the economy is doing good or excellent; that's almost twice as high as the number of whites that think so—even though Black unemployment is about twice that of whites. Eighty-one percent of Blacks say America is still a land of prosperity, while only 59 percent of whites think that way, even though Blacks make only 61 cents for every white dollar earned, the same as thirty years ago.

A 53 percent Black majority think that the economy is starting to recover. Only 40 percent of whites hold that opinion. Yet, for the average Black or white working-class person with a mortgage to pay, the situation is as bad as ever—and for Black people, that means roughly twice as bad. The Pew poll shows that 35 percent of Blacks report their homes are worth less than their mortgages, compared to just 18 percent for white people. Fifty-four percent of Blacks took a pay cut, worked reduced hours, or were forced to take unpaid leave during the Great Recession. Only 37 percent of whites suffered such employment trauma, yet Blacks are consistently—and insanely—more optimistic about the future and feel better about the present than whites do. Nearly a third of Blacks say they are in better shape than before the recession began, a figure with no basis whatsoever in real life, and a perception that is at total war with reality. Everything is worse for every major Black demographic since December 2007. There is nothing to be upbeat about—except, for Obama supporters, the election 0f 2008. From that point on, a large segment of Black America became disconnected from reality, numb to their own pain and to the pain of their children. They have been singing zip-a-dee-doo-dah while all around them Black America is in economic free-fall. These deluded Black folks have been rendered incompetent and politically useless to themselves and their families by the mere existence of a Black president. Obama's election was, besides the Great Recession itself, the worst thing that has happened to Black people in a long time.

July 6, 2010

GRIDLOCK IS A BLESSING: TO HELL WITH OBAMA AND HIS VAN JONESES

Saved, once again, by gridlock! In the absence of any serious social democratic presence in the U.S. Congress—a Progressive Caucus that went poof! years ago, a Black Caucus rendered ridiculous by Obamaism—glorious gridlock was the only force that could derail the SuperCommittee, just as gridlock saved us from Obama's $4 trillion "Grand Bargain" with House Speaker John Boehner this past summer.

Gridlock is not a dependable ally. It is what the condemned hope happens to traffic on their way to the execution site. But, with Occupy Wall Street only a very recent phenomenon, gridlock was all that stood in the way of Barack Obama finally consummating his long sought marriage with the GOP over the past year. Had the Republicans not repeatedly spurned The First Black President's offers of matrimony—for their own narrow reasons—the disgusting union would have long ago been accomplished.

The Obama train, which was always headed in the same fatal direction as the GOP juggernaut, has been stopped in its tracks, despite the president's vow to keep his hand on the throttle with a veto of any rollback of $1.2 trillion in automatic federal spending cuts. Having rejected a partnership with Obama, the Republicans will have great difficulty finishing off the last remnants of the New Deal and the Great Society in the coming election year. Instead, they will be consumed with keeping the military budget off the chopping block.

In the course of over six years of intense scrutiny of candidate and President Obama, we at *Black Agenda Report* have learned to read him like a (comic) book. Last November 3, when Republicans won control of the House, we wrote:

> We can only hope that the Republicans are so consumed with destroy-Obama fervor that they reject his entreaties to bipartisan collaboration, and rush to gridlock. . . . The best outcome that could result from Tuesday's Democratic debacle is that the Republicans overreach and, in their white nationalist triumphalism, make it impossible for President Obama and congressional Democrats to reach an accommodation with rampaging reaction and racism.

The Republicans were stupid enough to grant our wish, twice spurning Obama's shameless collaboration in catastrophic spending cuts, and finally leaving the matter to the doomed SuperCommittee.

BAR had Obama's number on December 15 of last year, when he defected to the GOP on the Bush tax cuts with not even a pretense of a fight. Obama, we wrote, had entered his "comfort zone" now that House Democrats were about to become the minority. He saw the defeat of his own party as putting him one step closer to a "Grand Bargain" with the Republicans.

In the twelve months since the Democrats' mid-term debacle, Obama has bared his naked corporatist butt for all to see. We predicted as much: "Obama is now in his element, where he can maneuver among fellow rightist Democrats and Republican Neanderthals, seeking the bipartisan nirvana he has craved his entire cynical, opportunistic career."

But within months, gridlock would thwart his plans. Hallelujah!

However, gridlock merely delays the trip to the guillotine. Only a mass movement can defeat massed capital, the master of both political parties. The Occupy Wall Street phenomenon, which only emerged in September and is not yet fully formed, is at constant risk of entanglement with the phony "movement" conjured up almost four years earlier in the delusional minds of so-called Progressives for Obama and their ilk—a "shake-and-bake" concoction whose only mission was election of a flim-flam artist as president.

The delusionists are at it again, gearing up to award their brown-skinned Ronald Reagan acolyte another four years to rut with Republicans. At the point-position of this well-heeled co-optation brigade is Van Jones, the Obama staffer who was fired as White House "Green Jobs Czar" on the ridiculous charge of being a closeted radical. Occupy Washington D.C. activist Kevin Zeese has issued a "Memo to Democratic Operatives" like Jones to "back off the Occupy movement":

> The former Obama administration official, who received a golden parachute at Princeton and the Democratic think tank Center for American Progress when he left the administration, is doing what Democrats always do—see the energy of an independent movement, race to the front, then lead it down a dead end and essentially destroy it. Jones is doing the dirty work of a Democratic operative and while he and other Dem front groups pretend to support Occupiers, their real mission is to co-opt it. . . .
>
> The Occupy Movement is not part of either corporate-dominated party and Van Jones is not our leader. It is corporate rule we oppose. The Obama administration and the Democrats as well as the Republicans maintain the rule of Wall Street. Occupiers have organized an independent movement that challenges the rule of the 1% and their Republican and Democratic lackeys. Bought and paid for with millions of dollars from Wall Street, the health insurance industry and big energy interests, Obama and the Democrats are part of the problem, not the solution.

The "problem" menacing all humankind is the rule of finance capital, backed by the imperial armament of the United States and its allies, who together account for 70 percent of all the military spending on Earth. The Sword of Damocles that hovers over the planet is Wall Street's $600 trillion-plus derivatives, financial nuclear bombs invented to satisfy the capitalist system's demand for ever-increasing rates of return on investment.

GRIDLOCK IS A BLESSING: TO HELL WITH OBAMA AND HIS VAN JONESES

In May of 2008—far too late to avert the impending catastrophe—a virtual Who's Who of European social democratic leaders, including former heads of state and ministers of treasury, posted an Open Letter in the French newspaper *Le Monde*, proclaiming that "Mad Finance Must Not Rule Us. " They were speaking of the $750 trillion in derivatives at large at the time: "Financial capital currently represents 15 times the gross domestic product (GDP) of all countries. . . . The world of finance has accumulated a gigantic mass of fictitious capital that does very little to improve the human condition and the preservation of the environment."

The nominally "socialist" politicians warned that, "when everything is for sale, social cohesion disintegrates and the system collapses." They urged immediate action to control financial markets, which "are incapable of self-regulation."

But of course, nothing of the kind occurred. The Meltdown followed a few months later, and today finance capital is eating Europe and the United States alive. Europe's faux socialists made themselves irrelevant—and are now paying at the polls—through their own decades of collaboration with the rise of all-powerful "Wall Street" structures. The cold, hard fact is that finance capital, which has seized hegemonic control of all economic, political, communications, and social mechanisms in the leading capitalist countries, is incapable of regulation. It must be overthrown, or it will destroy us all.

The current gridlock in the United States should be viewed as a temporary and fortunate respite, a chance to build the social movement that can save the people from the worst effects of the system's inevitable collapse. Humanity has no time for diversions—such as Democrats.

November 23, 2011

WHY BARACK OBAMA IS THE MORE EFFECTIVE EVIL

I made the following presentation at the Left Forum, Pace University, New York City, on March 17. On the panel were Gloria Mattera, Margaret Kimberley (of BAR), Suren Moodliar, John Nichols, and Victor Wallis. The discussion was titled, "The 2012 Elections: Lesser Evil or Left Alternative?"

Power to the people!

Let me say from the very beginning that we at *Black Agenda Report* do not think that Barack Obama is the Lesser Evil. He is the more Effective Evil.

He has been more effective in Evil-Doing than Bush in terms of protecting the citadels of corporate power, and advancing the imperial agenda. He has put both Wall Street and U.S. imperial power on new and more aggressive tracks—just as he hired himself out to do.

That was always Wall Street's expectation of Obama, and his promise to them. That's why they gave him far more money in 2008 than they gave John McCain. They were buying Obama futures on the electoral political market—and they made out like bandits.

They invested in Obama to protect them from harm, as a hedge against the risk of systemic disaster caused by their own predations. And, it was a good bet, a good deal. It paid out in the tens of trillions of dollars.

If you believe that what Wall Street does is Evil, then Obama's service to Wall Street is Evil, and there is nothing lesser about it. They had vetted Obama, thoroughly, before he even set foot in the U.S. Senate in 2004. He protected their interests there, helping shield corporations from class action suits, and voting against caps on credit card interest. He was their guy back then—and some of us were saying so, back then.

He was the bankers' guy in the Democratic presidential primary race. Among the last three standing in 2008, it was Obama who opposed any moratorium on home foreclosures. John Edwards supported a mandatory moratorium and Hillary Clinton said she wanted a voluntary halt to foreclosures. But Barack Obama opposed any moratorium. Let it run its course, said candidate Obama. And, true to his word, he has let the foreclosures run their catastrophic course.

Only a few months later, when the crunch came and Finance Capital was in meltdown, who rescued Wall Street? Not George Bush. Bush tried, but he was spent, discredited, ineffective. Not John McCain. He was in a coma, coming unglued, totally ineffective. Bush's bailout failed on a Monday. By Friday, Obama had convinced enough Democrats in opposition to roll over—and the bailout passed, setting the stage for a new dispensation between the American State and Wall Street, in which a permanent pipeline of tens of trillions of dollars would flow directly into Wall Street accounts, via the Federal Reserve.

And Obama had not even been elected yet.

Obama put Social Security and Medicaid and all Entitlements on the table, in mid-January. The Republicans had suffered resounding defeat. Nobody was pressuring Obama from the Right. When the Right was on its ass, Obama stood up and spoke in their stead. There was no Evil Devil forcing him to put Entitlements on the chopping block. It was HIM. He was the Evil One—and it was not a Lesser Evil. It was a very Effective Evil, because the current Age of Austerity began on that day, in January, 2009.

And Obama had not even been sworn in as president yet.

Who is the Effective Evil? I haven't even gotten into his actual term as president, much less his expansion of the theaters of war, his unique assaults on International Law, and his massacre of Due Process of Law in the United States. But I want to pause right here, because piling up facts on Obama's Most Effective Evils doesn't seem to do any good if the prevailing conversation isn't really about facts—but about intentions.

The prevailing assumption on the Left is that Obama has good intentions. He intends to do the Right Thing—or, at least, he intends to do better than the Republicans intend to do. It's all supposed to be about intentions. Let's be clear: There is absolutely no factual basis to believe he intends to do anything other than the same thing he has already done, whether Democrats control Congress or not, which is to serve Wall Street's most fundamental interests.

But, the whole idea of debating Obama's intentions is ridiculous. It's psycho-babble, not analysis. No real Left would engage in it.

I have no doubt that Newt Gingrich and Republicans in general have worse intentions for the future of my people—of Black people—than Michelle Obama's husband does. But that doesn't matter. Black people are not going to roll over for whatever nightmarish Apocalypse the sick mind of Newt Gingrich would like to bring about. But, they have already rolled over for Obama's economic Apocalypse in Black America. There has been very little resistance. Which is just another way of saying that Obama has successfully blunted any retribution by organized African America against the corporate powers that have devastated and destabilized Black America in ways that have little precedence in modern times.

Obama has protected these Wall Streeters from what should be the most righteous wrath of Black folks. To take a riff from Shakespeare's Othello, "Obama has done Wall Street a great service, and they know it." He has proven to be fantastically effective at serving the Supremely Evil. Don't you dare call him the Lesser.

He is the More Effective Evil because Black Folks—historically, the most progressive cohort in the United States—and Liberals, and even lots of folks that call themselves Marxists, let him get away with murder! Yet, people still insist on calling him a Lesser Evil, while he drives a stake through Due Process of Law.

I have not spoken much about the second half of Obama's first term in office. That is the period when the Left generally becomes disgusted with what they call his excessive "compromises" and "cave-ins" to Republicans. But that is a profoundly wrong reading of reality. Obama was simply continuing down his own Road to Austerity—the one he, himself, had initiated before even taking office. The only person caving in and compromising to the Republicans was the Obama that many of YOU made up in your heads.

The real Obama was the initiator of this Austerity nightmare—a nightmare scripted on Wall Street, which provided the core of Obama's policy team from the very beginning. That's why Obama's so-called Financial Reform was so diligent in making sure that Derivatives were virtually untouched.

The real Obama retained Bush's secretary of war because he was determined to re-package the imperial enterprise and expand the scope and theaters of war. He would dress up the war machine head-to-foot in a Chador of Humanitarianism, and march deep and deeper into Africa. He would make merciless and totally unprovoked war against Libya, and then tell Congress there had been no war at all, and it was none of their business anyway. And he got away with it.

Now, that is the Most Effective Evil war mongering imaginable. Don't you dare call him a Lesser Evil. Obama is Awesomely Evil.

Obama has advanced the corporatization of the public schools beyond Bush's wildest dreams, methodically constructing a national, parallel system of charter schools that, in practice, undermine and subvert the traditional public schools. In some places, they have replaced, or soon will replace, the public schools. The hedge funds and billionaires are ecstatic! The teachers unions then endorse their undertaker, foolishly believing he is the Lesser Evil.

So, what does the Left do in this election? The Left should do what it is supposed to do here in the Belly of the Beast at all times: disarm the Beast. This is their singular duty—not to advise the Beast, but to disarm it. At this time on the world historical clock, that means ripping the farcical "humanitarian" veil from the face of U.S. wars—and that face is Obama's face.

No genuine anti-war activist can endorse the war-maker, Obama. If you want to resist actual imperial wars, you must fight Obama. Period. Anything else is to endorse or acquiesce in his wars.

You can attend the United National Anti-War Coalition conference in Stamford, Connecticut next weekend, where you can meet with an array of organizations to begin a calendar of activities that will stretch past Election Day. You can join with UNAC in working to stop Obama from doing a repeat of Libya in Syria and Iran. If you can't bring yourself to do that, then I have no advice for you, because the alternative is acquiescence to Obama's cynical duplicities.

If the Green Party or any other party firmly opposes Obama's humanitarian, Orwellian farce, then support them. If they don't, then don't lift a finger for them.

If you are going to fight for anything, you've got to fight for the right to fight. That means fighting for the rule of law. So, if you don't plan to go underground or into exile anytime soon, you must fight the president who claims the right to imprison or kill any person, of any nationality, any place on Earth, for reasons known only to him. The man who excelled George Bush by shepherding preventive detention through Congress—Barack Obama, the More Effective Evil.

Fight him this election year. Fight him every year that he's here.

Power to the People!

March 21, 2012

FLETCHERISM AND FAKERY: GUARDING OBAMA'S LEFT FLANK

Bill Fletcher and Carl Davidson are two Left opportunists with a problem. Unlike four years ago, when Fletcher co-founded Progressives for Obama, their guy now has a record—and it is indefensible. Solution: nullify the issues right up front in the title to their reworked rationale for backing the Bill of Rights-destroying, Wall Street-protecting, Africa-bombing, regime-changing corporate Democrat. Their August 9 article, "The 2012 Elections Have Little To Do With Obama's Record . . . Which Is Why We Are Voting for Him" frames the campaign as a contest between "revenge-seeking" white supremacists and—well . . . those of us who are not revenge-seeking white supremacists. The facts of the Obama presidency—his actual behavior on war, austerity, and civil liberties—are deemed irrelevant, and the president himself becomes a mere stage prop in the battle against "Caligula," the Republicans.

Fletcher and Davidson want Blacks and progressives to respond with hysteria to GOP "irrationalism," to keep the traditional Democratic base in the Obama camp through raw fear. They claim the current campaign "will be unlike anything that any of us can remember." In truth, the abject Black failure to make a single demand of Obama, and the vapid excuses and rationalizations for the Left's political collapse in his presence, then and now, makes 2012 very much resemble 2008. Back then, Fletcher & Co. wrote:

> Barack Obama's very biography reflects the positive potential of
> the globalization process that also contains such grave threats

to our democracy when shaped only by the narrow interests of private corporations in an unregulated global marketplace. We should instead be globalizing the values of equality, a living wage and environmental sustainability in the new world order, not hoping our deepest concerns will be protected by trickle-down economics or charitable billionaires. By its very existence, the Obama campaign will stimulate a vision of globalization from below."

Four years later, we are admonished to forget the facts as they actually transpired—and as we at *BAR* predicted—and pretend the current campaign is a crusade against the Tea Party, with Obama as the incidental beneficiary. Right-wing populism is the bogeyman, in opposition to which we must re-embrace Obama. The GOP isn't just racist, it is "irrational," crying for "a return to the past." They write: "Obama represents an irrational symbol for the political right, and a potent symbol that goes way beyond what Obama actually stands for and practices. The right, while taking aim at Obama, also seeks, quite methodically and rationally, to use him to turn back the clock."

Of course, the meaning of the term reactionary is to "turn back the clock," a promise Republicans have been making for fifty years. And racism is fundamentally irrational, causing white supremacists to see that which is not there, be blinded to facts that are right in front of their noses, and to invent whole narratives of history. But this time is different, Fletcher and Davison insist, because the Right is so intensely focused on the symbolism of Obama, the Black man—and so "irrational" about it that they make up ridiculous things about him, like his non-citizenhood.

Therefore, our response, as progressives, must be to forge a "common front based on resisting white revanchism . . . on political misogyny, on anti-'freeloader' themes aimed at youth, people of color and immigrants, and a partial defense of the so-called 1%." The fact that Obama is demonstrably not a part of that common front must not dissuade us from joining his campaign. If the Right has made Obama its symbolic focus, we must, in response, make him the focus of our "common front." If the Right hates Obama with an irrational passion, we must hug him to our breasts.

Just in case the logic of such reasoning escapes you, Fletcher and Davidson remind us that the Republicans are not merely irrational—they are crazy like Caligula.

> November 2012 becomes not a statement about the Obama presidency, but a defensive move by progressive forces to hold back the "Caligulas" on the political right. It is about creating space and using mass campaigning to build new grassroots organization of our own. It is not about endorsing the Obama presidency or defending the official Democratic platform. But it is about resisting white revanchism and political misogynism by defeating Republicans and pressing Democrats with a grassroots insurgency, while advancing a platform of our own, one based on the "People's Budget" and antiwar measures of the Congressional Progressive Caucus. In short, we need to do a little "triangulating" of our own.

So, it's not about "endorsing the Obama presidency"—but about voting for Obama while claiming that the facts of what he did as president don't matter. It is about the nonsense of "creating space" so that the Left can do what it ought to do anyway, but which it didn't do in the two years leading up to the 2008 election, or in the first two and a half years of the Obama presidency, until the Occupy Wall Street activists came out of left field in disgust with both parties' subservience to finance capital. The anti-war movement seems largely to oppose only Republican wars.

The great fallacy, here, is that Democratic presidents in general, and Obama in particular, somehow create "space" for progressive activism. Movements create space for themselves, by acting. Only charlatans preach that progressive movements must install preferred personalities from the menus of the ruling circles before they can find space to move.

The great tragedy of the Obama era is that his presence has had the effect of shutting down progressive—and, most dramatically, Black—opposition to the prevailing order. This does not happen by the magic of charisma. Political operatives identified with the Left work diligently to maintain such silence—people like Fletcher and Davidson, who are once again guarding the left flank for Obama, whose great legacy has been to create vast political space for Wall Street and the Pentagon, with a minimum of resistance from white progressives, Blacks, and the rest of the Democratic base.

August 22, 2012

WHAT OBAMA HAS WROUGHT

Most people don't want to be a perceived as party-poopers, which is why the principled folks that have protested the evil antics of the corporate, imperial parties, in Tampa and Charlotte, are so much to be admired. Frankly, who wants to be the one to point out, in the middle of the festivities, that Michelle Obama was just a Chicago-Daley-machine hack lawyer who was rewarded with a quarter-million-dollar-a-year job of neutralizing community complaints against the omnivorous University of Chicago Hospitals? She resigned from her $50,000 seat on the board of directors of Tree-House Foods, a major Wal-Mart supplier, early in her husband's presidential campaign. But once in the White House, the First Lady quickly returned to flacking for Wal-Mart, praising the anti-union "death star" behemoth's inner-city groceries offensive as part of her White House healthy-foods-booster duties.

She also serves on the board of the Chicago Council on Global Affairs, the corporate foreign policy outfit to which her husband dutifully reported, each year, in his pucker-up to the presidency. The Obamas are a global capital-loving couple, two cynical lawyers on hire to the wealthiest and the ghastliest. They are no nicer or nastier than the Romneys and the Ryans, although the man of the house bombs babies and keeps a kill list. Yet, former "green jobs" czar Van Jones, a convention-night chatterer on CNN who was fired by Obama for no good reason, chokes up when he speaks of the Black family that fronts for America—a huge act of national camouflage.

It is as useless to anchor a serious political discussion to this year's Democratic and Republican convention speeches as to plan the liberation of humanity during Mardi Gras. Truth is no more welcome at the former than sobriety is at the latter. So, forget the conventions and their multilayered lies. Here are a few highlights of what Barack Obama has inflicted on the nation and the world:

Preventive Detention

George Bush could not have pulled off such an evisceration of the Bill of Rights, if only because the Democrats and an aroused street would not have allowed it. Bush knew better than to mount a full-court legislative assault on habeas corpus and, instead, simply asserted that preventive detention is inherent in the powers of the presidency during times of war. It was left to Obama to pass actual legislation nullifying domestic rule of law—with no serious Democratic opposition.

Redefining War

Obama "led from behind" a seven-month Euro-American air and proxy ground war against the sovereign nation of Libya, culminating in the murder, after many attempts, of the nation's leader. The president informed Congress that the military operation was not subject to the War Powers Act, because it had not been a "war" at all, since no Americans were known to have been killed. The doctrine was thus established—again, with little Democratic opposition—that wars are defined by the extent of U.S. casualties, no matter how many thousands of foreigners are slaughtered.

War Without Borders

Obama's drone war policies, greatly expanded from that inherited from Bush, have vastly undermined accepted standards of international law. This president reserves the right to strike against non-state targets anywhere in the world, with whatever technical means at his disposal, without regard to the imminence of threat to the United States. The doctrine constitutes an ongoing war against peace—the highest of all crimes, now an everyday practice of the U.S.

The Merger of Banks and State

The Obama administration, with the Federal Reserve functioning as a component of the executive branch, has funneled at least $16 trillion to domestic and international banking institutions, much of it through a virtually "free money" policy that could well become permanent. This ongoing "rescue" of finance capital is unprecedented in sheer scope and in the blurring of lines between Wall Street and the State. The routine transfer of multi-billions in securities and debts and assets of all kinds between the U.S. Treasury, the Federal Reserve, and corporate accounts has created de facto structures of governance that may be described as institutional forms of fascism.

These are world-shaking works of Obama-ism. Even Obama's "lesser" crimes are astounding: His early calls for austerity and entitlement-axing (two weeks before his inauguration) and determined pursuit of a Grand Accommodation with the GOP (a $4 trillion deal that the Republicans rejected, in the summer of 2011) reveal a politician intent on ushering in a smoother, more rational corporate hegemony over a thoroughly pacified civil society. Part and parcel of that pacification is the de-professionalization of teaching—an ambition far beyond de-unionization.

Of course, Obama begins with the delegitimization of Black struggle, as in his 2004 Democratic Convention speech—". . . there is no Black America . . . only the United States of America." To the extent that the nation's most progressive, anti-war constituency can be neutralized, all of Obama's corporate and military goals become more doable. The key to understanding America has always been race. With Obama, the corporate rulers have found the key that fits their needs at a time of (terminal) crisis. He is the more effective evil.

September 5, 2012

ANGELA DAVIS HAS LOST HER MIND OVER OBAMA

The "delusional effect" that swept Black America with the advent of the First Black President has warped and weakened the mental powers of some of our most revered icons—and it has been painful to behold. Earlier this month, Angela Davis diminished herself as a scholar and thinker in a gush of nonsense about the corporate executive in the White House. The occasion was an Empowering Women of Color conference in Berkeley, California. Davis shared the stage with Grace Lee Boggs, the ninety-six-year-old activist from Detroit. The subject was social transformation, but Davis suddenly launched into how wonderful it felt to see people "dancing in the streets" when Barack Obama was elected. She called that campaign a "victory, not of an individual, but of . . . people who refused to believe that it was impossible to elect a person, a Black person, who identified with the Black radical tradition."

There was a hush in the room, as if in mourning of the death of brain cells. Angela Davis was saying that Barack Obama is a man who identifies with the Black *radical* tradition. She said it casually, as if Black radicalism and Obama were not antithetical terms; as if everything he has written, said, and done in national politics has not been a repudiation of the Black radical tradition, as if his rejection of his former minister, the Rev. Jeremiah Wright, was not a thorough disavowal of the Black radical tradition. In his famous 2008 campaign speech in Philadelphia, Obama blamed such radicals for compounding the nation's problems. He viewed people like Rev. Wright as having been mentally scarred by battles of long ago, who were unable to see the inherent goodness of America, as he did.

This is the man who said he agreed with President Ronald Reagan that the '60s were characterized by "excesses." Can anyone doubt that Obama considers the historical Angela Davis, herself, to be a part of the political "excesses" of the '60s and early '70s that he so deplores?

And that is the saddest part of the story. Angela Davis, who retired as a professor of the history of human consciousness in 2008, seems not to be conscious of the fact that she is repudiating herself, her history, her comrades—all in a foolish attempt to artificially graft a totally unworthy Barack Obama onto the Black radical tradition—a place he not only does not belong, but most profoundly does not want to be. This is the guy who declared, at his first national broadcast opportunity, that "there is no Black America . . . only the United States of America."

How, then, did Angela Davis connect Barack Obama to the Black radical tradition? She didn't, because even an icon cannot do the impossible. Instead, Davis quickly told the crowd in Berkeley that "we need to figure out how to prevent somebody like Mitt Romney from getting elected." But the vast majority of Black people are going to wind up voting for Obama anyway, because he's not white and not Republican. There is no need to pollute the proud tradition of Black radicalism by dipping the corporate warmonger, Obama, into the historical mix. In doing so, Professor Davis has soiled herself, and done a terrible injustice to Black history and tradition. And, the biggest shame of all is, she has diminished herself and insulted our people for the sake of a president who doesn't give a damn for their history or their future.

March 28, 2012

BLACK AMERICA MORE PRO-WAR THAN EVER

Barack Obama has proven to be a warmongering thug for global capital, many times over. The question is: Have African Americans, his most loyal supporters, joined the bipartisan War Party, rejecting the historical Black consensus on social justice and peace (or, at least, the "peace" part)?

Ever since national pollsters began tracking African American public opinion, surveys have shown Blacks to be consistently clustered at the left side of the national political spectrum. More than any other ethnicity, African Americans have opposed U.S. military adventures abroad, by wide margins. Indeed, the sheer size of the "blood lust" gap between the races indicates that the Black international worldview differs quite radically from that of white Americans and, to a lesser but marked degree, from Hispanics.

That is, until the advent of Obama.

A *Washington Post*/ABC poll conducted between August 28 and September 1 showed 40 percent of African Americans supported President Obama's threats of airstrikes against Syria—two points more than whites and 9 percent more than Hispanics. Majorities of all three groups opposed bombing Syria—56 percent of Blacks, 58 percent of whites, and 63 percent of Hispanics—but African Americans were, for the first time in polling history, the most bellicose major ethnicity in the United States.

A Pew Research poll from the same period showed Blacks somewhat less supportive of airstrikes, with only 22 percent of African Americans and 29 percent of whites in favor. Fifty-three percent of Blacks and 47 percent of whites were opposed. (Hispanic data were not made available.) However, about one-quarter of both Blacks and whites were allowed to choose "undecided" in the Pew survey, without which option the results would likely have been more in line with the *Washington Post*/ABC poll, with large numbers of Blacks aligning themselves with Obama.

There is no doubt that this apparent decline in Black aversion to U.S. foreign aggressions has everything to do with the color (and party) of the commander in chief. For all the right historical reasons, African Americans have always been highly skeptical of U.S. motives abroad. With Obama nominally in charge, such righteous Black skepticism of "American" (meaning white) motives is less operative.

Only ten years ago, a Zogby poll revealed the vast chasm that existed between Blacks and the two other major ethnic groups on issues of war and peace. *The Black Commentator* for February 13, 2003 reported:

> An Atlanta Journal-Constitution/Zogby America poll released this past weekend shows that less than a quarter of Blacks (23 percent) support Bush's war against Iraq, versus 62 percent of the white public; 64 percent of Blacks surveyed "somewhat or strongly oppose" the planned attack, while 13 percent "aren't sure" what to think.
>
> The bloodthirstiness of white American males is astounding: 68 percent of men surveyed are gung-ho, indicating that the white male pro-war cohort soars somewhere in the high seventies. Less than half of all women favor war.
>
> Hispanics polled nearly as warlike as whites. When asked the general question on war, 60 percent support it.
>
> The lack of empathy with Iraqis as human beings marks white American males as a collective danger to the species. Zogby pollsters asked: Would you support or oppose a war against Iraq if it meant thousands of Iraqi civilian casualties? A solid majority of white men answered in the affirmative, as did more than a third of white women. Only seven percent of African Americans favored a war that would kill thousands.

Hispanics lost some of their bloodlust when confronted with the prospect of mass Iraqi civilian casualties; only 16 percent are willing to support such an outcome.

The fact that only a marginal proportion of Blacks (7 percent) favored an invasion in which thousands of Iraqi civilians would die—less than half the proportion of Hispanics and a small fraction of white belligerents of both sexes—speaks to African Americans' relatively deep empathy for other peoples as well as their disdain for U.S. militarism. It is central to the African American political-cultural legacy.

In the decade since the Iraq invasion, the general American populace has grown more wary of Washington's wars in the Mideast. Why, then, would the least militaristic ethnic group suddenly become relatively more warlike than whites? Have Black Americans undergone some accelerated ideological mutation in the intervening years?

Of course not, but Blacks have for almost six years been in the grip of a fundamentally unsettling experience for which African American history provides no defenses: the presence of a Black man at the helm of the Empire. The progressive, peace-seeking African American world-view is out of sync with the deep imperative to support the First Black President. Black skepticism of U.S. government motives is short-circuited by the fervent desire for Obama to succeed—since his success or failure is seen as Black America's collective legacy. Black politics crumbles under the weight of this massive contradiction, which is why Black America is in its deepest political crisis since Emancipation, unable to defend Black domestic interests or to be a force for peace in the world.

Black elected officials, overwhelmingly Democrats, act as role models of impotence, eunuchs in Obama's harem and, when required, cheerleaders in his wars. Had Obama not "postponed" his attack on Syria, there is every reason to believe that he would have gotten the support of about half the Congressional Black Caucus—just as when his war against Libya was challenged in June of 2011. Even after Obama is gone, the great task of Black progressives will be to sever the chains that bind Blacks to the Wall

Street-run Democratic Party, the incubator of future Obamas and, there-fore, unending Black political crises.

It is true that Black folks have lost their political bearings, if not their minds, in the Age of Obama, but that doesn't mean they can't recover their sanity and humanity once the maddening presence in the White House is gone. Mental breakdowns are not irreversible; otherwise, all the world's peoples would be permanently brain-damaged.

Perhaps the most curious and, in a sense, encouraging aspect of Obama-whipped Black political behavior is that most of those afflicted pay little attention to the First Black President's actual policies. The topic of Black conversation is usually not "*What* is Obama doing" but rather, "*How* is Obama doing?" His fans aren't concerned about his legislative agenda and are often shocked when informed that their icon engineered preventive detention laws and wants to cut Social Security. You are liable to be called a lying bastard, or even attacked, simply for citing his political record in Black settings where, typically, it is never debated or scrutinized. Instead, the subject of constant discussion is: *Who* is making trouble for Obama? What are *they* doing now to smear the man? In short, Black people aren't expressing their political convictions when giving tacit or active support to Obama, on the foreign or domestic fronts. They are, in fact, ignoring their own convictions in favor of upholding the icon.

As a result, what Cornel West calls the "Black prophetic tradition" slips into a coma. We know it will awake, but not without damage.

September 18, 2013

BLACK MADNESS UNDER OBAMA: AFRICAN AMERICANS MORE PRO-NSA, ANTI-SNOWDEN THAN WHITES AND HISPANICS

In yet another example of African American moral and political deterioration in the Age of Obama, a new Pew Research poll shows Blacks are more in favor of NSA spying on Americans than are whites or Hispanics. Moreover, the data indicate that Blacks are probably more likely to favor prosecution of Edward Snowden for his NSA spying revelations than are other ethnic groups.

Back in September, polling history was made when Black Americans were more in favor of air strikes against Syria than whites and Hispanics—the first time, ever, that African Americans were ranked as the most bellicose major ethnicity in the United States.

Something ugly has happened to Black America since 2008, eroding—if not reversing—the progressive Black historical consensus on issues of peace, civil liberties, and social justice that has prevailed since pollsters began soliciting Black opinion. One must conclude that either Black progressivism was a much shallower political current than previously believed, or the presence of a Black president has been such a shock to Black consciousness, so profoundly disorienting, that it has grievously distorted collective Black perceptions of reality. The African American worldview has been mangled beyond imagining.

Back in June of last year, when MSNBC's Black plantation hands Melissa Harris-Perry and Joy-Ann Reid were calling for Edward Snowden's head on a platter, and Black South Carolina congressman James Clyburn was telling people that Snowden's NSA revelations were nothing more than "an effort to embarrass the president," 60 percent of Blacks and an equal proportion of Hispanics approved of "the government's collection of telephone and internet data as part of antiterrorism efforts." Only 44 percent of whites wanted the NSA's metadata collections to continue. Pew Research pollsters asked the same questions after President Obama's speech on NSA spying last Friday. The survey showed that NSA's stock had fallen considerably over the past six months, but Blacks remain more NSA spy-friendly than whites and Hispanics. Forty-three percent of African Americans still approve of the agency's telephone and internet data collection, compared to 39 percent of whites and 40 percent of Hispanics, while majorities of whites (55 percent) and Hispanics (52 percent) opposed Obama on spying. Only 49 percent of Blacks would break with administration policy. In conventional political terms, African Americans—who are subjected to hyper-surveillance like no other group in the U.S.—are most heavily represented on the far Right on this issue, steadfast with "their" president.

Democrats are substantially more likely than Republicans to favor criminal prosecution of Edward Snowden, according to the Pew poll. Sixty-two percent of Democrats, versus 54 percent of Republicans, want to throw the book at Snowden. African Americans make up one quarter of the Democratic Party. The data indicate that Black zeal to protect Obama contributed significantly to the Democrats' lynch-mob mentality.

The polls show that the "Obscene Fourteen" Black lawmakers that voted to shield the NSA's meta-data trolling from congressional defunding in July, represented the majority of Black opinion at the time (60 percent). Put another way, Black majorities appear prepared to take even the most right-wing positions if they perceive it to be in defense of the First Black President. (The House effort to curtail the NSA's telephone and internet data-gathering failed by only 7 votes.)

Forty percent of Blacks told a *Washington Post*/ABC poll in late August and early September that they supported President Obama's threatened airstrikes on Syria. Although majorities of Blacks (56 percent), whites (58 percent), and Hispanics (63 percent) opposed Obama's air war, African Americans were the most supportive of war—the first time that has ever happened. Given that Blacks were far more pro-peace than either whites or Hispanics in the pre-Obama era, the conclusion is inescapable: substantial proportions of Black Americans are now more concerned with defending Obama than with preventing the death of thousands of innocents abroad at U.S. hands. In siding with the NSA's spies, Blacks have shown they are prepared to sacrifice their own civil liberties in order to safeguard the prestige of the icon in the White House.

If an individual exhibited such lifelong personality and values reversals, her relatives and friends would immediately suspect an emotional breakdown and seek professional help. Caregivers would try to identify the cause of the mental collapse and find ways to avoid further harm. A diagnosis of collective African American mental illness, brought on by the sudden and unexpected advent of a nominally Black president, is the kindest analysis available. The alternative diagnosis is that Black folks were always closet reactionaries just waiting for the emergence of a Black chief executive to show their true colors.

I'll go with sudden onslaught of collective mental illness. The second theory is even crazier than the first.

January 22, 2014

GRIDLOCK (ONCE AGAIN) RESCUES SOCIAL SECURITY FROM OBAMA AND THE GOP

President Obama now says that he won't include cuts in Social Security as part of his upcoming budget request to Congress. His apologists on the left, like MoveOn.org, quickly "thanked " Obama for the gesture, grateful that they wouldn't have to eat another Satan's Sandwich from the White House kitchen. But the Democratic loyalists should not be allowed to take credit for changing their hero's mind about Social Security. Obama hasn't paid them a bit of attention in the past five years, knowing that every time an election rolls around they will return to the Democratic Party fold like hungry puppies, or wayward children.

What saved Social Security—for the moment, at least—was the Republicans' continued refusal to join the First Black President in a Grand Bargain in which the two business parties would work hand in hand, in the spirit of bipartisanship, to dismantle what's left of the social safety net. Barack Obama fervently hoped that he would go down in history as the man who finally unraveled Franklin Roosevelt's New Deal and Lyndon Johnson's Great Society, through a consensus of the two major parties. He repeatedly stuck out his hand to his corporate colleagues on the other side of the aisle. Luckily for the rest of us, the Republicans always slapped his hand away, preferring gridlock to a shared victory.

And so begins Year Six of the Obama presidency, with another White House assault on entitlements frustrated, not so much by progressives but by the intransigent, racist Right. Gridlock, once again, to the rescue.

We at *Black Agenda Report* take some pleasure in saying we told you so. Specifically back in November of 2010, when the Democrats lost control of the House of Representatives. We concluded that, given the relationship of forces, gridlock was the best we could hope for. "Let us pray for gridlock," I wrote, "because all else is disaster."

Obama had already handpicked a deficit-cutting commission whose job was to create an austerity model that the Republicans and the right wing of the Democrats could agree upon. The more liberal Democrats would be cast into the dustbin of history, along with their favorite social programs. White House spokesman Robert Gibbs said those Democrats who balked at Obama's steady rightward course were "crazy" and "ought to be drug-tested." The liberals' feelings were hurt, but of course they kept coming home like little puppies. They suffered through 2011, when Obama put all entitlement programs on the grand bargaining table—only for the Republicans to reject the collaboration in favor of overreach and games of chicken.

Gridlock and its associated drama has prevailed on Capitol Hill ever since, preventing Obama and the Republicans from coordinating their strategies on behalf of the One Percent. Race plays a definite role in this and, for once, it has worked in the people's favor by keeping natural corporate allies, who share very similar agendas, at each other's throats much of the time. But this gridlock on the Right will end sooner rather than later. The people's domestic programs, international peace, and the viability of the planet must ultimately be saved by a people's movement, or it will not be saved at all.

February 26, 2014

OBAMA'S LAST PRESIDENTIAL LIES

Barack Obama has spoken to the nation as president for the last time. Hallelujah! The man I dubbed the "more effective evil" now gets a chance to make millions for himself, after spending eight years defending the wealth of the bankers and the rest of the One Percent.

Obama is going out like he came in: telling lies, with great style and skill. So many lies. He said he favored giving unions "the power to organize for better wages." He said the same thing when he was campaigning for his first term, promising to support the "card check" bill that would have allowed workers to rebuild their union membership. But he betrayed organized labor and did nothing to push the bill in Congress.

The outgoing president pointed out that "the effects of slavery and Jim Crow didn't just vanish in the '60s"—that these effects continue to plague Black people. But one hundred days after first taking the oath of office, Obama told reporters that he would not consider programs targeted at Black communities, that Blacks would have to depend on a rising tide to lift all boats, even though no such tide has ever risen for Black people in America.

Obama said the U.S. has "led the world . . . on the promise to save the planet." That's an outrageous lie. The U.S., China, and a few other powerful countries have been the problem, not the solution to climate change. Obama spent his first term sabotaging every effort to create mandatory limits on emissions.

The First Black President acknowledged that many Americans are "convinced that their government only serves the interests of the powerful." But he didn't take any of the blame, even though it was under his administration that Wall Street bankers were deemed "too big to jail," or even to indict. In the same dishonest fashion, Obama declared on Tuesday that "We need to uphold laws against discrimination . . . and in our criminal justice system"—when, on his watch, no federal charges were brought against any killer cops, except one who had already been indicted by local authorities.

Obama got downright cocky in defense of Obamacare, the right-wing Republican health program that Obama adopted as his own. The president said: "If anybody can put together a plan that is demonstrably better, I will support it." But don't bet any money on the letter and spirit of Obama's promises on health care. Back in 2003, when Bruce Dixon and I asked him if he favored a single-payer health care system, Obama answered that he favored "universal health care for all Americans" and intended to introduce or sponsor legislation toward that end. He kept saying that for the next five years, until he was elected president, and then proceeded to isolate and crush supporters of single-payer to the delight of the insurance and drug industries, which no longer had to fear. Obama is sneaky that way.

Finally, Obama bragged that the U.S. has "taken out thousands of terrorists, including bin Laden." What he didn't say was that his administration presided over the jihadist takeovers of Libya and much of Syria and Iraq. The truth is that tens of thousands of jihadists have been trained, armed, financed, and protected by the United States and its allies—not under Bush, but under Obama, making him fully responsible for the deaths of half a million people in those three countries alone. Not to mention Obama's other wars. But I've run out of time. The good thing is, so has Obama.

January 11, 2017

THE OBAMA LEGACY: A TEMPORARY DEFORMITY OF BLACK MINDS ON WAR AND PEACE

Eight years ago, Black America drank deeply from the intoxicating cup we at Black Agenda Report dubbed "ObamaL'aid," a mind-altering substance designed to dull Black folks' historical aversion to U.S. military adventures abroad and undermine their well-founded distrust of the motives of those that rule the United States. A million African Americans made pilgrimage to the Washington Mall in a "Great Black Hajj" to witness a near-miraculous event: the inauguration of the nation's First Black President. For far too many, and for far too long, the line between deliverance and delirium disappeared.

For the most profound historical reasons, Black people had always been skeptical of Power, which had always meant White Power. Most Blacks took for granted that racial dominance and aggression were facts of life in U.S. foreign policy, just as in domestic affairs. Ever since the '60s, when major polling organizations began tracking public opinion by race, Blacks have been the nation's most consistently anti-war constituency. But these vital Black political resistance mechanisms were compromised by the physical presence of a Black family in the White House. It was no longer a question of what "they"—white people—were up to in sending troops and bombs overseas, most often to kill people of color. Now the commander in chief of the world's most potent military was one of "us."

It was inevitable that a significant section of Black public opinion would be sucked into the dark side on issues of war and peace, in racial solidarity with a Black corporate militarist. As we at *BAR* feared and expected, the power-worshipping and image-obsessed Black misleadership class led the way in trashing Black America's collective legacy of empathy with the victims of U.S. imperialism—most horrifically with the unprovoked war against Libya.

In June of 2011, more than half the Congressional Black Caucus, twenty-four members, gave President Obama their full assent to the continued NATO bombing of Libya, which had already destroyed the infrastructure of what had been Africa's most prosperous nation. Thirty-one Black congresspersons voted to continue spending money on the regime change operation, with only six CBC members—John Conyers, Jr. (MI), Jesse Jackson, Jr. (IL), Barbara Lee (CA), Laura Richardson (CA), Bobby Scott (VA), and Maxine Waters (CA)—rejecting the aggression outright.[*] The "peace" faction in the CBC proved to be tiny, indeed only one-seventh of the caucus membership. (Back in 2002, only four members of the CBC voted in favor of giving George Bush war powers to invade Iraq. One month before the March 2003 invasion, just 7 percent of Blacks told the Zogby polling organization they favored "an invasion of Iraq that would result in the death of thousands of Iraqi civilians," while large majorities of whites supported that proposition.)

Among those in favor of continued funding for the 2011 Libya war was Atlanta Congressman John Lewis, a man who wraps himself in the aura of Dr. Martin Luther King, Jr., but who votes to continue the Unites States in its status as "the greatest purveyor of violence in the world today," as Dr. King put it in 1967.

Rep. Keith Ellison, the Black congressman from Minneapolis, a Muslim who now aspires to head the Democratic National Committee and is touted as one of the nation's leading "progressives," defended the U.S. aggression against Libya as a blow for "freedom and the right to self-determination." In reality, it was the opening salvo in Obama's military occupation of Africa and his hellish alliance with Islamic jihadists that would result in

---

[*]   See "Black Caucus on Libya War: The Good, the Confused, and the Hopeless," *Black Agenda Report*, July 2, 2011.

the death of half a million people in Syria and the destruction of that country's infrastructure.

In late August of 2013, Obama threatened to launch a direct air attack on Syria, supposedly in response to the Damascus government's alleged role in a chemical attack against civilians. According to a *Washington Post*/ABC poll, 40 percent of African Americans said they would support the airstrike—two points more than whites and nine points more than Hispanics. Although only minorities of Americans of all races were in favor of the bombing, it was the first time in polling history that Blacks registered as the most warlike constituency—due, no doubt, to the Obama Effect on Black political perceptions.

Prior to Barack Obama's two warmongering terms in the White House, it would have been impossible to imagine that virtually the whole of the Black political (misleadership) class, and an unknown portion of the African American rank and file, would be mimicking the CIA, ranting and raving about some bogus Russian threat to American "democracy." But this, too, shall pass. There is a deep *objective*, as well as historical, basis for broad Black opposition to U.S. imperial wars. We can expect the Obama era's gross deformity in Black attitudes towards war and peace to be corrected once the artificial aura of "Blackness" is removed from the White House. That is, when Black people no longer have strong emotional reasons to identify with U.S. State Power. The Black misleadership class, however, is utterly hopeless, having hitched its fortunes to a Democratic Party that is attacking a right-wing president-elect from even further to the right, in a rush toward all-out global war.

The ObamaL'aid has run out. Now it's time for Black folks to sober up and Fight the Power. And it ain't Russian.

January 19, 2017

PART VI

WARS IN AFRICA AND THE MIDDLE EAST

THE SHRINKING AMERICAN EMPIRE

The day before the U.S. invasion of Iraq in March of 2003, I wrote a piece called "They Have Reached Too Far"—"they" being U.S. imperialists. It was on that day, as U.S. tanks revved their engines in the sands of Kuwait, preparing to cross into what Washington thought would be a glorious future of global domination, that a crack opened up in time, and it was clear as a desert day that the U.S. empire would be swallowed up in that widening crack—maybe in my lifetime.

George Bush and his gang had rolled the dice, betting everything on a land and resource grab designed to save a parasitical system through world-defying theft and awesome—Shock and Awesome—intimidation. But there was not the slightest doubt in my mind that they would fail catastrophically, although no one could predict precisely how the disaster would unfold.

It was also clear that the U.S. aggression against Iraq should not be narrowly interpreted as all about Israel or about oil or about further expansion of U.S. spheres of geopolitical dominance or about beating back the challenge of the Euro. It was simultaneously about all of those things, and more. Empires seek to dominate the very planet, to set the terms for every human transaction. Nothing is beyond the ambitions of empire. Imperialists believe that *everything* can be made into a weapon with which to bludgeon the rest of humanity into submission.

So, back in 2003 I wrote that the impending Iraq war was "an oil currency war, a preemptive strike against the euro's potential to challenge the U.S. dollar as the sole denominator of petroleum purchases. By seizing the Iraqi oil fields and positioning itself to do the same in Saudi Arabia, Iran, and throughout the Persian Gulf, the Caspian Sea and South Asia, the U.S. can stop the euro cold and rule as its own OPEC, awesomely armed and dreadfully dangerous." The dollar would "remain supreme, backed by the oil reserves of the globe."

And that was part of the overall Plan: to set the terms of trade in oil and everything else on the planet, extracting wealth from all the world's people while creating nothing but terror and, hopefully, submission. But the American threat to humanity was so general, and so generally perceived and felt, it achieved the opposite of what Washington had wished. Rather than the world acclimating itself to the rule of the "New Rome," as the imperialists were openly calling themselves, much of the planetary community conspired to find ways to break the unequal ties that bound them to the empire.

The Iraq invasion greatly accelerated the process of U.S. imperialism's decline, so much so that only a few years later the American Lords of Capital found themselves turning to a Black man to put a dramatically different face on their imperial enterprise. But Barack Obama cannot save them. The U.S. dollar's days as the world's reserve currency are numbered, and when the dollar is finally dethroned only the military aspect of the imperial husk will remain.

July 8, 2009

RACE AND ARAB NATIONALISM IN LIBYA

Although a reawakened Arab nationalism "represents a catastrophe for U.S. imperialism," the conflict in Libya dramatically exposes an "endemic" racism in the North African Maghreb. This racism "is not just against other Africans, meaning non-Libyan Africans, but also within Libya itself." Its manifestations are immediately recognizable to African Americans.

U.S. corporate media are sure about certain things in Libya, and admit total ignorance of others, which makes for an uninspiring mix. They are sure that Muammar Gaddafi is hated by the vast majority of the Libyan people, whose sentiments, the western media all but unanimously believe, are expressed by the "rebels" that have taken Benghazi and other major cities. These same media, including correspondents that spend literally all their waking moments chronicling the rebels' every move and utterance, have no inkling of the politics that animates these people, beyond opposition to the regime and an undeniable Arab and Libyan nationalism.

What has become apparent from reports filtering out of the country is that many of the 1.5 million black African migrant workers trapped in Libya feel themselves under racial siege, hunted by what Black Americans would immediately recognize as lynch mobs—"pogrom" is another word that springs to mind—especially in the rebel-held areas.

The testimony of black African victims is most disturbing. "We were being attacked by local people who said that we were mercenaries killing people. Let me say that they did not want to see black people," sixty-year-old Julius Kiluu, an African building supervisor, told Reuters. Even in Tripoli, where the regime is not in full control of neighborhoods, Somalis told journalists they were "being hunted on suspicion of being mercenaries" and "feel trapped and frightened to go out." Ethiopians told of being "dragged from their apartments, beaten up and showed to the world as mercenaries." *ECAD Ethiopian News* reported that "Muammar Gaddafi haters are taking revenge on black Africans for money Gaddafi threw for many African dictators. The mob attacked and killed many Africans including Ethiopians for being only black."

A Turkish oil worker told National Public Radio's West African reporter Ofeibea Quist-Arcton, "We left behind our friends from Chad. We left behind their bodies. We had seventy or eighty people from Chad working for our company. They cut them dead with pruning shears and axes, attacking them, saying you're providing troops for Gaddafi. The Sudanese, the Chadians were massacred. We saw it ourselves."

An Associated Press report described twenty men held as "mercenaries" in a Benghazi jail cell as "looking disheveled and frightened." Outside, "three effigies were hanging from lampposts and flagpoles— all depicting mercenaries." A spokesman for the local rebel organizing committee said, "If people knew they were up there, they would tear down the door." He was clearly describing a lynch mob. But these men were "simply ordinary African workers who got caught up in the middle of this chaos," according to Peter Bouckaert of Human Rights Watch, who met with them.

A *Time* magazine story described videos that ". . . show the bodies of several dead, black African men killed by the protestors, including the corpses of two men being paraded on the hood of a car and driven through a crowd of demonstrators in al-Baida. Another video shows a black African man, who has been caught by the demonstrators, being hit and punched. A protestor asks: 'Who is giving you orders?' The man replies: 'They come from up high. I swear, I swear . . . orders, orders.' The protestor asks: 'They told you to fire at us?' The man replies: 'Yes, yes.'"

But a man calling himself Fazzani told France 24 International News, "I am very sorry to see these clips. One of the guys in the seen [sic] is black Libyan 'not from other African countries.' His family lives in EL Mansoura village in Elwadi shatty district about 200 KM from Borack Ashhati. (Borack AL Shatty is about 700KM south of Tripoli). I have not got permission to put his name here. Hope his family will see this and they will clarify." Fazzani described himself as a "Disappointed Black Libyan." He added a "few facts" of Libyan life: "Most of the residents of Fezzan (Southern part of Libya) are black skinned. Try to find photo of Libyan Embassordor [*sic*] to UN Mr Abdelrahman Shalgam (Is he mercenary?) Try to see photo of Top man of Gaddafi's Information office director (Bashir Saleh), he is more dark skinned than Nelson Mandela, does that mean he is a mercenary from Africa? I am not trying to be a racist but just to clarify few facts."

Any American—any *Black* American—can recognize the pattern of racial lynch law that treats all black Africans as alien, potential enemies. Racially motivated lynch mobs all act alike. Libyan Arab mobs can no more be defended as acting upon special, exigent circumstances (the mercenary "threat") than their American counterparts, who always had a ready excuse for their gruesome predations (Black crime, lust for white women, theft of white jobs, whatever). *The Christian Science Monitor*, in typical obfuscatory fashion, manages to convey useful information under a largely misleading headline: "How Qaddafi Helped Fuel Fury Towards Africans in Libya."

"I think that there are levels of racism within Libyan society that are quite problematic. But racism is not just against other Africans, meaning non-Libyan Africans, but also within Libya itself," Na'eem Jeenah, executive director of the Afro-Middle East Centre in Johannesburg, South Africa, told *CSM*. Another Johannesburg-based researcher, Issaka Souare, says that Libyans (presumably those who are lighter-skinned) may perceive Gaddafi as favoring the darker-skinned (and less developed) south of the country and resent his self-proclaimed "Pan-Africanism." Such sentiments are familiar to Black American ears, echoes of U.S. whites with the words "reverse racism" dripping from their twisted lips.

Hussein Zachariah, a metal worker for a Turkish construction company, told of traveling by car with another Ghanaian and two Chadians to the Egyptian border, after an anti-Gaddafi mob burned their migrant compound and all their belongings. The Chadians were forced out of the vehicle at an opposition roadblock, while the Ghanaians were allowed to continue their exit. Many Libyans, *CSM* explained, resent people from Chad because "Qaddafi has a known history of lavishing the nation's wealth to build connections" with leaders of his southern neighbor. The fate of Mr. Zachariah's Chadian co-workers is unknown. Hopefully, it was not the same as the "seventy or eighty" Chadian employees of a Turkish construction company whose slaughter was recounted to National Public Radio's Ofeibea Quist-Arcton.

Like virtually all black African migrants, Zachariah says he was often pelted with rocks and called a "slave" by Libyans on the streets during his three years working in Benghazi. The Arabic term is "abd," which means one who is subordinated, a servant or slave, but is deployed with the same contempt as "nigger" in the mouths of American racists. Gaddafi's "mercenaries" are no more to blame for Libya's latest paroxysm of anti-black violence than African American boxer Jack Johnson was responsible for the outbreak of deadly white riots after Johnson beat the Great White Hope, James Jeffries, in 1910. The underlying cause was racism, not the immediate event. Anti-black African riots claimed at least 150 lives in Libya in 2000, with no marauding black "mercenaries" as an excuse.

Col. Gaddafi has also played the "race card" in efforts to forestall European intervention in the Libyan conflict—the same tactic he used to cement business and diplomatic ties on the other side of the *Mediterranean.* As the *Huffington Post* reported on March 3:

> In his speech, Gadhafi lashed out against the freezing of his and other Libyan assets abroad and efforts by Europe to send aid to opposition-held Benghazi. In a pointed message to Europe, he warned, "There will be no stability in the Mediterranean if there is no stability in Libya. Africans will march to Europe without anyone to stop them. The Mediterranean will become a center for piracy like Somalia." . . . Gadhafi's regime has worked closely with Italy and other European countries to stop African migrants who use Libya as a launching point to slip into Europe.

The Arab reawakening, as I recently remarked, "will be plagued by fits and starts and disappointments and tragedies—but it cannot be rolled back." In the turmoil, what is also reawakened, or never really dormant, is a "problematic" form of anti-black racism that appears, at least in some parts of the North African Maghreb, endemic and woven into the fabric of Arab nationalism. The (re)emergence of Arab nationalism nevertheless represents a catastrophe for U.S. imperialism, which abhors all nationalisms except its own, as it seeks to bend every national aspiration to the will of capital and its war machinery. However, the racism that is clearly manifest in Libya's current dynamic is also a huge impediment to pan-African solidarity, inviting new waves of imperial mischief on the continent. On that score, we should have no illusions.

March 9, 2011

WESTERN MERCENARIES AND CORPORATIONS POURING INTO LIBYA

Western mercenaries are flocking to Libya, to protect the hordes of western businessmen that have descended on the country. A historic crime becomes a "gold rush" for those that destroyed the society's infrastructure and covet her resources.

Western security firms—a polite term for mercenary outfits—are cramming planes into Libya to make the country safe for an invasion of western capitalists, the real beneficiaries of NATO's war. So frenzied is the crush of war capitalists and their hired gunmen seeking to cash in on the Libyan catastrophe, the *New York Times* tells us a $5 cab ride from Tripoli's airport to downtown hotels now costs $800. The head of the U.S.-Arab Chamber of Commerce calls it a "gold rush," as officials of the government established by force of NATO airpower lay out the red carpet for the foreign hordes. Libya's nominal new rulers in the Transitional National Council are in a rush to sell off the nation's birthright before they've even got it in their hands.

The huge influx of big, burly western mercenaries is most ironic, since the so-called rebels' principal call to arms was that Muammar Gaddafi was maintained in power by paid gunmen from sub-Saharan Africa. They used the false specter of a black mercenary presence to turn the rebellion into a race war that claimed the lives of untold thousands of black Libyans and immigrant workers—an ethnic cleansing that no doubt still unfolds and will forever mark the new regime as racist to its core. That same regime now embraces a real world invasion of Euro-American mercenaries. White and money, indeed, makes right in the new Libya.

The bodies of the dead had not yet been buried in Sirte, the seaside city virtually leveled by months of NATO bombing—and where all the citizens' vehicles were stolen by riotous rebel gunmen—before trade delegations from France and Britain began descending on Tripoli. The French, who were so eager to be first in aggressive, unprovoked war, made sure they were also first in line to get a piece of the spoils. A delegation of businessmen from eight French companies arrived a whole week before their Libyan hosts' gunmen butchered Col. Gaddafi and scores of other prisoners. We're sure the French raised glasses of champagne to mark the occasion.

Of course, foreigners and their money were all over Tripoli before the Europeans and Americans decided that a Shock and Awe assault on Libya would put them in a better position to deal with the uncertainties of the Arab Spring. Foreign investment in Libya increased twenty-five-fold between 2002 and 2010. Gaddafi, by all accounts, had come to an accommodation with foreign capital. European and Asian corporations were transforming the face of Tripoli. Corporate logos on countless construction sites testified to Gaddafi's determination to "normalize" relations with the imperial powers and the world in general. In recent years, he released hundreds of Islamic fighters from prison as part of that "normalization." It would be his undoing.

So, before NATO's war, there was no question of western access to Libya, and certainly no threat of withholding oil. It is not access but the *terms* of access that makes the difference between war and peace with imperialism. For the Americans, the French, and the British, the price of peace is one's national sovereignty. Oh—and keeping out the Chinese, thirty thousand of whom were forced to leave Libya when the bombs started falling. It is doubtful that they will be back in such numbers, until after the current regime is, itself, overthrown.

November 1, 2011

A SECOND WAVE OF GENOCIDE LOOMS IN CONGO, WITH SUSAN RICE ON POINT

The 1996 invasion of the Democratic Republic of Congo by U.S. allies Rwanda and Uganda set in motion a genocide that left six million Congolese dead. Another wave of mass killings now looms with this month's capture of Goma, an eastern Congolese city of one million, by "rebels" under Rwandan and Ugandan control. "People need to be clear who we are fighting in the Congo," said Kambale Musavuli, of Friends of Congo. "We are fighting western powers, the United States and the United Kingdom, who are arming, training and equipping the Rwandan and Ugandan militaries." The main player in suppressing information on Congo's neighbors' role in the ongoing genocide is Susan Rice, U.S. ambassador to the United Nations.

Rice has fought a two-front battle to protect Washington's murderous clients, delaying publication of a U.N. Group of Experts report on Washington's clients' depredations in Congo, and at the same time subverting efforts within the State Department to rein in Uganda and Rwanda. Last week, Rice blocked the U.N. Security Council from explicitly demanding that Rwanda immediately cease providing support to M23 rebels who vowed to march all the way to Kinshasa, the Congolese capital.

Susan Rice has abetted the Congo genocide for much of her political career. Appointed to President Bill Clinton's National Security Council in 1993, at age twenty-eight, she rose to assistant secretary of state for African affairs in 1997 as Rwanda and Uganda were swarming across the eastern Congo, seizing control of mineral resources amid a sea of blood.

She is known to be personally close to Rwanda's minority Tutsi leadership, including President Paul Kagame. A ruthless soldier trained at the U.S. Army's Command and General Staff College at Fort Leavenworth, Kansas, Kagame was mentored by Ugandan strongman (and Reagan administration favorite) Yoweri Museveni, who is believed to have pioneered the use of child soldiers in modern African conflicts.

On the outside during the Bush years, Rice became a fierce advocate of "humanitarian" military intervention in Africa, urging air and sea attacks on Sudan and championing the U.S.-backed Ethiopian invasion of Somalia in 2006. A senior foreign policy advisor on Barack Obama's 2008 campaign team, Rice made it no secret she hoped to be named secretary of state. As U.N. ambassador, she is the administration's top gun on Africa, the focus of her outsized aggressions. Rice is widely credited with persuading Obama to launch NATO's bombing campaign for regime change in Libya. She parroted false media reports that Muammar Gaddafi's troops were raping Libyan women with the aid of massive gulps of Viagra, refusing to back down even when U.S. military and intelligence officials told NBC news "there is no evidence that Libyan military forces have been given Viagra and engaging in systematic rape against women in rebel areas." Yet, Rice said not a word about ethnic cleansing and racial pogroms against black Libyans and sub-Saharan African migrant workers, including the well-documented erasure of the black city of Tawergha.

Susan Rice's "humanitarian" instincts, like those of her boss, are highly selective—so much so, that a genocide equal to or greater than the Nazi liquidation of European Jewry is invisible to her. More accurately, Rice labors mightily to render the genocide in Congo invisible to the world, suppressing release or discussion of reports on Rwanda and Uganda's crimes.

The first, a "Mapping Report," described human rights violations in the Democratic Republic of Congo from 1993 through 2003. Finally published by the U.N. Office of the High Commissioner for Human Rights in October of 2010, after long delays, the document specifically charges Rwandan troops with engaging in mass killings "that might be classified as crimes of genocide." The more recent report by a U.N. Group of Experts concludes that M23, the Congolese "rebel" group that captured Goma, is actually "a Rwandan creation" embedded with Rwandan soldiers that take their orders from Paul Kagame's military. Uganda also supports M23.

Susan Rice, as an energetic protector and facilitator of genocide, should be imprisoned for life (given that the death penalty is no longer internationally sanctioned). But of course, the same applies to her superiors Hillary Clinton and Barack Obama. One would think that the Congressional Black Caucus would be concerned with the threat of a second wave of mass killings in Congo. Not so. A Google search fails to reveal a word of complaint from the Black lawmakers about genocide in Congo or suppression of documentation of genocide, or much of anything at all about Africa since the death of New Jersey Rep. Donald Payne, ranking member of the House Subcommittee on African Affairs, in March of this year.

Instead, incoming Congressional Black Caucus chair Marcia Fudge, of Cleveland, held a press conference with female Caucus members to defend Rice, "a person who has served this country with distinction," from Republican criticism of her handling of the killing of the U.S. Ambassador to Libya. "We will not allow a brilliant public servant's record to be mugged to cut off her consideration to be secretary of state," said Fudge. In the Congressional Black Caucus's estimation, Rice's "record" as chief warmonger in Africa and principal suppressor of the facts on genocide in Congo makes her a role model for African Americans, especially young Black women.

Her relationship to the women of Congo is more problematic. Said Kambale Musavuli, of Friends of Congo, which works tirelessly on behalf of victims of mass rape in eastern Congo: "Why should you want to help a Congolese woman who is raped, when your tax money is supporting the ones that are doing the raping? That's a contradiction." In the Age of Obama, the Black American relationship to Africa is suffocating from such contradictions.

November 28, 2012

OBAMA'S HUMILIATING DEFEAT

It was a strange speech, in which the real news was left for last, popping out like a jack-in-the-box after eleven minutes of growls and snarls and Obama's bizarre whining about how unfair it is to be restrained from making war on people who have done you no harm. The president abruptly switched from absurd, lie-based justifications for war to his surprise announcement that, no, Syria's turn to endure Shock and Awe had been postponed. The reader suddenly realizes that the diplomatic developments had been hastily cut and pasted into the speech, probably only hours before. Obama had intended to build the case for smashing Assad to an imperial peroration—a laying down of the law from on high. But his handlers threw in the towel, for reasons both foreign and domestic. Temporarily defeated, Obama will be back on the Syria warpath as soon as the proper false flag operations can be arranged.

The president's roiling emotions, visible through his eyes, got in the way of his oratorical skills. But then, he didn't have much material to work with, just an endless string of prevarications and half-truths strung almost randomly together. Obama, who was reluctantly asking permission from Congress to violate the most fundamental tenets of international law—permission that Congress is not empowered to give—framed Syria as a rogue nation because it has not signed a treaty on chemical weapons like "98 percent of humanity." This makes Syria ripe for bombing. The president does not explain that Syria's neighbors, Israel and Egypt—both U.S. allies—have also not signed the treaty. He does not suggest bombing Tel Aviv or Cairo.

THE BLACK AGENDA

Obama claims that the U.S. has proof that "Assad's chemical weapons personnel prepared for an attack near an area where they mix sarin gas. They distributed gas masks to their troops. Then they fired rockets from a regime-controlled area into eleven neighborhoods that the regime has been trying to wipe clear of opposition forces." Not a shred of evidence has been presented to back up this narrative which, under the circumstances, tends to prove it is fiction. On the other hand, there are credible reports (everybody's reports are more credible than the Americans'), that rebels under U.S. allied control were told to prepare to go on the offensive following an American retaliation to a chemical attack that would be blamed on Assad's forces—a story whose logic conforms to what actually occurred and answers the common-sense question, Who profits?

Obama will not for long accept diplomatic delays in his war schedule. On Tuesday night, he was already priming the public to accept Assad's guilt the next time chemical weapons explode in Syria. "If we fail to act," said the president, "the Assad regime will see no reason to stop using chemical weapons." American and allied secret services will gladly arrange a replay.

Early in the speech Obama raised the specter that, because of Assad's mad chemical predilections, "our troops would again face the prospect of chemical warfare on the battlefield." Moreover, "If fighting spills beyond Syria's borders, these weapons could threaten allies like Turkey, Jordan and Israel." At this point, the president was arguing for a punitive strike, and had taken on the persona of warlike Obama.

Near the end of the speech, Obama responds to those who want Assad "taken out" right away and permanently, rather than merely "degrading" his forces with calibrated strikes. Now speaking as the "moderate" Obama, the president makes the case that Assad has no "interest in escalation that would lead to his demise, and our ally, Israel, can defend itself with overwhelming force."

The two Obamas are matched with two corresponding Assads. One Assad is a menace to the whole neighborhood and to himself, while the other Assad knows who to mess with and takes no risks with his own survival. It would seem logical that the latter Assad, who is not prone to suicidal actions, would not launch a chemical attack just a few miles away from U.N. inspectors that had just arrived in the country at his government's request.

The point here is not to argue with Obama's logic, but to show how inconsistent, opportunistic, and at times incoherent his reasoning is. He has not the slightest interest in truth or simple logic, only in what sounds right in the immediate context. Obama mixes his personas, and those of his nemesis, at the drop of a hat because he is shameless and absolutely cynical—as befits a mass murderer.

Barack Obama pretends to believe—at least I *hope* he's only pretending—that it was his idea to wait for a congressional debate before blasting Syria to smithereens. "So even though I possess the authority to order military strikes, I believed it was right in the absence of a direct or imminent threat to our security to take this debate to Congress." He didn't take the debate to Congress; the congressional detour was forced on the White House on August 31, when it became clear that Obama lacked both domestic and foreign support for a speedy strike. That was Obama's first big defeat. The second was a knockout, after Russia and Syria seized on Secretary of State John Kerry's "joke" about Assad giving up his chemical weapons, at which point Obama's handlers advised him that his political position was, for the time being, untenable. He arrived in front of the cameras shaken, angry, and humiliated—with a patched-together script and a mouth full of crow.

The president who claimed that he could bomb the sovereign nation of Libya for seven months, overthrow its government, and kill its president, without triggering the War Powers Act—and, further, that no state of war exists unless Americans are killed—told his Tuesday-night audience that he opposes excessive presidential power.

"This is especially true," said Obama, with a straight face, "after a decade that put more and more war-making power in the hands of the president and more and more burdens on the shoulders of our troops, while sidelining the people's representatives from the critical decisions about when we use force."

In truth, it was the likelihood of rejection by American "people's representatives"— just as British Prime Minister Cameron's war plans were rejected by Parliament—that derailed Obama. It took more than 1,500 words before Obama acknowledged the existence of the real world, in which he was compelled to "postpone" a congressional vote on the use of force while the U.S., Russia, China, France, and Britain work on a U.N. resolution "requiring Assad to give up his chemical weapons and to ultimately destroy them under international control." Syria has already agreed to the arrangement, in principle. Obama must bear not only the bitter burden of defeat, but the humiliation of having to pretend that the U.N. route was his idea all along.

Expect him back on the war track in no time flat. What else is an imperialist to do?

September 11, 2013

RWANDA'S FORMULA FOR SUCCESS: MURDER YOUR NEIGHBORS AND STEAL THEIR WEALTH

In the years since 1996, at least six million people have died in the Democratic Republic of Congo as a direct result of an invasion by two U.S. client states: Rwanda and Uganda. It is the greatest slaughter since World War II, yet only a small fraction of the American public is even aware that the genocide occurred. The public remains ignorant of the ongoing crime—in which the United States is fully complicit—because the U.S. corporate media have successfully covered up the murder of millions of Congolese. More than that, organs like the *New York Times* act as PR agents for the perpetrators of the genocide, especially Rwanda—as exemplified by a puff piece that appeared in the *Times* this week titled "Rwanda Reaches for New Economic Model."

The article boosts Rwanda as an African economic success story, a country that is growing at 8 percent a year, even though it has "no oil, natural gas or other major natural resources" and no real industry. The *Times* takes us on a tour of Rwanda's fledgling little commodity and stock exchanges and quotes a government minister bragging that the country's development plan is to jump directly from an agricultural base to an information economy, "leapfrogging" over the industrial stage of development altogether.

In fact, the relative prosperity of the minority Tutsi political and business elite is built on the bones of six million dead Congolese and the natural resources looted from their country. Rwanda's so-called "New Economic

Model" is simply pillaging and massacre, theft and murder on a huge scale, in concert with multinational corporations and under the protection of the United States.

A U.N. panel of experts confirmed in 2001 that both Rwanda and Uganda were building up their own economies by looting eastern Congo's mineral resources—coltan, diamonds, copper, cobalt, and gold—and hauling away timber from Congo's forests. The investigators found that Rwandan and Ugandan militaries had appropriated Congo's wealth for themselves to such an extent that Uganda became a significant diamond exporter, even though it previously produced no diamonds at all. Ugandan gold exports increased fifty-fold between 1994 and 2000. Rwanda increased its gold production ten to seventeen times between 1995 and 2000. Rwanda's exports of coltan doubled and quadrupled, as did its production of cassiterite, another exotic mineral.

The U.N. report found Rwandan President Paul Kagame and Ugandan strongman Yoweri Museveni to be accomplices in the systematic looting of Congo, just as a later U.N. panel deemed both countries liable for genocidal acts against the Congolese people. Kagame and Museveni have built their economies on the extermination of their neighbors. Yet, the *New York Times* calls both countries African success stories. This week's puff piece notes the twentieth anniversary of the so-called Rwandan genocide of 1994—the cause, extent, and nature of which is in great factual dispute—while making no mention of the much larger loss of life right next door in Congo, which is the source of the Rwandan elite's prosperity. And because the New York Times and its fellow media whores cover up the genocide, the carnage and the looting continue to this very day.

March 26, 2014

THERE IS NO U.S. WAR AGAINST ISIS; INSTEAD, OBAMA IS PROTECTING HIS "ASSETS"

The U.S. claim that it is waging a global "war on terror" is the biggest lie of the twenty-first century, a mega-fiction on the same historical scale of evil as Hitler's claim that he was defending Germany from an assault by world Jewry, or that the trans-Atlantic slave trade was a Christianizing mission. In reality, the U.S. is the birth mother and chief nurturer of the global jihadist network—a truth recognized by most of the world's people, including the 82 percent of Syrians who believe "the U.S. created the Islamic State." (Even 62 percent of Syrians in Islamic State-controlled regions believe this to be true.)

Only "exceptionalism"-addled Americans and colonial-minded Europeans give Washington's insane cover story the slightest credibility. However, it is dangerous in the extreme for any country to state the fact clearly: that it is the United States that has inflicted Islamic jihadist terror on the world. Once the charade has been abandoned, once there is no longer the international pretense that Washington is not the Mother of All Terror, what kind of dialogue is possible with the crazed and desperate perpetrator? What do you do with a superpower criminal once you have accused him of such unspeakable evil?

President Vladimir Putin came closest last November, after Russia unleashed a devastating bombing and missile campaign against the Islamic State's industrial-scale infrastructure in Syria—facilities and transportation systems that the U.S. had left virtually untouched since

Obama's phony declaration of war against ISIS in September of 2014. The Islamic State had operated a gigantic oil sales and delivery enterprise with impunity, right under the eyes of American bombers.

"I've shown our colleagues photos taken from space and from aircraft which clearly demonstrate the scale of the illegal trade in oil and petroleum products," said Putin. "The motorcade of refueling vehicles stretched for dozens of kilometers, so that from a height of 4,000 to 5,000 meters they stretch beyond the horizon."

Russian bombers destroyed hundreds of the oil tankers within a week, and cruise missiles launched from Russian ships on the Caspian Sea knocked out vital ISIS command-and-control sites. Putin's derision of U.S. military actions against ISIS shamed and embarrassed Barack Obama before the world—an affront that only a fellow nuclear superpower would dare. Yet, even the Russian president chose his words carefully, understanding that deployment of jihadists has become central to U.S. imperial policy, and cannot be directly confronted without risks that could be fatal to the planet. Simply put, Washington has no substitute for the jihadists who have been a tool of U.S. policy since the last days of President Jimmy Carter's administration.

That's why President Obama admitted in August of 2014, "We don't have a strategy yet" to deal with ISIS. It had been thirteen years since 9/11, but none of the U.S./Saudi-sponsored jihadists had ever "gone off the reservation," spitting on the hands that fed them, attacking the al-Qaida fighters (al-Nusra) that are the real force behind so-called "moderate" anti-Assad "rebels," and threatening to overthrow the Saudi and other Persian Gulf monarchies. Obama had no strategy to combat ISIS because the U.S. had no strategy to fight jihadists of any brand in Syria, since all the other terrorists worked for the U.S. and its allies.

Obama is still not waging a "war" against the Islamic State—certainly not on a superpower scale, and not nearly as vigorously as did the far smaller Russian forces before their partial withdrawal in March of this year. The *New York Times* published an article last week that was half apology, half critical of the U.S. air campaign in ISIS territory. The

Americans blamed their lackadaisical air campaign on "poor intelligence," "clumsy targeting," "inexperienced planners," "staffing shortages," "internal rivalries," and—this from a nation that has caused the deaths of twenty to thirty million people since World War II—"fear of causing civilian casualties." However, the Pentagon now claims to have hit its stride and is concentrating on blowing up the Islamic State's money, targeting cash storage sites, resulting in reductions in salaries of about 50 percent for ISIS troops. The U.S. military says it has destroyed about four hundred ISIS oil tankers. (The Russians claim to have destroyed a total of two thousand.)

As a counterpoint, the *Times* quoted David A. Deptula, a retired three-star Air Force general who planned air campaigns in Afghanistan in 2001 and in the Persian Gulf in 1991. He called the current U.S. air campaign against the Islamic State "symbolic" and "anemic when considered relative to previous operations."

The U.S. has averaged 14.5 air strikes a day in the *combined* Syrian and Iraqi theaters of war, with a peak of seventeen a day in April. That's far lower than NATO's fifty strikes a day against Libya in 2011, eighty-five strikes a day against Afghanistan in 2001, and eight hundred a day in Iraq in 2003. It's way below Russia's fifty-five Syrian strikes a day—nine thousand total strikes over a five-and-a-half-month period—by an air force a fraction of the size of the 750 U.S. aircraft stationed in the region (not counting planes on aircraft carriers, or cruise missiles).

The numbers tell the tale: the U.S. is not carrying on a serious "war" against ISIS troop formations, which remain aggressive, mobile, and effective in Syria. The Pentagon's claim of fear of inflicting civilian casualties should be dismissed outright, coming from an agency that has killed between 1.3 million and two million people since 9/11, according to a 2015 study by Physicians for Social Responsibility.

American excuses concerning "poor intelligence," "clumsy targeting," "inexperienced planners," "staffing shortages," and "internal rivalries" might even contain some kernels of truth, since one would expect gaps in gathering intelligence and targeting information on jihadists that were considered U.S. assets, not enemies. And, there is no question that "internal rivalries" do abound in the U.S. war machine, with CIA-sponsored jihadists attacking Pentagon-sponsored jihadists in Syria. The point being, the U.S. backs a wide range of jihadists that have conflicts with one another.

The U.S. plays up the killing of Islamic State "leaders" and the blowing up of money caches. This is consistent with what appears to be the general aim of the Obama administration's jihadist policy, now deeply in crisis: to preserve the Islamic State as a fighting force for deployment under another brand name, under new top leadership. The Islamic State went "rogue," by the Americans' definition, when it began pursuing its own mission two years ago. Even so, the U.S. mainly targeted top ISIS leaders for elimination, allowing the main body of fighters, estimated at around thirty thousand, to not only remain intact, but to be constantly resupplied and to carry on a vast oil business, mainly with NATO ally Turkey. (The U.S. has also been quite publicly protecting the al-Qaida affiliate in Syria, al-Nusra, from Russian bombing, despite U.S. co-sponsorship of a U.N. resolution calling for international war against al-Nusra.)

To a military man like retired general Deptula, this looks like a "symbolic" and "anemic" campaign. It's actually a desperate effort to balance U.S. interests in preserving ISIS as an American military asset, while also maintaining the Mother of All Lies, that the U.S. is engaged in a global war on terror, rather than acting as the headquarters of terror in the world. To maintain that tattered fiction, at least in the bubble of the home country, requires the maintenance of a massive and constant psychological operations apparatus. It's called the corporate news media.

June 2, 2016

YES, OBAMA AND CLINTON CREATED ISIS—TOO BAD TRUMP CAN'T EXPLAIN HOW IT HAPPENED

Donald Trump has backtracked—sort of—on his assertion that President Obama and Hillary Clinton are "the founders" of ISIS, or the "most valuable players" on the Islamic State team. "Obviously, I'm being sarcastic," said the self-styled "America-Firster," quickly adding, "but not that sarcastic, to be honest with you."

Trump cannot articulate or fully grasp the horrific truth of his original statement because that would require a much more fundamental indictment of U.S. imperial policy in the Muslim world since the last days of 1979, when Zbigniew Brzezinski convinced President Jimmy Carter to set the jihadist dogs loose in Afghanistan. As stated in his memoir *From the Shadow*, Brzezinski advised Carter to aid the right-wing Muslim resistance to the leftist, secular government in Afghanistan in order to "induce a Soviet military intervention" and thus embroil the USSR in a Vietnam-like quagmire. Brzezinski viewed the so-called Mujahadeen as potential foot soldiers of U.S. global policy. "What is most important to the history of the world? The Taliban or the collapse of the Soviet empire? Some stirred-up Moslems or the liberation of Central Europe and the end of the cold war?" Brzezinski asked, rhetorically, decades later.

Having acted in accordance with Brzezinski's counsel, President Carter can accurately be described as a founding "creator" of al-Qaida, along with fellow "most valuable player" Ronald Reagan whose CIA partnered with Saudi Arabia to spend billions drawing Muslims from around the globe into the war in Afghanistan. Together, the U.S. and the Saudis gave birth to the international Islamic jihadist movement—a phenomenon that had not previously existed in world history. The jihadists would become an essential weapon in the U.S. imperial armory, a ghastly tool for regime change in the Muslim world which also doubled as justification for the never-ending American quest for planetary dominance, now that the Soviet boogeyman was gone.

Brzezinski became Barack Obama's foreign policy guru, with consequences that should have been predictable for U.S. Middle East policy but were largely ignored by liberals and so-called progressives in their euphoria at the exit of George W. Bush.

Clearly, the U.S. public would not tolerate another episode of massive, direct U.S. troop involvement in the region; that was no longer an option. But what force, then, was available to execute Washington's unfinished agenda for conquest in this part of the world? In 2011, Obama launched the Mother of All Proxy Wars, first against Muammar Gaddafi's government in Libya, then swiftly mobilizing the totality of the international jihadist network that had been created out of whole cloth under Carter and Reagan nearly thirty years before. Washington and its NATO partners in the Libya aggression, in close concert with Saudi Arabia, Qatar, and the United Arab Emirates, turned Syria into a cauldron of death, funneling billions of dollars in weapons to literally hundreds of Salafist and outright mercenary militias, with al-Qaida's regional affiliate, al-Nusra, at the core. This was Obama's idea of a "smart" war: a frenzied terror offensive cloaked in lies and deception.

The criminal foreign policy pursued by Obama and Secretary of State Hillary Clinton is rooted in the same worldview arrogantly articulated by Brzezinski when he derided those who fretted over the blowback that might result from deploying "some stirred-up Moslems" as foot soldiers of imperialism. As the U.S. and its allies literally *competed* to flood Syria with the weapons, funds, intelligence resources, and diplomatic and media cover to bring down the government in Damascus, they collectively created both the material basis and political space for the jihadists to pursue their own ideological objectives. ISIS emerged, to establish a caliphate of its own in Syria and Iraq. No one should have expected otherwise.

Back in July of 2014, we at *Black Agenda Report* described the rise of ISIS as signaling "the final collapse of U.S. imperial strategy in the Muslim world—certainly, in the Arab regions of Islam." We wrote:

> Think of it as a Salafist declaration of independence . . . from the Arab monarchies and western intelligence agencies that have nurtured the international jihadist network for almost two generations. The Caliphate threatens, not only its immediate adversaries in the Shiite-dominated governments of Syria and Iraq, but the potentates of the Arab Emirates, Qatar, Kuwait, and the Mother of All Monarchist Corruption in the Arab Sunni heartland, the Saudi royal family. The threat is not inferential, but literal, against "all emirates, groups, states and organizations" that do not recognize that ISIS in its new incarnation is the embodiment of Islam at war.

ISIS did not exist when President Obama took office and put Hillary Clinton in charge at Foggy Bottom. His (and her) regime change in Libya and massive, terroristic pivot to Syria "created" ISIS. And, let's get the history right on this score: the U.S. did not reject the jihadist death cult that became ISIS; rather, the Islamic State divorced itself from the U.S. and its European and royal allies. Yet it still took the Russian intervention in Syria in September of last year to push Washington to mount more than token air assaults against ISIS. Apparently, the U.S. wants to avoid killing too many Islamic State fighters in hopes that there will be lots of them left to join U.S.-sanctioned jihadist outfits when it gets too hot for ISIS. (Al-Nusra has changed its name and resigned from al-Qaida—with the blessing of al-Qaida's leadership in Pakistan—so as to better blend in with the other jihadist outfits on western payrolls.)

You don't need to take Donald Trump's word for it that Obama and Clinton have been "most valuable players" for ISIS. The U.S. military's Defense Intelligence Agency (DIA) came to much the same conclusion back in 2012. The military spooks' reports, declassified last year, showed the DIA had warned that "the West, Gulf countries, and Turkey [which] support the [Syrian] opposition" believe "there is the possibility of establishing a declared or undeclared Salafist principality in eastern Syria (Hasaka and Der Zor), and this is exactly what the supporting powers to the opposition want, in order to isolate the Syrian regime."

The DIA was alarmed that:

> . . . the deterioration of the situation has dire consequences on the Iraqi situation and are as follows: This creates the ideal situation for AQI [al-Qaida in Iraq, which became ISIS] to return to its old pockets in Mosul and Ramadi, and will provide a renewed momentum under the presumption of unifying the jihad among Sunni Iraq and Syria, and the rest of the Sunnis in the Arab world against what it considers one enemy, the dissenters [meaning, Shia Muslims]. ISI could also declare an Islamic State through its union with other terrorist organizations in Iraq and Syria, which will create grave danger in regards to unifying Iraq and the protection of its territory.

Thus, a year after Obama and his European and Arab friends brought down Libya's Gaddafi and shifted their proxy war of regime change to Syria, U.S. military intelligence clearly saw the imminent rise of ISIS—and that "this is exactly" what "the West, Gulf countries and Turkey . . . want, in order to isolate the Syrian regime."

Yes, Obama created ISIS, with the enthusiastic assistance of Hillary Clinton, and he is still nurturing al-Nusra, the erstwhile affiliate of al-Qaida, which was midwifed into existence by Jimmy Carter and Zbigniew Brzezinski. In the intervening years, the jihadists have become indispensable to U.S. imperial policy, but especially so since George W. Bush's defeat in Iraq, which soured the American public on "dumb" wars—meaning, in Obama-Speak, wars in which large numbers of Americans die. Proxy wars are ideal—"smart" because only Arabs and Africans and people that Americans have never heard of die. Libya wasn't even a war, according to Obama, since no U.S. personnel perished.

The truth about ISIS and the Obama administration is so obvious that even Donald Trump has a hazy idea of what happened in Syria and Libya.

However, the spoiled man-brat white nationalist billionaire from Queens is incapable of putting the Obama/Clinton/ISIS connection in the historical context of U.S. imperial policy. Sadly, most "liberals" and far too many "progressives" (including Black ones) are afflicted with the same disease as Trump: extreme imperial chauvinism—which is practically inseparable from white supremacism. Extreme imperial chauvinism allows Americans to send to the White House people that should, instead, be sent to the gallows or a firing squad (after a trial, of course). It allows Americans who claim to be on the "left" side of the spectrum to recoil in horror at Donald Trump (who hasn't killed anybody that we know of, and who says he will not engage in regime change as president), yet they will vote for a woman whose career is soaked in the blood of hundreds of thousands in the Middle East and the northern tier of Africa, and whose husband set in motion a genocide that has killed six million people in the Democratic Republic of Congo.

One candidate, Trump, most resembles the late Alabama governor George Wallace with a "let's make a deal" foreign policy. The other, Clinton, is a genocidal maniac whose crimes as president will be Hitlerian in scale.

What is scarier than Clinton or Trump is that Americans seem to have no visceral aversion to genocide (of nonwhite peoples). But, unless you're a Green or some shade of Red, genocide isn't even an election issue.

August 17, 2016

PART VII

FOUNDATIONAL LEADERS: JAMES BROWN, MALCOLM X, AND MLK

JAMES BROWN: THE MAN WHO NAMED A PEOPLE

In death, James Brown last weekend vied for headlines with two other passing luminaries: a former US president, Gerald Ford, and the man a generation of Americans has been taught to hate, Saddam Hussein. That's world-class celebrity—no doubt about it. However, despite all the accolades, I believe the historical James Brown has been shortchanged. Even Brown's many, mostly self-authored titles—"Hardest Working Man in Show Business," "Godfather of Soul," "Soul Brother Number One," to mention just a few—fail utterly to convey the Barnwell, South Carolina native's seismic impact on the modern age. James Brown can arguably be credited with a feat few humans have achieved since the dawn of time:

He named an entire people: *Black* Americans.

More accurately, James Brown was the indispensable impresario who chose the moment and mechanism that allowed Black Americans to name *themselves*. He was the Great Nominator who in 1968 put forward for mass consideration the term that the descendants of former slaves would voluntarily and by acclamation adopt as their proud, collective designation. "Say It Loud, I'm Black and I'm Proud" set in motion a tsunami-like process—breathtaking in speed and scope—that for the first time in their North American history created a mass social forum through which slave descendants could loudly register their ethnic-name preference. Overnight, it seemed, the great bulk became "Black" people—with an attitudinal clause: get used to it.

The uniqueness of the Brown-impelled nomenclature change lay in its referendum-like character. With "Say It Loud," Mr. Brown, who had earned a powerful bullhorn by forging direct, cultural connections to the masses—which is, of course, what popular entertainers do—cracked open the social space in which a whole people could quickly affirm or reject their Blackness. The phenomenon built upon, but was more far-reaching than, Stokely Carmichael's popularization of "Black Power" two years earlier. Carmichael's slogan called for—demanded—power for Black people. But James Brown's anthem empowered ordinary Black folks to signal to their leaders and oppressors—the whole world, in fact—the fundamental terms of any dialogue: how they were to be addressed.

To be sure, group nomenclature had been a near obsession among Africans/Negroes/Coloreds/Blacks as far back as intra-Black debates have been recorded. But the late '60s, the point in history seized by James Brown to introduce his plebiscite, was a time of both unprecedented mass Black political action (including urban rebellions) *and* the emergence of Black-oriented media that could reach into every nook and cranny of the national Black polity. For the first time, the Black call-and-response could be national—that is, people-wide—and, in political terms, near-instantaneous. Through the medium of Black-oriented radio, which was then a one-sound-fits-all Black demographics affair, the Black call-and-response was no longer limited to the literate classes, or to the realm of the church. Thanks to Black radio, everybody got a chance to declare whether or not they were "Black and proud." Most voted, "Yes." It was a landslide. The skeptical minority were drowned out by the Black and newly-Black, or borne along by the backbeat of James Brown and the Famous Flames.

A Name Is No Game

One vastly beneficial effect of the James Brown Black popular referendum was to clear away the historical-rhetorical nomenclature underbrush that had built up over generations—to collectively say, in effect: We're Black now, let's get on with more productive discussions. Until James Brown definitively split Black history in two—BB and AB; Before Black and After

Black—the terms Colored, Negro, Black, and some variant of African had coexisted (though not necessarily capitalized), with varying degrees of friction and tolerance. Clearly, the folks that founded the African Methodist Episcopal and African Methodist Episcopal Zion churches were not repelled by the term African, despite the fact that "The Race" was despised by the broad masses of whites. By taking their faith in their own hands, building their own church, these early congregations empowered themselves to speak on their own terms—at least with one another. More important than *what* folks called themselves, was the effective right to decide the question. Within the proscribed parameters of Black life in AME and AME Zion—and later, Colored Methodist Episcopal and other denominations—Black folks could, by voluntary association, "name" themselves.

However, Black preferences—or Negro, Colored, or African preferences—meant nothing to whites, who called Blacks by whatever terms or epithets they chose because they had the power to do so. Emancipation did not break the white monopoly on power, yet the post-Civil War freedmen's nomenclature debate seemed to escalate, to take on a life of its own. Frustrated by the death of Reconstruction and the rise of Jim Crow, many Blacks got caught up in a current of thought that argued, in chicken versus egg fashion, that Black powerlessness was caused by failed nomenclature. If only Black folks would take on an identity that best befitted their heritage and aspirations, they might find a way out of the tightening racial vise.

Others saw somewhat more clearly that the power to name a people was only an extension of the real sources of power: wealth, a savage white citizenry willing to kill for the sake of perceived privilege, and the might of the state. Such Black citizens saw that use of language was simply an acting out of actual power relationships, not the cause—or even a significant contributing factor—in racial disparity. Words, names, can be wielded as whipping sticks against those who are already powerless to resist. It is the power and intentions of the word-wielder—his ability to define the Other as he sees fit—not the word, that is operative.

Respect, the need to show or withhold it, is an outgrowth of power relationships, not the other way around—a real-world fact well understood by

Black lawyer Ferdinand Lee Barnett, founder of the Chicago Conservator. In 1878, the newspaper's first year of operations, Barnett wrote an editorial titled, "Spell It With a Capital."

> We have noticed an error which all journalists seem to make. Whether from mistake or ill-intention, we are unable to say, but the profession universally begins Negro with a small letter. It is certainly improper, and as no one has ever given a good reason for this breach of orthography, we will offer one. White men began printing long before Colored men dared read their works; had power to establish any rule they saw fit. As a mark of disrespect, as a stigma, as a badge of inferiority, they tacitly agreed to spell his name without a capital. The French, German, Irish, Dutch, Japanese, and other nationalities are honored with a capital letter, but the poor sons of Ham must bear the burden of a small n.
>
> To our Colored journalistic brothers we present this as a matter of self-interest. Spell it with a capital. To the Democratic journals we present this as a matter of good grammar. To the Republicans [the party to which most Blacks were allied at the time] we present it as a matter of right. Spell it with a capital. To all persons who would take from our wearied shoulders a hair's weight of the burden of prejudice and ill will we bear, we present this as a matter of human charity and beg you SPELL IT WITH A CAPITAL."

Note that Barnett uses the capitalized term "Colored" twice, but "Negro"— the subject of his editorial—only once, an indication that he may have been more comfortable with the former. But Barnett did not quibble over the use of either. Rather, he asked—begged—that his people be accorded at least the nominal respect of a capital letter, whether as Negro or Colored. Barnett recognizes that the lower case is reserved for people who can be treated as lower beings; that non-capitalization is intended as "a mark of disrespect—a stigma—a badge of inferiority." It is not the relative merits of "Negro" or "Colored," but the small *n* (or small *c*) that is meant to diminish The Race as a whole—a reinforcement and reminder of Black powerlessness.

By today's standards Barnett's editorial may seem groveling, but that is a misapprehension. He was simply informing Power that he knew what they were up to. In the absence of countervailing power, there could be no expectation that whites would be forced to change their behavior. Barnett was not one to grovel, by the way; he later became the husband and collaborator of Ida B. Wells, the crusading journalist and anti-lynching activist whose militancy often worried her colleague W. E. B. DuBois' "last nerve."

For a century after Emancipation, the terms Negro, Colored, Black, variants of African, plus periodic outbreaks of obscure, short-lived, and now-forgotten nomenclature, were cohabitants of the ghetto. (The *Baltimore Afro-American* newspaper began publication in 1892, preceding by more than seventy years Malcolm X's Organization of Afro American Unity.) None of the group names was enforceable as a standard, not even among Blacks, who nevertheless periodically expended precious time and energy engaging in name disputes largely disconnected from actual power relationships, and without benefit of a movement strong enough to make the conversation relevant to the Black masses.

Fifty-two years after editor Barnett's appeal, the *New York Times* finally deigned to upgrade "Negro" to capital status. "[This] is not only merely a typographical change, it is an act in recognition of racial self-respect for those who have been for generations in the 'lower case,'" the paper announced to its readership in 1930. Of course, this was the *Times'* decision to make, in keeping with the spirit of what Barnett called "human charity"—not to be mistaken as some great victory for "Negro" self-determination. That would come almost two generations later, and the word would be "Black."

Black Power

By the early '60s, "Black" was clearly in ascendance among *some activist circles* of former Negroes. The emergence of a roiling national Freedom Movement, the African decolonization process, the observable fact that the descendants of slaves were now poised for numerical dominance of cities across the country—a multiplicity of world-altering factors—had converged to make a new day imaginable; some thought, inevitable. The imminence and necessity of a great change in power relationships required new nomenclature, both to clarify emerging realities and to accelerate the movement that was making these new realities possible.

But the new word was *not* new. "Black" is as ancient a part of the American racial lexicon as "Negro," a derivative of the Portuguese word for "black." Both terms crossed over long ago from descriptive adjectives to nouns denoting an entire people who were articles of commerce or social proscription. Only the deliberately obtuse could deny that Coloreds, Negroes, and Blacks were proper nouns for what Barnett maintained was one of the "nationalities" resident in the United States. What set "Black" apart from its foreign-derived counterpart "Negro," or from the ambiguous "Colored," was the sheer weight of racist, victim-internalized cultural values embedded in the English term. Black was bad, incorrigibly bad, bottomlessly bad—bad to the bone.

Certain elements of Black folks (by any name) have always deployed an inversion formula to turn their racist-dominated world right side up. "Bad" became "good." They embraced "bad"—"bad" as you wanna be! The Stagger Lee philosophy of life in the ghetto boiled upward through the thin layer of "Renaissance" Negroes in Harlem. The March 19, 1935 "civil disturbance" widely recognized as the beginning of the modern Black urban riot (or rebellion) cycle was an historical break from the pattern of murderous white mob invasions that had punctuated Black folks' previous existence in the U.S.

The Negro, formerly pictured as a lone, mindless brute or passive "uncle" was now perceived in his growing numbers as a "time bomb" ticking away in the nation's cities. By the '60s, Stagger Lees were assembled on every street corner, a palpable political presence. Watts, Los Angeles, 1965, confirmed that there were now multitudes of "bad" Negroes eager to break out of the old racial paradigm. Somehow, the old nomenclature didn't fit anymore. The massed Negro had acquired the power to frighten the rulers in America's centers of commerce.

It was past time for a popularizer to synthesize—sloganize—the objectively transformed relationship between slave descendants and the majority culture and its rulers. Finally, after so many generations of near irrelevance, the never-ended nomenclature discussion could occur in the presence of a vibrant national political movement, amidst a radically changed urban environment. Most importantly, the conversation was now connected to concrete questions of power relationships, questions of direct relevance to an entire people.

"We want Black Power," Stokely Carmichael declared in 1966. Carmichael was by no means the first to define both a people and their aspirations in the two-word phrase. "Black Power" had been around for a while, promulgated by Congressman Adam Clayton Powell, Jr. and author Richard Wright, among others. But the time was now right, and the cameras were rolling. Many future historians would note that the Black Power Era had begun.

But not quite. The various branches of the movement were not in agreement—not about the nature of the "power" that was sought, and not about "Black."

And nobody had effectively posed the question to the people.

R.I.P. Negro and Colored

James Brown was uniquely situated in the new media environment that had evolved since Memphis radio station WDIA became the first to employ an all-Black announcing staff in 1949. By the late '60s, Black-oriented radio had penetrated every city with a substantial Black population—and lots of smaller ones as well. James Brown, constantly on tour and *always* on the charts, delivered his unadulterated sound to everyday folks who worked up almost as big a sweat during the performance as he did. Brown also generously greased the palms of disc jockeys and program directors throughout the land, securing a permanent place on nearly every R&B station's playlist. In 1967, Brown bought radio stations in Knoxville, Tennessee;

Baltimore, Maryland; and Augusta, Georgia, making him the biggest radio mogul of his race at the time.

Brown was the ultimate hook-master, musically and lyrically—a genius that came to full flower with his 1965 release "Papa's Got a Brand New Bag." Brown dropped hooks like Einstein dropped science, with perfectly integrated musical and lyrical phraseology that embedded itself in the mind and body more indelibly than any commercial advertisement. Had he lived in a more just world, James Brown could have earned tens of millions of dollars on Madison Avenue, outclassing so-called classic ads like "Flick my Bic," "Sometimes you feel like a nut, sometimes you don't," and "Coke: It's the Real Thing" with his far more elegant, concise, and powerful "I feel good (I knew that I would), I got you," "This is a man's world," and "I break out in a cold sweat." Increasingly, the James Brown sound came to be defined by his magnificent hooks—his inimitable and irresistible people-catchers.

Four months after Martin Luther King's assassination and the resulting rebellions in more than one hundred American cities, Brown would drop the hook that definitively and inarguably named a people. Appropriately beginning with the words "uh, with your *bad* self," "Say It Loud—I'm Black and I'm Proud" sealed the fate of "Negro" and entombed "Colored" in its moldy crypt.

The linguistic sea change wrought by "Say It Loud" was made possible by the confluence of a genuine national political Movement, the swirling global currents of decolonization, concentrated urbanization, unprecedented mass civil rebellion, and a new and dynamic radio and records communications network with near-universal reach—factors that had never before in Black American history existed, collectively or severally. But it took the unassailably authentic, "super-bad," quintessentially "Black," hook-master supreme James Brown to seize the moment, and set it off.

Self-Determination

Brown's greatest gift was to allow masses of Black people to participate in the process of self-determination. Nothing like it had happened before, or has happened since. By submitting the declaration "I'm Black and I'm Proud" directly to the people, for them to affirm or reject, Brown took the name issue out of smoke-filled strategy rooms and away from the machinations of self-selected "spokespersons." James Brown called out, and the people responded—democracy in action.

The effects of Brown's plebiscite were far more profound than a simple change in ethnic appellation. By embracing "Black," the people stripped the term of its historical negative baggage—something only the people themselves can do, not their "leaders" or preachers or soothsayers. Coming only months after the dramatic crescendo of the '60s—King's death and cities in flames—the popular response to Brown's referendum can also be seen as an affirmation of the previous decade's struggle.

Ten years later, an entirely different exercise was imposed on Black America, one that had no relationship to self-determination or any notion of democracy. Seventy-five self-selected "representatives" of the race locked themselves in Washington hotel meeting rooms in December 1988 for a conference that was supposed to hatch a political agenda for the '90s. After two days in conclave, Rev. Jesse Jackson emerged to inform the press that a decision had been reached. Henceforth, Black folks would be known as "African Americans."

Was that it? A unilateral name change declaration? From the press coverage, it appeared to be so, although the usually well-informed Richard Prince, columnist for the Maynard Institute for Journalism Education, later insisted that "one reporter—Lillian Williams of *the Chicago Sun-Times*—made the so-called 'name change' the news story from the meeting." Whether Ms. Williams was capable of manipulating the Washington press corps or not, the following decade saw no evidence of the existence of any "African American Agenda" except the name imposition.

The whole sorry process was emblematic of how far Black politics (yes, "Black" with a capital "B") had devolved since JB's referendum. In the absence of a real movement, with no mandate from the people directly concerned, no mechanisms for popular review, and in total secrecy, less than one hundred mostly unelected people conspired (yes, that's the appropriate term) to substitute their own choice of name for an entire people, who had only a decade before affirmed by acclamation their preference for "Black."

The merits of "African American" are irrelevant. The conferees had no *right* to impose their preference on Black people. By their secretive and monumentally presumptuous actions, these self-selected spokespersons proved beyond doubt that they do not respect those they claim to represent, and have not a clue as to the meaning of self-determination. Nearly twenty years later, there is no reason to suspect that the surviving conferees have learned a thing about popular democracy.

James Brown had many flaws but he respected his audience, which at the time was damn near all of us. He submitted his contributions—lyrical, musical, and political—to the judgment of the masses. He treated Black people as active agents in their own lives, with full knowledge that his personal fortunes were always subject to the people's verdict.

The term "Black" remains the people's default preference, overwhelmingly so in Black informal speech.

Thank you, Mr. Brown, for giving us the opportunity to choose.

January 9, 2007

DRAGGING MALCOLM X TO OBAMALAND

Manning Marable's rendition of Malcolm X's life should be read very carefully, so as not to confuse Malcolm's evolving worldview with the late Columbia University professor's left-reformist politics. The author's mission is to discredit revolutionary Black nationalism as outdated and primitive. Black Democratic Party activity and support for President Obama are hyped as the new Black Power.

In packaging the life of Malcolm X for a wide audience, Dr. Manning Marable has presented us with an opportunity to reignite the debate over the meaning of Black self-determination, a discussion-through-struggle that effectively ended when the Black Freedom Movement became no longer worthy of the name. Unfortunately, it appears this was not Dr. Marable's intention, since *Malcolm X: A Life of Reinvention* is largely an attempt to render useless the vocabulary of Black struggle. Essential terms such as "self-determination," "Black nationalism," "revolutionary," and "empowerment" lose their meaning, abused and misused for the purpose of portraying the great Black nationalist leader as inexorably evolving into a "race-neutral" reformer on the road to Obamaland.

This article does not address the complaints of those angered by Marable's insistence that Malcolm X had a youthful homosexual relationship with an affluent white man, although it is shocking that Marable would throw this in the mix based on wholly inferential evidence and the author's own psychological speculations. Our overarching concern is that Malcolm's *politics* have been distorted by often clumsy, sometimes clever manipulation of the language of struggle, so that the politics of today's left-reformers and Obama supporters, like Marable, appear vindicated.

Marable's interventions in Malcolm's mental processes begin in earnest on page 285, in the "Chickens Coming Home to Roost" chapter. It is early 1964, and Malcolm is contemplating a final break with the Nation of Islam. Marable takes over as the Black icon's muse, deconstructing Black Muslim theological doctrine, as he speculates Malcolm must have struggled to do, and concluding that "a new religious remapping of the world based on orthodox Islam would not necessarily stigmatize or isolate the United States because of its history of slavery and racial discrimination. Instead of a bloody jihad, a holy Armageddon, perhaps America could experience a nonviolent, bloodless revolution."

While Malcolm was certainly questioning the catechism of inevitable, white man-scorching, Allah-directed Armageddon, it is another thing entirely to have Malcolm pondering a "bloodless revolution" in America. Malcolm derided those who conceived of revolution as anything other than bloody, and he was speaking in secular, not religious, terms. His best-known speech on the subject is "Message to the Grassroots," delivered in October 10, 1963.

> There's no such thing as a nonviolent revolution. [The] only kind of revolution that's nonviolent is the Negro revolution. The only revolution based on loving your enemy is the Negro revolution. The only revolution in which the goal is a desegregated lunch counter, a desegregated theater, a desegregated park, and a desegregated public toilet; you can sit down next to white folks on the toilet. That's no revolution. Revolution is based on land. Land is the basis of all independence. Land is the basis of freedom, justice, and equality.

Malcolm never did accept the notion of revolution as bloodless, nor did he recognize the fight against segregated public accommodations as revolutionary. But Marable tries to convince us that Malcolm must have contemplated a reformist political path *in his mind*, if not in practice. This is

William Styron-style biography, as Morgan State University's Dr. Jared Ball has suggested, with Malcolm forced to play Styron's Nat Turner.

By 1964 Malcolm had made a strategic decision to support Black integrationist efforts, at least rhetorically, but there is nothing that leads us to think that integration had become his end goal, or that he believed integration was revolutionary. He had decided to become part of the broad "movement" to both influence and benefit from it. Marable would have us believe (page 298) that Malcolm's public endorsement of desegregation and voter drives signified that he had scaled down his liberationist aspirations, or that he thought voting equals or leads to African American self-determination—some very faulty logic. Revolutionary Marxists have also seen the value in electoral politics at certain junctures, but that didn't mean they stopped preparing for the forceful overthrow of the bourgeoisie. Nevertheless, Marable tells us that Malcolm's movement activities "marked an early, tentative concession to the idea that perhaps blacks could someday become empowered within the existing system."

The clear inference is that Malcolm was wilting in his desire to wipe "the existing system" off the map. What existing system does Marable refer to, precisely? White supremacy? Capitalism? Bourgeois electoral pay-for-play democracy? Marable keeps Malcolm's mind vague and cloudy, although in his actual historical voice the "evolving" Malcolm hates capitalism and U.S. imperialism more intensely than did the "old" Nation of Islam Malcolm. Marable also introduces his trick word "empowered," which he will use repeatedly in the book to confuse rather than clarify. Blacks "could someday become *empowered* within the existing system"— to do what? To determine their collective destinies? To defy white majorities? To push aside the rule of capital? Marable tries to cage Malcolm, while assuring us that the revolutionary Black nationalist was "tentatively" becoming a liberal reformer.

Gratuitous, non-defensive violence, in Malcolm's NOI talks, always came from the hand of Allah. Malcolm never rejected the right of self-defense; otherwise, he would not have become Malcolm the icon. Marable knew this, so he again invades Malcolm's mind (page 302): "By embracing the ballot, he was implicitly rejecting violence, even if this was at times difficult to discern in the heat of his rhetoric."

What kind of violence was Malcolm rejecting? Certainly not defensive violence, and Malcolm had never publicly urged Blacks to commit unprovoked aggressions against whites. The purpose of Marable's sentence can only be to show alleged *movement* by Malcolm toward some state of non-volatility, which we are expected to associate with political moderation: reform.

Marable grows so bold in pushing his back-to-the-future reformist fantasies that by page 333 he describes a Malcolm X who has become "race-neutral." On May 21, 1964, Malcolm spoke at Chicago's Civic Opera House, telling a crowd of 1,500 people, "Separation is not the goal of the Afro-American, nor is integration his goal. They are merely methods toward his real end—respect as a human being." Malcolm went on to say, "Unless the race issue is quickly settled, the twenty-two million American Negroes could easily adopt the guerrilla tactics of other deprived revolutionaries." Not that he necessarily advocated that (wink).

Three days before he was assassinated, Malcolm said, "I'm man enough to tell you that I can't put my finger on exactly what my philosophy is now." But not to worry, Dr. Marable has the vision and the answer. He concluded that Malcolm had "made his race-neutral views clear in Chicago . . . ." There is no rational basis for Marable's amazing interpretation, other than he thought it moved his political storyline on Malcolm's evolution (or race-neutralization) forward.

The opposite of race-neutral, Malcolm lived and died a Race Man, meaning simply that he put the Race first. As he wrote (page 368) to an Egyptian Muslim Brotherhood luminary who was disappointed that Malcolm was so decidedly non-race-neutral, "As a black American, I do feel that my first responsibility is to my twenty-two million fellow black Americans."

In the final "Reflections on a Revolutionary Vision" chapter, Marable speaks for himself, in the process confirming that he has been sneaking his own words, thoughts, and politics into Malcolm's head for four hundred pages. The Columbia University professor of African American Studies claims to know what Malcolm really, really wanted: "What Malcolm sought was a fundamental restructuring of wealth and power in the United States—not a violent social revolution, but radical and meaningful change nevertheless."

Although the description is so vague, wishy-washy and—damnit!!— so soft and noncommittal as to bear no resemblance to any incarnation or developmental stage of Malcolm X, it fits the self-image of Manning Marable and his circle perfectly. They are the Black left Obamites, purported radicals who have a perpetual love affair with Power. Such people cannot imagine that others are not as enamored of Power as they are and are eager to graft their own vacillations and corruptions onto others, by rhetorical hook or literary crook.

If this assessment seems harsh, it is certainly not as outrageous as Marable's gall in superimposing his politics on Malcolm X. Even when Marable speaks in his own voice, he manages to intimate that Malcolm would agree with him. "If legal racial segregation was permanently in America's past," writes Marable on page 486, "Malcolm's vision today would have to radically redefine self-determination and the meaning of black power in a political environment that appeared to many to be 'post-racial.'"

Marable appears to think these are heavy questions, but they're products of an unfocused, but deeply biased, mind. First of all, legal segregation was defeated before Malcolm's death, and no sane person at the time thought it would be brought back. Malcolm had time to find out what life was like for Black southerners without state-sanctioned Jim Crow. Marable's question is badly put. If he means, what would Malcolm think about today's levels of segregation, then the answer would be that the northern cities would remain very familiar to him in their racial composition and are, in fact, blacker than in Malcolm's day—which might tend to indicate to Malcolm that self-determination was an even more critical concern.

Still, Marable insists that Malcolm would be forced to redefine self-determination and its sibling, Black Power. But self-determination, as a foundational principle of relations among peoples, requires no redefinition. Marable understands it as "the right of oppressed nations or minorities to decide for themselves their own political futures," and he agrees that Malcolm "never abandoned" the "ideal." Why, then, would Malcolm in 2011 have to "redefine" self-determination and the "meaning of black power?" Because the political environment "appeared to many to be post-racial?" Who is it that thinks the environment appears post-racial? If Marable is speaking of white people, or any non-African American people, their opinions cannot be cause for "redefinition" of another people's right. If he means that Black people in the mass believe we live in a post-racial nation, he is a damn fool. But even if such Black folks existed, that would not require a redefinition of self-determination. African Americans would simply "determine" that they love post-racialism and want to do nothing to change it, as is their self-determinationist right.

Marable risks making himself look stupid simply to make the intended point that Malcolm and his Black Nationalism and self-determination talk are passé and should be dismissed except as historical artifacts. For Marable and his Black left Obamites, Malcolm's only other use is to somehow authenticate today's reformers—and even President Obama!— as heirs to yesterday's revolutionary Black nationalists. This is the purpose put to Malcolm by Peniel Joseph, the Tufts University professor of history and author of *Dark Days, Bright Nights: From Black Power to Barack Obama*, which attempts to draw a straight-line historical connection between Malcolm X and the corporate politician in the White House.

Manning Marable is up to the same trick. "Given the election of Barack Obama," Marable writes on page 486, "it now raises the question of whether blacks have a separate political destiny from their white fellow citizens." He does not explain why Black destinies have changed just because a Black Democrat who raised more corporate money than the Republican won a presidential election. How did that electoral fact entwine Black/white destinies in ways that did not previously exist? How were the Black masses empowered by Obama's victory, and if they were somehow empowered, why would that draw them closer to whites? It would have been better if Marable had left the final chapter out of his book—it reflects badly on his powers of reasoning.

Finally, Marable attempts to create artificial space between Malcolm X and his direct political progeny, the Black Panther Party for Self Defense. On page 403 he writes: "Had Malcolm continued to mainstream his views, it is unclear how he would have negotiated relations a few years later with the Black Panthers, a group born of much of the intellectual framework Malcolm had assembled in the early to mid-1960s."

It is nearly impossible to conceive of a Black Panther Party had there not been a Malcolm X. Marable insults a generation of Blacks that came into political consciousness in the '60s—a cohort to which he chrono-logically belonged. He substitutes his imagined, inferred, reinterpreted Malcolm for the man whose words and bearing called forth and virtually sculpted the youthful Party that debuted in the year following his death. Marable projects Malcolm as if he would be a stranger to the Panthers, with whom he would have to "negotiate," when Malcolm's life tells us it is far more likely that the emergence of a militant revolutionary nationalist youth movement that spoke his language—because they learned it largely from him—would compel Malcolm to take the struggle to an even "higher level."

April 27, 2011

MLK AND OBAMA: TWO DIAMETRICALLY OPPOSED LEGACIES

The following is an edited version of remarks I delivered at a panel discussion, "Remembering Past Wars and Preventing the Next," organized by World Beyond War *on April 3 at New York University.*

When we invoke the memory of Dr. Martin Luther King, it is usually in the context of "civil rights" and "human rights." Today, it is in the context of peace. I like to think of Dr. King's work as part of the civilizational project of humanity. That is, how human beings construct a world in which they can coexist and thrive in the bosom of nature.

The civilizational project is a justice project. Civilization is not just about technology; it is not just about wealth and the accumulation of surplus. It's about what people collectively do with that surplus. It's about justice.

The Black Radical Tradition is about justice; it is a civilization-building tradition. Justice is the measure of civilization, and there can be no peace without it. Of necessity, the Black Radical Tradition speaks to the broad sweep of human historical development. There is nothing narrow or parochial about it. And sometimes, the Black Radical Tradition finds that perfect voice, at the pivotal time. On April 4, 1967, that was Dr. King's voice, when he told his audience at Riverside Church that their country was "the greatest purveyor of violence" on Earth, and that there was a damnable system in place that had created this nightmare, and that right-eous men and women had no choice but to oppose it.

Dr. King spoke of the Triple Evils: racism, militarism, and materi-alism—meaning, in contemporary society, capitalism. The sum total of these evils is U.S. imperialism, the global system that was committing the violence he came to that church to oppose, the system of capitalism as it actually exists, that is headquartered in the United States, and whose violence is the greatest obstacle to the construction of a humane civilization.

When Dr. King said that "the arc of the moral universe is long, but it bends toward justice," he was expressing confidence that humanity would throw off—overthrow—these evil systems. That did not sit well with the captains of imperialism, and Dr. King was dead exactly one year later. But that did not silence the voices of Black anti-imperialism. Those voices, including Dr. King's own, had gotten even louder and more defiant after the assassination of Malcolm X three years earlier.

SNCC, the Student Non-Violent Coordinating Committee, which some folks thought of as the children of Dr. King's Southern Christian Leadership Conference, was agitating against the war and the draft years before King. They had taken up the anti-imperialist banner in the years after the exile of W. E. B. Dubois and the erasure of Paul Robeson from public life—men who were giants of anti-imperialism. When Dr. King was shot down, there erupted the greatest wave of Black rebellion in the history of the United States. That rebellion fueled the explosive growth of the Black Panther Party for Self Defense, whose appeal was so compelling that its chapter infrastructure could not absorb the tens of thousands of Black youth that wanted to join.

It was a revolutionary Black nationalism that was profoundly anti-im-perialist—proudly and loudly socialist—a movement determined to join with a world that was up in arms against the empire. It was Malcolm's child—out to avenge Dr. King.

Therefore, it had to be crushed by the massive repressive forces of the State, in a dirty war that reached its most savage peak in 1969 with a merciless campaign of political imprisonment and assassination, including the murder of Black Panthers Fred Hampton and Mark Clark by Chicago police and the FBI. The Party was driven into retreat, back to its founding turf in Oakland, California.

However, the decisive blow to the Black movement for self-determination and against U.S. imperialism was delivered by forces internal to the Black community. It came from a class that had not been concerned about justice in any civilizational sense, but only about getting rid of Jim Crow—American apartheid—so that they could also walk the halls of the empire and live the corporate life. Their vehicle—the only one that was open to this Black aspiring class—was the Democratic Party, because the other party was busy transforming itself into the White Man's Party. With very few exceptions, this was a class for itself, consumed by a mission of "representationalism." They wanted no part in social transformation; they wanted only to be represented in the upper echelons of corporate, governmental, and symbolic media power. Their agenda was solely concerned with their own upward mobility. They were not about justice or peace.

Here are two examples—founding members of this new, Black misleadership class:

Carl Stokes, the first Black big city mayor, elected in Cleveland in 1967. The first thing he did was to appoint a Black retired general as police chief, and the first thing the general did was to arm the cops with hollow point bullets.

Maynard Jackson, the first Black mayor of Atlanta, elected in 1973. Four years later he fired one thousand striking sanitation workers—the same folks that Dr. King had gone to Memphis to support nine years earlier and died trying.

The rise of a selfish, servile, corporate ass-kissing Black class, combined with murderous application of state power, snuffed out the Black Liberation Movement, which was anti-imperialist at the core. There was a brief resurgence of Black "movement" politics with the campaign against South African apartheid. But, only briefly.

For two generations, Black movement politics was smothered by the hegemonic power of the Democratic Party, whose tentacles strangled the militancy out of virtually every Black civic organization. The churches, the fraternities, the sororities—all behave like annexes of the Democratic Party. They invoke Dr. King's name and use the word "justice" a lot—and the word "peace" every so often—but justice and peace cannot possibly find a home in one of the two parties of war.

So, the question becomes: Do two generations without a real peace and social justice movement in Black America mean that the Black Radical Tradition has been crushed? Have Black people, the historically most left-leaning constituency in the United States, shed their anti-imperialism and embraced war? The most definitive answer that I have seen to that question came in a Zogby poll, conducted in late February 2003. It was only a few weeks before George Bush crossed into Iraq—a war that everyone knew was coming. The Zogby poll asked a straightforward question. Here it is, verbatim:

"Would you support an invasion of Iraq if it resulted in the death of thousands of Iraqi civilians?"

A super-majority of white males said, "Hell yes, let's get it on." A bare majority of white females felt the same way. Sixteen percent of Hispanic Americans said they would invade, even if it meant killing thousands of civilians. However, only 7 percent of Blacks agreed with that statement—meaning, only a marginal segment of Black America had any willingness to kill Iraqi men, women, and children. This shows that the Black worldview is worlds apart from that of most white men and women. It's also very strong evidence that Black people remain anti-imperialist, despite two generations without a movement that was loudly and proudly and defiantly anti-imperialist.

But, then came the First Black President: Barack Obama.

We at Black Agenda Report feared, correctly, that a pro-war, Black Democratic president would have a profound effect on Black political behavior. We were very anxious about the rise of this guy who we knew would be a war president. We worried about the effect that his presence in the Oval Office would have on the Black worldview. We expected, and got, the worst.

We feared that Black people, for the first time in history, might begin to identify with U.S. national power if one of their number was the personification of that power. That is a very, very heady brew for a people who had been rendered invisible for most of their sojourn in North America. There was never any question of how the Black misleadership class would react to having a Black Democrat in the White House. Their agenda is to stick as close to Power as possible, and to celebrate Blacks being represented in the halls of power, even if that person is engaged in crimes against humanity and crimes against peace. And so, the Black misleadership class did not surprise us in terms of their behavior under President Obama.

Back in 2002, when President George Bush was asking for War Powers permission to attack Iraq, only four members of the Congressional Black Caucus went along with him. But by June of 2011, when the United States and NATO were doing their regime change mission in Libya, more than half of the Congressional Black Caucus—twenty-four members—gave their full permission and assent to Obama's continued bombing of Libya. And thirty-one of the forty or so voting members of the Caucus opted to continue spending money on the Libyan operation. That number includes John Lewis, who tries to cloak himself in all the vestments of Dr. Martin Luther King. He also voted to continue funding for that war, AFRICOM's first war on Africa. Keith Ellison called that war "a blow for freedom and self-determination."

But what about the masses of Black people? There was some disturbing evidence of the effect that Barack Obama's presence in the White House was having on Black people's historical, bedrock anti-imperialism. Back in late August of 2013, Obama threatened to launch airstrikes against Syria. Polls showed that 40 percent of Black Americans would have supported such an airstrike, compared to only 38 percent of whites and a smaller percentage of Hispanic Americans. It is true that only minorities of any American ethnicity supported Obama's threatened strike, but this was the first poll in the history of polling in which more Black people were for a warlike action than white people. Compare that to the only 7 percent of Blacks that supported an invasion of Iraq a decade earlier. Obama has had his effect.

With the current hysteria about Russia, we see the entirety of the Congressional Black Caucus and the Black misleadership class bad-mouthing the Kremlin with the same intensity and insanity as their white counterparts. What really disturbed me, however, was a conversation I had with a brother who styles himself as a revolutionary. He's head of the Revolutionary Black Panther Party. I was interviewing him after the police "vamped" on some of their members in Milwaukee. All of a sudden, out of the blue, he starts talking about those damn Russians! And he's supposed to be a revolutionary Black Panther!

Dr. Gerald Horne speaks of the "Putin Derangement Syndrome" that afflicts the ruling circles in the United States, who fear the U.S. is losing its dominant position in the world. But, somehow, this insanity has filtered down, even to folks that call themselves Black revolutionaries. The First Black President has left us with a deep and lingering problem. Even out of office, he packs a weaponized legacy.

April 5, 2017

PART VIII

TODAY'S LEADERS: TRUMP, BIDEN, SANDERS

NONE OF THEM HAS EVER BEEN MY PRESIDENT

As a revolutionary Black nationalist whose socialism predates my facial hairs, I have no problem saying Donald Trump is not my president. Neither is the current occupant of the White House, nor were any of the Democrats, Republicans, and Whigs that preceded him.

On a chilly November day in 2009 a newly created coalition, of which I was a co-founder, marched on the White House to denounce and renounce Barack Obama as a tool of white supremacy and the imperial war machine. "Obama, Obama, you can't hide. We charge you with genocide," we shouted, indicting the First Black President for the crimes he was busily committing in service to his masters on Wall Street. The Black is Back Coalition for Social Justice, Peace, and Reparations had been formed less than two months before, largely to demonstrate that not all Black people were bamboozled by the slick corporate politician from Chicago, elected one year earlier in the nation's first billion-dollar presidential campaign. As the Coalition's founding press release stated: "Black and Brown people continue to suffer the brunt of un/under-employment and predatory loan scandal crises. Military spending under Obama has increased as have the warfare this nation continues to export to Iraq, Afghanistan, Pakistan, Venezuela and Colombia. Mass incarceration, police brutality and political imprisonment remain rampant. . . . "

The Black is Back Coalition warned of the "traps set by Obama's so-called 'post-racial' politics that perpetuates the same oppressive militarist agenda well known during the Bush regime."

To paraphrase Fidel Castro, history has vindicated us.

Obama mobilized NATO air forces and jihadist proxies to destroy Libya, which had previously enjoyed the highest living standard in Africa. He redeployed these same al-Qaida terrorists to Syria, killing four hundred thousand people, displacing half the surviving population, and bringing the U.S. to the very brink of nuclear war with Russia. This so-called "Son of Africa" has effectively occupied most of the continent through a U.S. Military Command (AFRICOM) that was less than a year old when Obama was sworn into office. The African Union provides diplomatic cover for the CIA-run "peace keeping" mission in Somalia, while U.S. conventional forces have infiltrated the militaries of all but two African nations. The holdouts, Eritrea and Zimbabwe, are under constant threat of regime change. Obama joined George Bush and Bill Clinton in perpetuating the twenty-year-long slaughter in the Democratic Republic of Congo that has claimed more than six million lives, the worst genocide since World War Two ("Obama, Obama, you can't hide. We charge you with genocide!")

With the eager assistance of Secretary of State Hillary Clinton, Obama baldly abetted a Nazi-spearheaded coup against the elected government in Ukraine—and then blamed Moscow when Russian-speaking Ukrainians resisted, provoking a "New Cold War" that could turn hot in an instant. At the same time, Obama "pivoted" to militarily confront China, whose economy is already, by some measures, larger than that of the U.S. The jihadist war in Syria should also be seen as a theater of imperialism's last-ditch offensive to encircle "Eurasia" in hopes of preserving U.S.-based multinational corporate domination of a "rigged" system of dollar-based world trade.

Just as the Black is Back Coalition warned, Barack Obama was the Black face of imperialism—a change of color without a difference. He tried to hand off the controls to Hillary Clinton, who got six million votes less than he did, and lost.

Back in 2007, when Obama and Clinton were pretending to be ideological opponents—as cookie-cutter corporate Democrats often do—we at *Black Agenda Report* wrote that "There's not a dime's worth of difference" between the two. Every decent, peace-loving person on Earth should be glad to be rid of both of them. Humanity would probably not survive another year of either one.

Donald Trump is also a danger to humanity, like every other U.S. chief executive since Truman nuked Hiroshima and Nagasaki. If words mean anything, Trump starts off as less of a doomsday international menace, since he claims to want to establish talking, rather than shouting, threatening, nuke-rattling relations with Russia and China, while Clinton's version of "reset" was an armed confrontation with Russia over the skies of Syria. Of course, all that could quickly change. Trump may be a "party of one" among Republicans in Congress and even in his own cabinet.

For those who fear Trump's "fascism," the threat level depends on how he uses the arsenal of repressive tools bequeathed to him by the Obama administration. These legal, infrastructural, and technological instruments of the national security state are fascist in their intent; they were made for the purpose of tracking, disorganizing, neutralizing, and locking up dissidents, and disinforming the public at large. Thus, President Obama and his predecessors were fascist-*minded*, whether you call their administrations operatively fascist or not. The Obama administration would not have pushed a bill through Congress allowing the U.S. military to detain American citizens without trial or charge if he had not anticipated using it. He would not have feverishly upgraded an omnipresent national and global surveillance apparatus if he had not anticipated putting it to the task of martial rule. Fascist-minded is all that can be said of Trump, at this point, as well.

Black Lives Matter activists have been under FBI surveillance since day one. Ever since Ferguson, the federal government has taken the lead in over-charging "rioters" in rebellious cities. New York City cops have used social media surveillance as the basis for conspiracy charges against groups of more than one hundred young Black people in separate sweeps in Manhattan and the Bronx. The "fascism" that correctly described Jim Crow rule in the pre-Civil Rights South lives on at the core of the mass Black incarceration regime put in place with the crushing of the Black Liberation Movement two generations ago. The current movement against police terror, which ultimately demands Black community control of the police, put activists in direct confrontation with the coercive arm of the State. There is no retreat from this response to the demands of Black people "on the street," who bear the daily brunt of repression and are also among the most effective organizers.

The Black movement against police terror didn't need a Donald Trump waiting in the vestibule of the White House to get "mad." The movement has already crossed the Rubicon of confrontation with the State. The moment occurred in the second term of the First Black President, when a new generation learned that liberation cannot be vicariously experienced. The twenty-first century Black movement emerged with the knowledge that Black corporate Democrats are not their allies, nor are Black police chiefs, or Black preachers whose real loyalties are to the Democratic Party and its Wall Street patrons.

If the Black movement were afraid of the likes of Donald Trump, it never would have gone up against the militarized police that occupy Black communities. You can't scare people with a specter if they have already been in combat with the real thing.

To the extent that electoral activity is useful to the movement, it should be employed with special vigilance close at hand, against misleaders like the thirty-two members of the Congressional Black Caucus who failed to support the Grayson Amendment that would have halted Pentagon transfers of weapons and equipment to local police departments. The "Treasonous Thirty-Two," comprising 80 percent of full-voting Black Democrats in the House, cast their shameful votes in June 2014, just two months before Michael Brown was shot down in Ferguson, Missouri. (Rep. William "Lacy" Clay, representing Michael Brown's district, was among them.) If the movement is to have any special targets for electoral vengeance, it is these homegrown enemies, who turn Black people's votes against themselves.

Trump or no Trump, the Black movement must continue to press and refine its demands—or Power will concede nothing. On November 6, after their annual march on the White House, the organizations of the Black is Back Coalition ratified a nineteen-point document that puts self-determination at the heart of the broadest range of issues confronting Black America: "Every central demand, every strategy of struggle, must be formulated with the goal of self-determination in mind. Otherwise, the movement will allow itself to be drowned in reformist schemes and projects that bind Black people even more tightly to structures of outside control." The points range from "Black Community Control of Police" to "Halting Gentrification" and "Nationalization of the Banks." They were compiled during Barack Obama's time in the White House and will remain relevant under a President Donald Trump.

We've *been* mad. Let's get organized and get free.

November 16, 2016

CRIMINAL NATION: OBAMA AND TRUMP BOTH SHOULD BE JAILED FOR WAR CRIMES

It is as if the Gambino and Genovese crime families were arguing their turf disputes in the courts and the news media. The Democrats are screaming bloody murder over President Trump's firing of FBI director James Comey, whom Hillary Clinton still blames for her defeat at the polls and whom the bipartisan War Party has never forgiven for his earlier hesitancy to blame the Russians for the same offense. Now that Trump has cut Comey loose—ostensibly for his handling of the Clinton emails scandal, according to three letters sent by Trump and his two top Justice Department officials—the Democrats have stepped up calls for a special prosecutor to continue the evidence-less crusade against the Kremlin.

It's the Saturday Night Massacre all over again, cry the Democrats, harkening back to the weekend in 1973 when President Nixon fired Watergate special prosecutor Archibald Cox. But this is not about the rule of law; quite the opposite, it's about continuing the momentum of the U.S. military offensive begun in 2011 under President Obama, a wholly illegal aggression that has destroyed Libya, killed half a million Syrians, delivered vast regions to the control of the two feuding factions of al-Qaida, and brought the world closer to nuclear annihilation than at any time since the Cuban missile crisis.

The War Party is determined to make the offensive permanent, to keep up the pressure on the ultimate targets, Russia and China, until they break or capitulate to U.S. domination of the world. The current, rabid anti-Russian hysteria adds another layer of fake news on top of the wholly fictional U.S. "War on Terror" scenario. But these mega-lies can no longer mask the great obscenity of the twenty-first century: that the U.S. is allied with al-Qaida, whose jihadists act as imperialism's foot soldiers in the Middle East.

Donald Trump thought last month's attack on Syria had bought him immunity, or at least a respite, from the wrath of the War Party, which was determined to burn him at the political stake—not for his raging racism and hostility to civil liberties, but for his previously stated opposition to "regime change" and never-ending tensions with Russia. Trump's fifty-nine-missile salvo against a Syrian airbase was supposed to wipe the slate clean and forgive his heresies against the extralegal rights of the "exceptional" U.S. empire. But apparently, there is no statute of limitations on even the suggestion of peaceful coexistence with targeted states.

And now, in an almost laughable legalistic perversion, a group of lawyers from the Obama White House, of all places, is suing the Trump administration for failing to provide sufficient legal rationale for last month's Tomahawk hit on Syria. The lawyers at United to Protect Democracy claim their insider knowledge of "how the federal government works" gives them unique insights on "implementing and enforcing the norms that have constrained presidential power for decades"—although they never constrained Obama from his own lurch towards apocalypse in 2011. Indeed, these legal hit men for empire acknowledge as much, admitting (or bragging?) that "we defended past presidents against legitimate oversight and illegitimate attacks."

The self-styled "watchdog" group does not list its board or members on its website, but their admission implicates them in Obama's legal defense of his regime change assault on Libya. The U.S.-NATO bombing campaign, which killed an estimated fifty thousand people, destroyed the country's infrastructure, resulted in the murder of its chief of state, empowered jihadist militias, and unleashed a torrent of arms across Africa and the Middle East, nevertheless did not violate the War Powers Act because "U.S. operations do not involve sustained fighting or active exchanges of fire with hostile forces, nor do they involve U.S. ground troops," wrote Obama's lawyers. When challenged by Congress, Obama maintained that the war on Libya was not a war at all, because no Americans were killed.

Like synchronized dancers, the U.S. and its allies pivoted immediately to Syria, where they attempted to use much the same formula—jihadists + arms + financing + CIA training + political protection at the U.N.—to overthrow the Bashar al-Assad government. This "proxy war," which involved U.S. military and intelligence personnel on the ground from the very start, was never a secret and was always a clear violation of the United Nations Charter, which the U.S. is legally obligated to uphold. Nations are forbidden to use force against other nations except in self-defense or with the authorization of the U.N. Security Council. Unlike in Libya, the U.S. did not have the fig leaf of enforcing a U.N.-authorized "no-fly zone" in Syria. Yet, there was hardly a peep from any but a handful of Democrats, and therefore no need for Obama's in-house lawyers to defend their chief against charges of aggressive war, the most serious of international crimes.

In 2013, after Syria was falsely blamed for a chemical attack on civilians, Obama threatened to directly bomb Syrian forces. His lawyers were prepared to argue that an attack on Syria could be justified—like Bill Clinton's bombing of Kosovo in 1999—on vague grounds of eliminating a threat to peace. But of course, the greatest threat to peace is aggressive war, of which the United States was already—and chronically—guilty. In the end, Obama decided to ask Congress for authorization to bomb, and then changed his mind when the Russians offered to broker destruction of Syria's chemical weapons stockpiles. But like all U.S. presidents, and with no grounds under international law, Obama insisted that commanders in chief have the right to bomb other countries to defend U.S. "national security" based on their own judgment—another legal nonsensicality.

So, the legal mercenaries of United to Protect Democracy, veterans of Obama's 2011 military offensive, have no problem with violating international law. Their beef with Trump appears to be that he did not provide sufficient legal *rationale* for his bombing Syria, which is different than actually obeying international law. Trump's people issued what are described as "talking points" to explain his actions against Syria. But former White House lawyer Justin Florence, the group's legal director, wrote that this is not enough: "The U.S. government must publicly articulate its legal theory in order to uphold the international legal framework we have relied on for so many years as a constraint on other states."

The U.N. Charter is clear on what constitutes aggression. Trump is an aggressor. So were Obama and Bush (the U.N. Secretary General said so), and so was Clinton. Since the U.S. is a superpower and a permanent member of the U.N. Security Council, the United Nations will never authorize the international community to punish the U.S. for its crimes. But that does not absolve the U.S. of criminality—and humanity's collective memory and conscience will never forgive the United States for the crushing of nations and the death of millions. The Democratic Party hacks with law degrees at United to Protect Democracy are concerned not about peace, but that U.S. presidents go through the motions of rationalizing their imperial crimes. Say *something* that sounds good, they urge. Convince the American public that it's OK for the U.S. to claim life and death powers over the rest of humanity. Make an *effort*, why don't ya?

The real problem these "watchdogs'" have with Trump is that he has not bothered to commission creative lawyers like themselves to provide lofty wordage to justify the indefensible. He has not taken care to skillfully *market* U.S. imperial aggression to its home population. This may not be impeachable, but it is embarrassing and unbefitting of an "exceptional" empire.

Ajamu Baraka, the 2016 Green Party vice presidential candidate and an editor and columnist at *Black Agenda Report*, wrote in *BAR*, "The absence of any real opposition to the reckless use of U.S. military force— the attack on Syria, the macho demonstration bombing in Afghanistan, the provocations toward North Korea—exposed once again the unanimity among the U.S. ruling class and the state on the use of military force as the main strategy to enforce its global interests."

The American public does not think of itself as bloodthirsty, but it has a huge tolerance for the spilling of other people's blood. Americans also have a peculiar sense of entitlement. "Imperial privilege is this strange ability on the part of the U.S. public to 'shrug off' the consequences experienced by people impacted by the direct and indirect result of U.S. militarism," Baraka writes.

Obama's former lawyers at United to Protect Democracy understand that Americans demand only that politicians use pretty words to justify the barbarities committed in their name. If you stick with the formula, the template, and make Americans feel exceptional, then you can bomb the hell out of the rest of the world at will.

May 10, 2017

BERNIE SANDERS CAN'T SHAKE HIS IMPERIAL PIGGISHNESS

Donald Trump's performance last week at the U.N. General Assembly set the rhetorical bar for U.S. imperial piggery at a twenty-first century low—although Hillary ("We came, we saw, he died") Clinton is surely his equal in moral depravity. At about the same time that Trump was threatening to incinerate a whole nation of people, Bernie Sanders attempted to fill in the vast holes in his own foreign policy profile in a speech at Westminster College in Fulton, Missouri. This is the same venue where Winston Churchill, the twentieth century's prototypical western imperial pig politician, delivered his Cold War-initiating "Iron Curtain descending on Europe" speech in 1946. It is deep swine territory, and Sanders could not help but wallow in it.

Churchill was an arch racist, an admirer of fascists until they threatened his home island and its global colonial empire, and a great innovator in war crimes against civilian populations—and, therefore, a hero of the Wild White West. Sanders revealed his own swinish predilections in Westminster. The Vermont senator reverently quoted Churchill's "strategic concept" to provide "nothing less than the safety and welfare, the freedom and progress, of all the homes and families of all the men and women in all the lands." What these words actually mean, in the mouth of an imperialist, is eternal subjugation of the darker races while rich white men bear the "burden" of global governance. But Sanders chose to give the most benign interpretation to Churchill's colonial pig-talk, claiming the British prime minister's "challenge" to current society means moving "toward a global community in which people have the decent jobs, food, clean water, education, health care and housing they need."

Churchill would never dream of providing a welfare state for Britain's colonial captives, nor is Sanders proposing to do so for the far-flung subjects of the U.S. empire. However, imperialists reserve for themselves and their "exceptional" home countries the right—no, the *obligation* (or "burden")—to shape the destinies of the rest of the human species, if only in their imaginations or to garner cheap speechmaking points. President George W. Bush also wanted to bring "freedom and progress" and safety and welfare and all those other good things to Iraq in the wake of Shock and Awe—and doubtless meant it. Donald Trump has a vision of prosperity for the world, too—embossed with his own golden logo. The Japanese empire imposed an Asian "Co-Prosperity Sphere" under the armed guidance of Tokyo.

Bernie Sanders is an imperialist, and therefore of the same general political species as Churchill, Clinton, and Trump. Many of Sanders' leftish supporters cannot fathom how anyone could describe their hero as "an imperialist pig," as I did in a June 15 article. They think imperialism is a personal characteristic, a kind of meanness—the same misconception they have about racism—rather than a global system centered in their home country. That's why not only nearly every self-styled "patriot" is an imperialist, as are many, if not most, U.S. "progressives"—especially the white ones. They truly cannot fathom the meaning of other people's right to self-determination but see themselves as benevolent vectors of human progress—which is why "liberals" are so prone to crimes of "humanitarian" military intervention, the imperialist hoax-of-choice since Bill Clinton's presidency.

A disturbing proportion of Black Americans have caught the same disease after eight years of identification with U.S. power under Obama, who, I wrote "was among the most aggressive defenders of white supremacy in history," having waged seven simultaneous wars to preserve the U.S.-based multinational corporate empire. Obama handed off those wars to Trump, who is vigorously pursuing all of them and threatening more aggressions.

Foreign policy was largely an afterthought in the Bernie Sanders presidential campaign, which is a kind way of saying that he did not challenge Barack Obama's foreign policy and was, therefore, in tacit agreement with the First Black President's global depredations. Certainly, Sanders backed sanctions against Russia ("that means tightening the screws on them") and supported the near-genocidal Obama-Clinton regime-change war "to get rid of this guy [President al-Assad]" in Syria. That's more than enough to qualify the 2016 Sanders as a world-class imperialist pig.

The 2017 version is much the same. Like virtually the entire Democratic Party, Sanders eagerly foments anti-Russian hysteria, embracing CIA tales of Russian "efforts to undermine one of our greatest strengths: the integrity of our elections, and our faith in our own democracy." He vows to "work in solidarity with supporters of democracy around the globe, including in Russia"—code words for continuation of the Obama-Hillary Clinton policy to foster regime change in Moscow. No serious advocate for peace talks like that—and if you do not advocate for peace, you are not a progressive.

Sanders' anti-Russia rhetoric negates much of the progressive-sounding wordage in Sanders' speech. At any rate, his remarks contained very little of substance on the burning issues of the day. Sanders delivered mostly pablum to signify that he is the Not-Trump, and takes strong stands only on long-dead issues. "The goal is not for the United States to dominate the world," he said. "Nor, on the other hand, is our goal to withdraw from the international community and shirk our responsibilities under the banner of 'America First.'" But even Trump can say nice things about the United Nations, and did last week, even as he displayed complete contempt for and ignorance of international law. And Barack Obama broke every international law and covenant in the book, while grandiloquently playing the globalist.

Sanders said the U.S. should not have overthrown the elected Iranian government of Prime Minister Mohammed Mossadegh in 1953 and shouldn't have deposed Chile's Salvador Allende in 1973. He was against the Vietnam War, and the Iraq War—George Bush's, not the current Obama-Trump Iraq war, about which he has nothing to say.

Sanders claims to oppose the U.S.-backed Saudi Arabian war against Yemen, although last year he was encouraging the Saudis to become more aggressive in the region. (He apparently meant more aggression against Syria—a violation of international law with which Sanders had no quarrel, since President Assad is a "bad guy" and the Russians are trying to subvert "our democracy.")

"The Global War on Terror has been a disaster for the American people and for American leadership," said Sanders. "We must rethink the old Washington mindset that judges 'seriousness' according to the willingness to use force. One of the key misapprehensions of this mindset is the idea that military force is decisive in a way that diplomacy is not."

The "new Washington mindset" Sanders fuzzily proposes has no room for the universal principles of self-determination, national sovereignty, and international law. It should be understood that Sanders is talking about use of American military force against sovereign nations; "diplomacy" does not apply to al-Qaida and its ISIS offshoot. Sanders fails to once mention the legality of U.S. violations of other nations' sovereignty— because *he is an imperialist who does not respect international law.* Sanders says, "Military force is sometimes necessary, but always—always—as the last resort," but he does not recognize that only the U.N. Security Council can legally authorize attacks on sovereign nations. Plus, even Trump will claim that he only unleashes the military as a last resort.

Bernie Sanders supports the Iran nuclear deal. So do lots of Republicans. But, the "deal" is an imperialist instrument based on lies that even the U.S. intelligence agencies rejected. In 2007, all of the U.S. spy agencies joined in assessing that Iran had dismantled its nuclear program in 2003. This National Intelligence Estimate outraged the Bush regime and probably prevented them from launching a full-scale military attack on Iran. But the Obama administration ignored the Estimate, despite another intelligence assessment in 2011 that determined Iran was still on a non-weapons nuclear track. The U.S. and Israel nevertheless waged an assassination campaign against Iranian scientists and unleashed the world's first massive cyberattack on the country's installations, finally threatening a full-scale military attack to force through the current "deal" on nuclear weapons.

Donald Trump, the unilateralist imperialist, threatens to break the deal. Sanders says the U.S. should honor it. But the Iran agreement is itself an imperial imposition based on threats of armed aggression. Whoever supports that type of "diplomacy" is as much an imperialist pig as Trump.

Sanders wants the Iran agreement to serve as a model for dealing with North Korea; in other words, bully Pyongyang until it buckles under. The difference between Sanders' approach and Trump's "fire and fury" is that the Democrat would "look for ways to tighten international sanctions" through "the international community working together." But, it's the same lawless blackmail. Sanders says nothing about direct talks with North Korea, the North's key demand, which would amount to actual diplomacy. But that would smack of equality among nations—an anathema to imperial powers, and to would-be imperial presidents, Bernie Sanders included.

In his entire speech on foreign affairs, Sanders did not utter the word "Africa" once, nor did he say the word "Israel." Yet the U.S. virtually occupies the continent of Africa, through its African Command, while Israel practically occupies U.S. foreign policy. Does that mean Sanders has no policy on Africa or Israel? No, it means he goes along with the general direction of U.S. imperial policy as it exists—because *he is an imperialist.*

September 28, 2017

HOW DONALD TRUMP RODE IN ON "DARK MONEY"

A team led by University of Massachusetts professor emeritus Thomas Ferguson reveals that "a giant wave of dark money" flowed into Donald Trump's campaign coffers in the last months of the 2016 election, enabling him to go heads up with Hillary Clinton's $1.4 billion juggernaut in the final stages of the contest. The identity of Trump's late-campaign godfathers is "shrouded," according to a paper authored by Ferguson and his collaborators Paul Jorgensen and Jie Chen, but all signs point to "a sudden influx of money from private equity and hedge funds." The cash infusion brought Trump's total spending up to $861 million. Although that's still substantially less than Hillary's total outlays, Trump's dark money arrived just in time to capitalize on Clinton's failure to mount an effective blitz in Michigan, Wisconsin, and Pennsylvania.

Thus, it wasn't the Russians that brought us Trump, but the usual suspects: private equity and hedge fund bandits. Ferguson notes that a number of private equity managers "who do not appear in the visible roster of campaign donors" began to show up "prominently around the President" after his upset win—masters of dark money, creeping into the light to claim their rewards.

Prof. Ferguson specializes in tracing corporate money to deduce the political leanings and schemings of the various corporate sectors. During the Obama administration, Ferguson's research showed Silicon Valley and the high-tech sector were Barack Obama's most reliable corporate allies, in terms of campaign contributions and political support. (And he, in turn, dutifully served the digital oligarchs.) The new study indicates that Trump owes a huge debt to the vultures of financial speculation. But then, virtually every corporate sector is seeing its wish lists fulfilled under this president, who over the past year has proven his loyalty to his class.

Or, some would argue that he has been bludgeoned into that posture. Certainly, the bulk of the ruling class and their attendants, interpreters, and enforcers were horrified that the Orange Menace might destabilize the two-capitalist-party system, undermine the free global flow of capital and jobs, and allow the momentum of the military offensive begun by Barack Obama in 2011 to falter. That threat to the imperial order has passed. Trump's savage assault on the very concept of regulation, his willingness to renegotiate NAFTA and the Trans Pacific Partnership, and the rise of the generals, as both day-to-day and overall policy managers in his White House, are "normalizing" Trump. The Republican tax cut—a looting spree—although not engineered by Trump, redounds to his benefit in 1 percent circles. As their unearned gains accrue, the Lords of Capital appreciate the uses of The Donald. Orange is the new normal—a measure of how insane late-stage capitalism has become.

Democrats are not happy, sensing that their partnership with the clandestine services to eject Trump by non-electoral means is losing steam by the day. After almost two years, the predicate offense—that Trump and the Russians colluded in hacking the Democrats—has not been proven or even convincingly presented. By now, the media-CIA-Democrat version of "resistance" is hoping that Trump will somehow self-destruct through some act or statement that is beyond the pale—except that nobody knows where "beyond" is.

Decent people thought Hillary Clinton had stepped beyond civilized discourse when she greeted news of Libyan leader Muammar Gaddafi's murder, cackling, "We came, we saw, he died." Nothing so vile and savage had passed the lips of any ranking diplomat of a major power since World War II, yet Clinton not only kept her job, but would have become president were it not for the late campaign cash infusions from hedge funders to Donald Trump. Clinton's murder-drenched cackle was a more shocking affront to civilization than any outburst yet recorded by Trump—a man not clever enough to paraphrase Julius Caesar—including his barroom cracker commentary on "shithole" countries.

The corporate Demo-press case for a Trump-Putin axis looks more and more like a Potemkin construct, a daily assemblage of front-page portals to nowhere, all façade with no back. One must eat and breathe manure to pull the likes of Donald Trump even deeper into the muck, from *below*—but that has been the mission the premier corporate media have assigned themselves. Whatever aura of fairness and credibility that still clings to their filthy corporate carcasses is irrevocably fading. And that is a good thing, just as it is a good thing that President Trump is despised by about half the country, and that Hillary Clinton is even less popular than Trump, and that the global public's trust in the United States has plummeted dramatically under Trump's presidency. What true radical does not wish for the dissolution of the mad pox of U.S. imperialism and all its interlocking institutions, with hope that this will signal the end of half a millennium of Europe's rapacious wars against the rest of the planet and of capitalism's war against the Earth itself?

In truth, imperialism, internally and externally, shudders under the weight—not of Donald Trump's orange mane, but of its own contradictions. Trump is an excretion of the system. Late-stage capitalism is the mother of monstrosities, subverting science itself—the sum total of humankind's acquired knowledge and labor—to the enslavement of the species, the path down which Amazon, Google, Apple, and the other techno-omnivores are rushing, propelled by the same for-profit engine that carved up our ancestors' worlds into edible chunks for a rich, white few.

The unraveling of this system is the overarching story of our times, a saga of great crime—and real resistance. The oppressors' media cannot tell this story, so they must smother reality with a daily narrative of lies: "counter-speech," as Google, Twitter, and Facebook have dubbed their new policy. They want to monopolize (and, of course, monetize) the human story—no dissenting versions allowed. One immediate aim is to disappear *Black Agenda Report* and a short list of other left publications and, then, move on to other white-outs.

(It is really quite amazing that senior and junior imperial heads of state—Obama, Merkel, Macron, May—and titans of industry—Bezos, Zuckerberg, Pichai—were so quick to affix their own imprimaturs to the crude hit piece put out by the red-baiters at *PropOrNot*, and showcased on the front page of the *Washington Post* back in late November 2016. The combined audiences of the dozen or so targeted lefty sites would have little impact on a national electoral contest. But again, empire demands a monopoly.)

The main objective is to make endless war palatable, as imperialism attempts to bomb, blockade, occupy, and bluster its way out of a cascade of crises. Unable to compete with the Chinese command economy, its "soft" power exhausted, the U.S. empire plays the only strong card it has left: its massive military, now centered on a special operations force roughly as large as the entire French Army. War becomes both the means of imperial survival and justification for its continued existence: the how and the why of empire.

That's why there is no such thing as a "resistance" that is not loudly and consistently antiwar.

January 31, 2018

MASS MANUFACTURERS OF SLANDER AND LIES

Chastened by the long-awaited Mueller report—or at least what we've learned about the two-year probe into "Russiagate" from Attorney General William Barr—the U.S. corporate media have been forced to partially abandon their ludicrous claim of "collusion" between Donald Trump and Vladimir Putin. Or maybe the hysteria-makers were finally exhausted by their marathon of lies. But the civil war within the U.S. ruling class will continue to simmer, because it is rooted in real contradictions—primarily, a fear that Trump cannot be depended on to keep up the momentum of President Obama's global military offensive and thus disrupt the rise of China and its strategic ally, Russia.

The Lords of Capital are painfully aware that U.S. imperialism has been drained of whatever "soft" power it once had in the world and left with only two cards to play: multi-theater, unremitting military aggression and full-spectrum weaponization of the dollar. "Regime change" is the local-ized manifestation of Washington's desperate bid to upend and disrupt the emerging new global order, as China returns to its historical place at the center of the world—the position it held when Columbus embarked on his pillages. Therefore, although Donald Trump has gotten a respite from Mueller, the orchestrated demonization of Russia, China, Venezuela, Syria, and "socialism" will remain the daily fare of the U.S. propaganda machine that masquerades as journalism. In other words, a step back to "normal."

The *New York Times* can thus continue to personalize its New Cold War hysteria with Putin-bashing, while leaving Trump out of it. For example, in an article this week titled "Russia's Military Mission Creep Advances to a New Front: Africa," the *Times* claims that "expanding Moscow's military sway on the continent reflects Mr. Putin's broader vision of returning Russia to its former glory." The piece is sheer polemics disguised as journalism, citing recent Russian military "cooperation with Guinea, Burkina Faso, Burundi and Madagascar" and Russian "major oil and gas interests in Algeria, Angola, Egypt, Libya, Senegal, South Africa, Uganda and Nigeria" as grave threats to stability in Africa. Yet, in a 1,500-word article, the *Times* fails to even mention AFRICOM, the U.S. military command that has virtually occupied the entire continent since its inception in 2008, climaxing with President Obama's 2011 assault on Libya that plunged the whole northern tier of the region into flames. By 2017, according to journalist Nick Turse, AFRICOM was "conducting 3,500 exercises, programs, and engagements per year, an average of nearly 10 missions per day, on the African continent," a "signal of America's deepening and complicated ties" in Africa.

Nothing Russia has done in Africa comes close to Washington's deep penetration of the continent, yet the *Times* writes that "the United States military has a relatively light footprint across Africa." The U.S. and Europe fund and oversee every African "peace-keeping" mission, including the conflict in Somalia, where the CIA directs a full-scale drone war that has been dramatically escalated under President Trump. In the eight years that Barack Obama was president, "AFRICOM went from three military bases to 84 bases" on the continent, said Paul Pumphrey, co-founder of Friends of Congo. Six million Congolese have died as a result of interventions by U.S.-backed regimes in neighboring Rwanda and Uganda, with the full complicity of Washington. Under U.S. and Israeli tutelage, Africa's largest nation, Sudan, was split in two in 2011, only to see South Sudan erupt in a civil war two years later that has killed nearly four hundred thousand people. The United States and France overcame their imperial rivalry in Africa and have partnered to occupy Mali and Niger, where four U.S. Special Forces troops were killed in 2017, and the U.S. is building a huge drone base, to be staffed by at least eight hundred American personnel.

The U.S. military footprint is heavier and wider, by far, than any other nation, but *Times* reporter Eric Schmitt apparently feels confident in stating, as fact, that the U.S. has a "light footprint" in Africa because that's what AFRICOM's top brass has been saying since 2012. Therefore, it must be true, despite the numbers that say differently. Nick Turse, whose reporting got him blackballed by AFRICOM's high command, wrote in 2018 that the U.S. maintained "34 sites scattered across the continent, with high concentrations in the north and west as well as the Horn of Africa." The biggest military facility is located in Djibouti, a desperately poor country that has been turned into a foreign base farm for the U.S., France, Italy, Saudi Arabia, Japan, and China (Beijing and Tokyo's only bases in Africa), purportedly to patrol against piracy on the Somali coast.

Russia has no bases in Africa, but is said to be exploring establishing one in the Central African Republic, the former French colony where the U.S. briefly imprisoned Haitian president Jean Bertrand Aristide after overthrowing his elected government in 2004. The talks between Moscow and Bangui have caused consternation in Washington and Paris, anxieties that have been relayed to the *New York Times* with full confidence that the paper's private sector propagandists are better liars than any military press spokesperson. The *Times* dutifully writes that France's minister of armed forces is unhappy. "We feel very much concerned by the growing Russian influence in a country that we know well, the Central African Republic," Florence Parly told reporters during a recent visit to Washington.

France knows the country well because it oppressed and exploited the Central African people for generations—an expertise that white Americans tend to respect.

So, Africa is swarming with U.S. troops stationed at bases throughout the continent, second only to the French presence in the region, but the *Times* can say with a straight face that the U.S. Africa Command has a "light footprint," while the baseless Vladimir Putin dreams of "returning Russia to its former glory" through "a more militaristic approach in Africa," in the words of an American general. There should be little doubt that

Russia, the second biggest arms merchant in the world, behind the U.S., is actively seeking African markets for its weapons. What scares the U.S. is that African nations like Guinea, Burkina Faso, Burundi, and Madagascar want to do arms and training deals with Russia, to diversify their defense suppliers and create a "multi-polar" environment in Africa.

U.S. imperialism tolerates only one pole—its own—and instructs its media mouthpieces to vilify all competitors. But the U.S. cannot compete economically with Russia's partner, China, whose trade with Africa surpassed the United States in 2009. African states are eager to become part of China's New Silk Road, or Belt and Road Initiative, the world's greatest public works, transportation, and trade project, which offers Africa unprecedented "connectivity" to the planet's economic center in the East. The U.S. has nothing to offer Africa but guns, drones, and an extended half-life for the neocolonial order—and Russia can cut a better deal on the guns.

The *New York Times* and the rest of the corporate media tell tales that only Americans believe, in service of a crumbling imperial, racist order. The U.S. media bubble is a scary place, populated by demons and villains that are determined to steal or destroy an "American way of life" that most Americans—especially Black folks—have never lived.

Having nothing to offer the people but endless war and austerity, the Lords of Capital invent enemies, complete with full-blown fictitious pathologies, conjured histories, and fabricated motives. Amid the imperial rot, the oligarchs turn on each other, as they did in 2016 in a fit of panic called Russiagate. A Deep State referee named Mueller has called for a pause in the fratricide among the corporate brethren, but that can only signal an intensification of the lies that corporate media tell against external "enemies" and actual dissidents on the home front.

In decline, the Lords of Capital have no good stories to tell. To the extent that they control the domestic narrative, everything becomes slander.

April 3, 2019

SANDERS VS. THE ENDLESS AUSTERITY REGIME

Corporate Democrats have had great success in smothering Bernie Sanders' challenge to the capitalist austerity regime that has eroded U.S. working class incomes and economic security for two generations. Just two years ago, in the wake of his astounding bid to deny Hillary Clinton the Democratic presidential nomination, the Vermont senator was the most popular politician in the country. Although some Democrats blamed Sanders for Donald Trump's even more surprising 2016 election, by the next year the septuagenarian Medicare for All champion's favorability ratings exceeded all others—including among Black voters. Most astonishingly, Sanders had almost single-handedly removed the stigma from the word "socialism," an amazing feat for a New Deal Democratic reformer who has never advocated anything remotely resembling the overthrow of the rule of capital, and who remains an "imperialist pig" in foreign affairs.

As the 2020 campaign season approached, a great sense of foreboding was evident within the U.S. ruling class. Sanders was by now associated with a whole menu of issues—Medicare for All, free public college, a $15-an-hour minimum wage, and more—that had become popular with majorities of all voters and super-majorities (80 or even 90 percent) of Democrats. With the Clinton machine in tatters and Sanders' supporters presumably eager for another shot at seizing the commanding heights of the Democratic Party, 2020 was looking like a very problematic year for capitalist duopoly politics. The system was already under the deliberately-induced stress of Russiagate, as corporate Democrats and their allies in media and the national security state daily delegitimized the Trump regime. Corporate Democrats were confident—just as they were in 2016—that they could win the White House by making Trump, himself, effectively the sole issue of the campaign. But first they had to neutralize Bernie and his austerity-busting, super-majority issues, to clear the way for an economic issues-less anti-Trump crusade—the corporate Democratic ideal.

So, they simply threw all the shit at hand into the game, simultaneously mobbing and co-opting Sanders with the biggest, most multicolored crowd of Democratic politicians ever assembled for a presidential race—even larger than the horde that Republican moneybags financed in hopes of derailing Donald Trump four years earlier. Dollar-drenched corporate hacks like Senators Cory Booker and Kamala Harris claimed to endorse Sanders' signature Medicare for All legislation, and Senator Elizabeth Warren, once considered anathema by corporatists—the Bride of Berniestein—was suddenly a darling of party leaders and media.

Sanders has gotten lost in the slosh, as intended. The corporate strategy was to ensure that the super-majorities of Democrats that support Sanders' issues were split among the "progressive" pretenders, while Joe Biden soaked up the nervous-nellie voters that are desperate to beat Trump with someone—anyone—"electable." The corporatists' nightmare scenario, that Sanders would rev up his highly energized and youthful 2016 machine, funded by tens of millions in small-contributions, and smash his way to a first ballot victory at the convention, seems far less likely. The corporate media—now supremely acclimated to close-order political drill by Russiagate—have acted in near-unison to alternatively ignore or malign Sanders, often pretending he is just not there as they fawn over his mimics, who can be counted on to retreat from corporate-opposed issues once the Bernie-bear has been contained.

In their desperation to blunt Bernie, the Lords of Capital gave Kamala Harris permission to ambush Old Man Biden, who personifies Barack Obama's partially successful Grand Bargain with Republicans as well as an earlier accommodation with Dixiecrats. Harris rose to the occasion in the last debate, miraculously losing her signature tic-giggle as she committed euthanasia on screen. But it's all in service to the higher corporate purpose. Harris' strategy to diffuse the Sanders vote is much like the "close as a man's belt" battle doctrine employed by the Vietnamese, who would attack the Americans from such close quarters that it was impossible for the U.S. to effectively deploy its awesome artillery and air power without hitting their own troops' positions. Harris hung around Sanders' belt on Medicare for All, even raising her hand when the corporate debate instigator/moderator asked who among the candidates would abolish private health insurance. (Naturally, she reneged afterwards.) As the emerging Great Corporate Black Hope (Booker is clearly hopeless), Harris offers the African American supermajority that supports Medicare for All a Black face (and a woman) to vote for. At the end of the process, Harris will revert to corporate form.

There is only one escape from this fetid and flooded corporate swamp for Sanders. He must very quickly get serious about building a grassroots movement-type politics on the ground, that creates issue-based events that cannot be ignored, involving tens of thousands of people, and that disrupts the corporate-managed pace, coverage, and content of the primary season. In short, Sanders must subvert the corporate process and start acting like he really is leading a "revolution," as he tells his supporters. Otherwise, he will be effectively marginalized, despite the super-majorities that support his issues and the transparent dishonesty of his mimics.

If you think this column is supportive of the Sanders candidacy, then you haven't been reading *BAR* all these years. We are socialists and Black liberationists who do commentary and analysis, and have never backed corporate parties or candidates. The Democratic Party serves its ruling class financiers and is the main agency of their control over Black America, where the Republicans are irrelevant. As one of the two parties of capitalist governance in the U.S., the Democratic Party will self-destruct before it bucks its corporate bosses. That's why purported "socialists" like Sanders, or the Democratic Socialists that always wind up supporting Democrats, are delusional if they think they can usurp control of the devil's machine— or they are trying to fool the rest of us.

However, Bernie Sanders' non-socialism isn't really important at this juncture in history. The ruling class isn't scared of his socialist pretensions, but will viciously resist New Deal-type reforms that threaten their austerity regime, a global Race to the Bottom that ruthlessly diminishes the living standards and economic security of the masses of people, so that they will accept any job, under any conditions of employment. Capitalist austerity is designed to provide working people with no options but to take what the bosses offer. Austerity regimes gut the social safety nets, not to save money, but to impose abject desperation on working people so that they will accept the "shit jobs" that are now the norm even in the "most-developed" capitalist countries. The Lords of Austerity are creating a global precariat, defined as "a condition of existence without predictability or security, affecting material or psychological welfare."

The Lords of Capital oppose single-payer health care, not so much in solidarity with their capitalist brethren in the insurance and pharmaceutical industries (capitalists have no problem devouring or sacrificing each other), but because single payer erases the connection between employment and health care, eliminating medical precarity and reducing the bosses' power. Thus, capitalists oppose single payer even though it would dramatically reduce the costs of labor for most businesses. That's why corporate Democrats resist Sanders' menu of reforms despite the fact that 80 to 90 percent of Democratic voters support them.

The ruling class agenda for the future is quite simple: endless war and austerity. Since they have no other vision, and have done fabulously well for themselves over the past forty years of austerity and war, they tolerate no deviation from the corporate order and will lash out lethally against those that threaten their war-making and austerity-imposing prerogatives. It is unthinkable that the rulers would allow one of their governing parties to fall into the hands of austerity busters. Rather, the Lords of Capital would be compelled to destroy such a party—and govern from another platform—rather than surrender the institution to folks that actually want to give the people what they want.

The people need to see that contradiction played out in the Democratic Party, the duopoly party whose constituencies are actually eager to make substantive demands on the state. (Republican rank-and-file whites desire only that their government affirm white supremacy.) It would have been a great political lesson if Sanders' momentum was such that corporate Democrats have to steal the nomination from him in broad daylight, hopefully prompting a mass exit from the party and creation of a new social democratic formation (or a much bigger Green Party). Or, if somehow Sanders won the nomination, we could all watch the corporate players pick up their marbles to form a new "centrist" party, leaving leftish Democrats encamped in the hollow shell. As things stand at this early stage in the process, Sanders may simply wind up an also-ran—allowing the corporate spinners to write the obituary on his "far left" escapades.

Or maybe Bernie will catch fire again, and propel us to the next contradiction.

July 10, 2019

THE ISSUE-LESS IMPEACHMENT: THE CORPORATE DEMOCRATS STAND FOR NOTHING, SO THEY IMPEACH FOR NOTHING

The impeachment of Donald Trump has nothing to do with social justice at home and abroad, global environmental stability, or the rule of law anywhere on the planet. Rather, the corporate Democrats have methodically narrowed the scope of the indictment to exclude all the actual crimes of this president against humanity, peace, the environment, and the rule of law—for the obvious reason that both corporate parties and all modern U.S. presidents are collectively and individually guilty. In limiting the indictment to Trump's attempted political extortion of Ukraine for the purpose of influencing a U.S. election—a laughable charge, since the Kiev regime is the creature of the U.S. (Democratic) engineered overthrow of the previous, elected Ukraine government—the Democrats are effectively exonerating themselves and their Republican brethren of the full spectrum of lawlessness that is everyday politics in the belly of the racist, imperial beast.

Trump will be put in the dock for a (relatively) minor offense as a kind of purgative of the whole corporate system's rotten innards. It's like indicting the mass-murdering, criminal war-waging South African apartheid regime for gerrymandering elections in which Blacks, by law, could not vote. The cited offense is meaningless, and all the rest is forgiven.

The corporate Democrats have used the vile, childishly compulsive, and overtly racist Trump as a straw man ever since he announced for the

2016 presidential race. They desperately needed an opponent as personally "deplorable" as The Donald, to make themselves appear "progressive" by comparison. When you're running against The Devil, simply not being Lucifer is enough. With Trump as her opponent, Hillary Clinton could campaign on a platform of—not much of anything. The Democrats reasoned that, given a choice between the status quo (endless austerity and war) and rule by a dangerously unpredictable, race-baiting clown, the people would opt for the status quo. It was a miscalculation.

Thanks to WikiLeaks (whose founder Julian Assange languishes in prison for revealing mega-crimes of the United States under both parties) we know that the Democratic National Committee urged its operatives and friendly media to encourage Trump's quest for the nomination. It worked like a charm, or a curse. The Age of Trump, as defined by who dominates the corporate airwaves, began long before the Orange Con Man seized control of half of the duopoly electoral system. By the time Trump squeezed out an Electoral College victory over the Democrats, corporate media had awarded him *$5 billion* in free air time—more than his Republican opponents, Hillary Clinton, and Bernie Sanders combined. The Democrats should have been more careful about what to wish for.

Having inflicted Trump on the nation and the world, the Democrats, through Uberlord Hillary Clinton, blamed it on The Russians and Putin's "assets" within the U.S. polity—meaning *Black Agenda Report* and other left-wing web sites slandered by the *Washington Post* and its otherwise anonymous source, *PropOrNot*. But, despite their surprise loss at the polls, the Democrats were still in need of Trump as a straw man. During the course of the 2016 campaign most of the ruling class and their media had crowded into Hillary Clinton's big fat tent—along with the scariest denizens of the national security state—in panic at the prospect of the unpredictable Trump at the helm of American Empire. Clinton's defeat became an opportunity to purge the U.S. political conversation of meddlesome Left voices and to reclaim the political narrative for American Exceptionalism—an imperial version of white supremacy that is versatile enough to accommodate a nominally Black president.

With the Russiagate-endorsing CIA as a public partner, the Democrats became the premier Party of War, while Trump solidified the GOP's long-time status as the White Man's Party—a true Devil's Duopoly, within whose sulphuric confines Black voters feel little choice but to huddle with the less overtly racist of the Beelzebubs (even when "less racist" means Joe Biden, the mass incarcerator and friend of Dixiecrats). Trump still gets more airtime than anybody else, or any *issue*—because the Democrats and the corporate media have made *him* the sole issue of public discourse, along with the Russians. The demonization of foreign enemies has come home to roost. The U.S. ruling class is split, creating a crisis of legitimacy in the U.S. political order for all the world to see, but which is blamed on the Russians, in furtherance of endless war and to continue the purge of the Left.

It is a bizarre impeachment, nothing like the attempt to rid the nation of Andrew Johnson after the Civil War. Johnson was a racist Democrat who was unalterably opposed to Black political equality through Radical Reconstruction of the defeated Confederacy. His successful impeachment might have strangled Jim Crow in its cradle. The odious and ridiculous Donald Trump is highly unlikely to be removed by the Senate, but the Democrats' issue-less impeachment charade is yet another opportunity to extend Trump's usefulness as straw man, with Democrats hoping once again that this will be a winning electoral strategy. But even if Trump is reelected, he will still be the corporate Democrats' straw man, whose very presence is used to drown out demands for an end to constant warfare and the Race to the Bottom.

December 11, 2019

THE CORPORATE DEMOCRATS' (AND ALICIA GARZA'S) GET-SANDERS SLANDERS

Once upon a time not so long ago the U.S. corporate media was a livelier place, where the rich people that owned the presses argued among themselves about the destiny of the nation and the world through the pages of their publications. They allowed some leeway for lowly reporters to disseminate pertinent facts, even if such information sometimes tended to favor politicians, movements, and countries disliked by the ruling classes. Of course, "Reds" were always demonized and Black public opinion disregarded unless backed up by Molotov cocktails. But elements of truth could eventually be found between the lines and in stray articles of corporate media, providing more reason to read the *New York Times* and the *Washington Post* than simply to find out what the ruling classes were thinking and planning.

The War of/on Terror and Russiagate—both involving mass psychological warfare operations to stamp out domestic resistance to the global U.S. imperial offensive—signaled that the Lords of Capital's tolerance for dissent was approaching zero. The contradictions of late-stage capitalism and the increasing precariousness of U.S. empire squeezed all vestiges of liberality out of the boardrooms, as was reflected in the content of their ever-consolidating media.

Finally the internet, that vast digital outback where the Left's survivors had sought refuge from corporate monoculture, was targeted for political cleansing. McCarthy-era censorship was resurrected, with publications like *Black Agenda Report* at the top of the blacklist. However, it's not just us real radicals that have been rendered non-persons in the headquarters nation of the "free" corporate-ruled world. Bernie Sanders, a U.S. senator, has joined the ranks of those whose name will not be spoken by corporate media, except in the negative.

Sanders' mission is anything but revolutionary: it is to "sheepdog" back into the Democratic Party fold the millions of stray, leftish Americans that despair of the duopoly electoral system. Sanders believes that the "more inclusive" half of the corporate duopoly will allow itself to become the vessel that will enact single-payer health care, free higher education, a dignified minimum wage, and confiscatory taxes on billionaires, whom he proclaims "should not exist." But the billionaires that actually control the Democratic Party's structures have decreed that it is Sanders whose existence will not be acknowledged in the pages of their properties, unless it is to pillory him.

Corporate media vengeance against Sanders has been fierce and comprehensive—approaching the anathema that has been heaped on Trump, the overtly racist billionaire that took over the GOP and made it a purer White Man's Party, and who converted the previously bipartisan Deep Imperial State into Deep Blue Democrats with his questioning of U.S. regime-change and "free trade" policies. The Democrats and their corporate media partners thought Trump would be easy to beat in 2016, and to make sure he was the Republican nominee, they provided him with billions of dollars in free airtime.

The GOP, an imperial and "free trade" party like the Democrats, tried to mob Trump. They threw every party notable and vote-getter into the primaries, sixteen in all—precisely as the Democrats would do to head off Sanders' second bid for the presidency four years later, with twenty-six contenders assembled with the party's blessing. Joe Biden, the consummate but rapidly fading corporate shill, was their Great Hope, but they had plenty of minions in reserve.

It would also take a unified corporate media to stop Sanders, who in 2017 was the most popular politician in the United States, eclipsing all others in favorability. His core policies were backed by two-thirds of all voters and even larger super-majorities of Democrats. But the rich man's press was up to the challenge. Having been drilled for three years in the daily delivery of a unitary, Democrat-spook-concocted Russiagate scenario, the corporate media had been disciplined to the task of no-holds-barred political assassination.

It was a blitzkrieg. Every minor Democratic presidential contender in the Party-summoned menagerie had a more interesting story for the press to tell than Sanders, who was buried at the end of articles, most often in a negative context, or not mentioned at all despite his long-time second place ranking to Joe Biden. CNN and MSNBC hated Sanders 24/7—as if he were Trump—with MSNBC permitting its legal analyst, Mimi Rocah, to exclaim that Sanders "makes my skin crawl." Polls were rigged, in that few of them were capable of reaching statistically viable numbers of the under-forty voters that strongly favored Sanders but use only cell phones—a fatal professional flaw often acknowledged in the fine print, but pollsters then made up numbers anyway, to Sanders' detriment.

Sanders and his super-majority-supported issues must be defeated, because they represent the clearest threat yet to the forty-year-long bipartisan policy of "austerity"—which, in plain language is the dragooning of the American workforce into the Race to the Bottom that capitalism has imposed on all of the global working class within its reach. The aim is to remove every social support that might allow workers to reject participation in the "gig" economy of low-paid, contracted, part-time jobs—the "shit" work that makes up the majority of "new jobs" under late-stage capitalism and fuels the phenomenal growth of the billionaire class. Deindustrialization is austerity = Race to the Bottom. The Lords of Capital have no other strategy for the future and neither do their minions in the Democratic Party. So they reject Sanders, the social democratic reformer, like the plague. But Sanders' issues are not so easily slandered, side-tracked, or buried.

The deliberately overcrowded Democratic primary field is designed to dilute the austerity-busting agenda introduced by Sanders, through the diversion of multiple personalities. When it became clear that Biden was not a good bet for the ruling class to stake its systemic life on, the corporate media fell in love with Sanders' mimic Elizabeth Warren, who had already signaled her loyalty to "the Party" and an openness to gradualism on Medicare for All and the rest of her agenda. For the time being, until Sanders is effectively neutralized, that's reassuring enough to make Warren a favorite of much of corporate America and their media. Once the Sanders threat has subsided, however, Warren will be required to further neuter herself to allay the fears of billionaire Democratic donors, who threaten to withhold their money or even support Trump if the capitalist boat is rocked. Every indication is that she will try to present as little problem as possible to the rulers.

Warren and the corporate Democrats were vastly assisted in their get-Sanders campaign by Alicia Garza, the Black Lives Matter nameholder and disburser of capitalist political philanthropy, who organized a shameful slander against Sanders after the Working Families Party board engineered an endorsement of Warren. Although Sanders and his campaign officials said nothing at all of a racial nature in response to the questionable actions by the WFP (80 percent of whose board and membership backed him in 2016), and despite the fact that Sanders has polled consistently second to Biden in Black support and has the most diverse backing of any candidate, Garza pretended that a racial crime had been committed. (See Margaret Kimberley and Danny Haiphong's articles on this travesty.)

Donald Trump, the Democrats' FrankenCracker, who won the presidency partly on the strength of the billions in free airtime the corporate Democrats guided his way ($5 billion worth by Election Day), remains useful to the Party, which may be why Nancy Pelosi took so long to give the nod to impeachment proceedings. The Democrats still want to run against Trump and his roaring racism, just as they did in 2016, because it allows them to avoid economic issues. "Anyone Blue Will Do" is a corporate Democratic slogan designed to blunt resistance to the Race to the Bottom and to protect the billionaires.

Sanders' quest for the nomination is probably doomed if he continues to play by rules while the corporate media (and Warren) conspire in a dirty game against him. His best hope is to attempt to turn his campaign into a "movement"—to take to the streets with his rallies and march on the nearest iconography of the 1 percent, to make such noise and motion that the corporate media cannot ignore him. That, too, would be cause for shrieks from both the Party and the press, but at least Sanders' anti-Race to the Bottom message would be heard, and maybe a real movement would outlive his candidacy, organized outside the oligarchy's bought-and-paid for property: the Democratic Party.

October 2, 2019

TRUMP IS A CRIMINAL BUT THE DEMOCRATS BELONG TO THE SAME MAFIA

The grievously wronged Iranians have apparently fired a purposely harmless salvo of missiles into several U.S.-occupied bases in Iraq to avenge last Friday's U.S. drone assassination of Revolutionary Guards commander Qassi Suleimani. Although the Fars News Agency claimed, for Iranian popular consumption, that "at least 80 US armed personnel have been killed and around 200 others wounded," American and other NATO forces in Iraq report no casualties, giving Trump an opportunity to claim victory and back off from further aggressions. Trump followed the Iranian lead, holding a press conference on Wednesday to dance away from continued armed hostilities.

Since there is no "peace party" with any influence on governance in the United States, a U.S. retreat from Armageddon is the most that the world can hope for in the near term. Trump's mafia-style hit on the revered Iranian general—yet another Nuremburg-level U.S. crime against peace and humanity, for which death by hanging is the historical punishment—seemed designed to set the stage for a reprise of George Bush's 2003 "Shock and Awe" demonstration of U.S. imperial firepower, this time with an orange tinge.

Iranian national pride required a pantomimed military response, but the U.S. has provoked a far worse punishment by the Iraqis, on whose territory Suleimani was ambushed. The Iraqi parliament swiftly voted 170-0 to kick the five thousand U.S. troops out of their country, an exodus that would render Washington's foothold in neighboring Syria untenable, thus sealing the fate of the remaining U.S.-backed al-Qaida "rebels" holed up in Idlib province and hastening the demise of ISIS forces currently shielded from Russian air attack by U.S. firepower. Donald Trump, who (correctly, but incoherently) charged Barack Obama with "founding " ISIS, may well have fast-forwarded the definitive end of the U.S.-Islamic jihadist presence in Syria and Iraq.

Not that this was Trump's intention. The Republicans and Democrats are united under the American imperial banner, and only differ on details of strategy to maintain Washington's global domination. As *BAR* contributing editor Danny Haiphong writes, "There may be two political parties in the United States, but there is only one ruling class agenda."

Yet there is a profound split in the U.S. ruling class—not about the necessity to preserve the empire, on which there is no debate among the rulers, but over how Washington should manage relations with its junior imperial partners in Europe and elsewhere, and over the modalities of 1 percent governance within the United States. On foreign policy, the Democrats have since 2016 positioned themselves as the more aggressive War Party, constantly goading Trump to attack Russia and its Syrian ally and to "stand up" to North Korea to prove he is not a "dupe" of Vladimir Putin. As the party of Barack Obama, the previous Super-Sanctioner of rebellious nations, the Democrats are vicious in maligning Venezuela. And as the party of Hillary Clinton the Democrats have killed hundreds of thousands in U.S.-directed and financed jihadist wars in Libya and Syria. They are the puppeteers and paymasters of terror on a scale that Donald Trump has yet to match, an orgy of sectarian beheadings, torture, rape, and mass murder that Trump's assassination of General Suleimani may inadvertently bring to a close with U.S. ouster from the region.

At home, the Democrats have spent the last three years constructing a New Cold War censorship of the Left, starting with *Black Agenda Report* and other radical websites targeted only weeks after the 2016 election. As Black Alliance for Peace national organizer (and *BAR* editor) Ajamu Baraka writes, the Democratic "opposition," including the Democrat-leaning corporate media, is not anti-war—it's anti-Trump. The Democrats, like their corporate and banking masters, are determined to preserve the neoliberal economic order—the global Race to the Bottom in which U.S. workers compete with super-exploited workers in the developing world. The only difference is that the Democrats would "integrate" the management of this dwindling wage economy through a policy of racial and ethnic "diversity." Same downward destination, but with multi-colored overseers. Same police occupation of Black communities, and same racialized gaps in earnings and wealth for the masses of Blacks and browns—but rewards aplenty for the misleadership classes of the oppressed, whose job is to keep the social peace while oligarchs swallow society whole. Most of the Congressional Black Caucus joined other Democrats in awarding Trump yet another record-breaking military budget. Seventy-five percent of the Black Caucus voted in 2018 to make police a protected class and assault on cops a federal crime. Eighty percent of the Black Caucus voted five years ago to keep the Pentagon's 1033 program funneling military weapons and gear to local police departments—and the Caucus has become even more reactionary and treacherous since then.

Although many of the issues have changed since Malcolm X's day, Blacks remain locked into much the same power relationships as half a century ago. Malcolm's "foxes" and "wolves" of 1963 are still on the prowl: *"The white liberals are more dangerous than the conservatives; they lure the Negro, and as the Negro runs from the growling wolf, he flees into the open jaws of the 'smiling' fox. One is a wolf, the other is a fox. No matter what, they'll both eat you."*

There is one big difference in the political landscape, fifty-seven years after Malcolm spoke those words. The "Black misleadership class"—a term coined at BAR and its predecessor, *The Black Commentator*—now plays a pivotal role in the electoral workings of the Democratic half of the corporate duopoly system of governance. As I explained two years ago, the Black misleaders are *"those Black political forces that emerged at the end of the '60s, eager to join the corporate and duopoly political (mostly Democrat) ranks, and to sell out the interests of the overwhelmingly working-class Black*

*masses in the process. It is both an actual and aspirational class, which ulti-
mately sees its interests as tied to those of U.S. imperialism and its ruling
circles. It seeks representation in the halls of corporate power, and dreads
social transformation, which would upset the class's carefully cultivated relationships with Power."*

Malcolm's "foxes" and "wolves" are still on the prowl. Blacks are still
at the bottom and racing deeper into the abyss. But an opportunistic
sliver of the Black population has aligned with banksters and oligarchs in
Democratic boardrooms. They join with corporate Democrats in screaming
that Trump is the existential threat, not U.S. imperial wars, in which most
Democrats are complicit; not the Race to the Bottom, which is as much a
Democrat as Republican project; not the Mass Black Incarceration State,
which is mainly enforced by urban Democratic regimes of all colors; and
not capitalism, a system that was born like the white settler United States
in Native genocide and Black chattel slavery.

The Black misleadership class has no solidarity with anyone. They are
hustlers, who have hijacked the aspirations of a proud, brave, and inde-
pendent-minded people—a people who have historically sought social
justice and peace for not only themselves but all mankind. That people
needs a new party, with themselves in the leadership, a party that will
Fight the Power. There is a world of allies out there, sharing the same aspirations. But none can be free of the scourge of war—the ultimate crime
against humanity, from which all others flow—while the war-makers are
in power in the Citadel of Capital.

The key to unlock all of our chains is right here, in the belly of the
beast.

Power to the People!

January 9, 2020

SHAKY JOE BIDEN, BILLIONAIRE BLOOMBERG, AND THE GLOBAL RACE TO THE BOTTOM

U.S. oligarchs have begun to panic at the prospect that they will lose control of the other half of the American electoral duopoly. With the GOP in Donald Trump's unreliable hands, the Democrats four years ago became the de facto ruling class party, and thus the favored brand of the national security state and most of the corporate media. Although there is not even one genuine anti-imperialist among congressional Democrats—certainly not Bernie Sanders or Elizabeth Warren—the party's popular base is in revolt against a forty-year domestic austerity regime that offers nothing but ever-declining real wages, non-existent job security, and a visibly decaying nation-scape. It has finally dawned on most Americans that they have been conscripted into a Global Race to the Bottom, and they want out of the downward spiral.

Sanders and Warren are running for president on austerity-busting issues supported by super-majorities of Democrats (and up to half of Republicans). In previous eras, the corporate rulers would embrace milder versions of reform in health care, wages, job security, educational costs, and environmental protection, in order to blunt demands for more transformative measures. But those days are over. The Lords of Capital are committed to the Race to the Bottom—locked in by the nature of capitalism-in-decline.

Despite their vise-grip on media and corporate donor control of the Democratic Party machinery, all the oligarchs' eggs are in Joe Biden's basket this election year. The numbers show that, were it not for all-consuming fears of Trump among older Black voters, who cling to the notion of Biden's "electability," Sanders and Warren would collectively sweep the primaries. The corporate consensus on austerity—and, therefore, the shape of capitalism, at home and globally—is in dire peril. That's why Michael Bloomberg has thrown his $55 billion hat into the ring—not because he has any prospect of winning the nomination (his presence in fact helps the anti-austerity candidates), but as the first stage in what Bloomberg has determined will be an epic battle to preserve the austerity regime and its hold on the Democratic Party machinery—the favored party of the ruling class as long as Trump runs the GOP.

Bloomberg is signaling to his fellow oligarchs, through his blaring commitment of up to a billion dollars, that they must become deadly serious about containing the economic populist wave among the Democrats, or face collapse of the austerity regime. The fate and fortunes of the oligarchy cannot be allowed to depend on Old Shaky Joe. Bloomberg has put himself and his fortune into the contest to rally his (ruling) classmates to the task of shoring up corporate control of the Party if Sanders, or some Sanders-Warren combination, seizes the top spots on the ticket.

Winning the nomination, or even the presidency, doesn't automatically get you control of the party. But the Democratic Party is a political organism with an institutional life. Although probably only twenty House members, and less than a handful of senators, can at this moment be counted on to support Sanders' full agenda, that cohort would immediately swell if Sanders wins the nomination in Milwaukee—and will explode if he is elected president in November. Former New York mayor Bloomberg, the most electorally attuned of the oligarchs, knows this. He understands that Democratic politicians will only remain fully dependable corporate servants if they are provided with an assured source of funds, through reliable structures. Bloomberg's gambit is to enlist his ruling class fellows in an all-out push to further consolidate their dollar dominance of the institutional Democratic Party—the only electoral vehicle left to preserve austerity capitalism with a racially "diverse" face. Although Bloomberg cannot expect to win a decisive number of delegates, he is conducting a "demonstration-effect" campaign to fully engage his uber-class fellows in the fight to maintain the corporate nature of the Democratic Party.

But Shaky Joe Biden remains the first line of corporate defense. If he does poorly in New Hampshire and Iowa, his aura of "electability" will be shattered. Black voters are not ideologically wedded to Biden. If they voted their economic agenda, Blacks would be overwhelmingly for Sanders. Only the existential threat of a Trump re-election keeps older Blacks in Biden's corner. That will change in a flash if Biden does not win strong approval from whites in the first two contests—the corporate nightmare that terrifies and energizes Bloomberg. Biden's long career as a gladiator for austerity has now moved to center stage, as he defends his role in Barack Obama's attempt at an across-the-board, slash-in-entitlements "Grand Bargain" with the Republicans, a betrayal of the Democratic base that ended—blessedly—in gridlock at the end of Obama's first term. Sanders will have to be careful in his condemnation of Biden, to avoid indicting The First Black President.

The best outcome in 2020 would be a break-up of the Democratic Party, creating space for a genuine political debate in the belly of the imperial beast. It now appears that such a rupture is at least as likely to come from the right, from Bloomberg-organized billionaires, as from the left, through a mass defection by Sanders supporters infuriated by yet another round of the Party's dirty tricks. I believe Bloomberg is preparing to launch a kind of "Third Way" party structure to shore up corporate Democrats and isolate and deny endorsement to Sanders should the Vermont senator win the nomination—leaving Sanders with only the rump of a party behind him.

If that happens, we at *Black Agenda Report* will celebrate the end of duopoly and a new scenario of struggle.

January 23, 2020

FEAR PERVADES BLACK POLITICS, AND MAKES US AGENTS OF OUR OWN OPPRESSION

Black voters in South Carolina kicked off Joe Biden's political resurrection last Saturday and stuck with the worthless corporate hack through Super Tuesday's primary contests. Although the craven Black misleadership class will no doubt shout hallelujahs that "hands that picked cotton now pick presidents" and claim Black voters exercised brilliant "strategic" judgment in making themselves indispensable to the corporate Democratic party establishment, the true motivator of Black Biden supporters is a pervasive and deeply corrosive fear. Not just dread of four more years of Trump, although that is central to Black political behavior, but abject terror at the very thought that the Democratic Party—"our" party, in many Black folks' minds—might fracture under the challenge of the Sandernistas.

Voluminous data over many years has shown that African Americans are to the left of Hispanics on issues of bread and butter and, especially, war and peace, and far to the left of white Democrats. But, unlike Hispanics, Blacks cannot be depended on to uphold their own historical political consensus in Democratic Party primary elections for fear of weakening the chances of defeating The White Man's Party. Hyper-conscious of their minority and despised status—and surrounded by hostile, race-obsessed white Republicans in the southern states—older Blacks cling to Democratic Party structures as if their lives depend on it. The ascent of Donald Trump has only tightened the duopoly trap, causing Blacks to invest their votes in candidates they perceive as "good for the party," as if that is synonymous with Black interests.

Ruling-class panic at the prospect of losing control of the top of the Democratic ticket has deeply infected the party's most loyal constituency. Thus, Black folks over forty, and many younger ones, are behaving like Malcolm X's "house Negro," who asks with genuine concern, "Is we sick, boss?" when the master is feeling poorly. The screechingly raucous, out-of-control Democratic debate in Charleston just days before the South Carolina primary appears to have scared the hell out of Black voters— and lots of white ones, too—who perceived "their" party coming apart at the seams and blamed the mayhem on Bernie Sanders. With Sanders and Michael Bloomberg bearing the brunt of the assault, Joe Biden appeared like the tranquil eye of the storm, a safe haven for fearful party loyalists. Biden's endorsement by Amy Klobuchar and Pete Buttigieg on the eve of Super Tuesday enveloped Obama's former vice president in an aura of consensus.

Bloomberg's presidential persona was punctured, but he wasn't really in it to win it. The odious oligarch knew he couldn't win the nomination of a party whose rank-and-file overwhelmingly support Sanders' austerity-busting agenda, even if they doubt Bernie's chances against Trump or his ability to get his program through Congress. The formerly Republican Bloomberg's candidacy was a necessary (and affordable) charade to certify him as a born-again Democrat, thus legitimizing his billion-dollar bid to buy control of the party's machinery to insulate it against infection by more upstarts like Alexandria Ocasio-Cortez (AOC) and her mentor, Sanders.

On Tuesday night, CNN pundit and former Virginia governor and Democratic National Committee chairman Terry McAuliffe confirmed that the party welcomed Bloomberg's billions. Bloomberg had already promised to pay the cost of five hundred political operatives answerable to the DNC through the November election, no matter who wins the nomination. McAuliffe looked forward to Bloomberg putting his entire state-of-the art New York City headquarters in service to the party. The aim is to progressive-proof the Democrats by making the party a hostile environment for leftish politics.* Bloomberg's presidential run is a way to "launder" his billion-dollar purchase of the party infrastructure. Other oligarchs can be expected to make it a joint venture to shore up their class's hegemony over the U.S. electoral system, to safeguard the ruling class agenda of endless war and the global Race to the Bottom.

The allure of Bloomberg's gold has exposed the cockroaches of the Black misleadership class, hordes of whom scurried across the linoleum to enlist as mercenaries of Obscene Capital. This is the undiluted essence of Black Democratic "strategic" politics. Four members of the Congressional Black Caucus—Meeks (NY), McBath (GA), Plaskett (VI), and Rush (IL)—plus the despicable former Tennessee congressman Harold Ford and the Black mayors of Little Rock, AR; Compton, CA; San Francisco, CA; Stockton, CA; Charlotte, NC; Columbia, SC; Houston, TX; and Washington, D.C., plus former mayors of Columbus, OH; New York City; Baltimore, MD; Philadelphia, PA, and Flint, MI whored for Bloomberg, and can be expected to be at his and the other oligarchs' service for the duration of the party's battles with leftish interlopers.

Bloomberg's withdrawal from the race and endorsement of Biden only further sanctifies his larger mission to purge the party of any taint of leftism. Elizabeth Warren will now choose how she will express her "capitalist to the bone" sentiments. The Black Lives Matter elements, notably Alicia Garza, that joined the party when they left the "movement" will follow.

The rot is deep, a product of generations of capital-subordinate Black politics that followed the violent suppression of Black self-determinationist movements and the imposition of a counterinsurgency, mass incarceration regime at the end of the '60s. Rather than resist the New Jim Crow/Same Old Rich White Man's Rule, the Black misleadership class eagerly offered themselves as co-managers of oppression—for a small cut of the spoils and the privileges of racial "leadership."

---

* See "Bloomberg Wants to Swallow the Democrats and Spit Out the Sandernistas," *Black Agenda Report*, Feb. 19, 2020.

FEAR PERVADES BLACK POLITICS, AND MAKES US AGENTS OF OUR OWN OPPRESSION

It has always been clear to *Black Agenda Report* that the post-'60s betrayals of the Black misleadership class necessitated that a future Black liberation movement must be largely an internal Black struggle to uproot the corrupted elements in our polity. False unity has become Black folks' Achilles Heel, allowing Black charlatans free rein in our communities and reserving most elected positions for servants of Capital. The Democratic Party is a predatory edifice of Black disempowerment from which our people must either free themselves, or become agents of their own perpetual oppression, and accomplices in the degradation of humanity worldwide.

Black youth see the truth and will act on it, we are certain.

March 4, 2020

PART IX

COVID-19 AND LOCKDOWN

TIME OF PLAGUE AND MELTDOWN: MASS MURDER BY CORPORATE DUOPOLY

Tens of thousands of people, disproportionately Black and brown, are marked for death by coronavirus in the coming weeks and months because the United States' political system allows only corporate parties to govern. By ensuring that the Dictatorship of Capital is immune to effective electoral challenge, the duopoly system has made the people of the United States less healthy than the rest of the developed world and far more vulnerable to epidemics of all types. As dutiful servants of Capital, the Democratic and Republican parties have for more than forty years facilitated a Race to the Bottom (austerity) that has steadily lowered working people's living standards and slashed social service supports, including the number of hospital beds, which have declined by more than half a million since 1975 despite a population increase of 114 million.

Barack Obama and his Democrat-controlled Congress saved the oligarchy from self-destruction in the Great Recession, and then collaborated with the resurgent Republicans in a "Grand Bargain" to ensure that social services, including local and state public health systems, would never recover lost revenue and personnel. The pruning and hyper-privatization of medical care was overseen mainly by Democrats in the big cities and largely by Republicans on the state level, with both parties in general agreement that the public health sector was less "efficient" and "innovative" than for-profit medicine. The public health sphere became even more dependent on private suppliers, including overseas sources. Inventories of ventilators, masks, and other equipment and gear were kept to a minimum, in line with the private sector's "just-in-time" profit-maximizing philosophy. But time ran out when the coronavirus hit, and there is now no possibility of avoiding many tens of thousands of deaths due to a shortage of equipment, beds, and health care personnel.

The shrinking of the public health sector is a capitalist crime, abetted by the two corporate parties. Not content to lessen the life-chances of their own citizens, the duopoly parties screamed for sanctions that have crippled the health sectors of Venezuela and Iran, killing tens of thousands before anyone had heard of COVID-19. The United States is a global vector of suffering and death, through the policies of its corporate party tag team. When deadly diseases are set in motion, the crime becomes mass murder-suicide.

Donald Trump is singularly stupid, incompetent, and self-dealing, but these very qualities make him incapable of effecting any fundamental change in national *systems*, for good or ill. Congress rebuffed his attempts to cut funding of the Centers for Disease Control and Prevention, but that matters little in the current crisis because *there is no national health system for the CDC to bolster, direct, and rally*. U.S. health care has been shrunken, privatized, and made wholly incapable of coping with mass contagion—which never arrives "just in time."

It was too late long before Trump. And, if Fast-Talking-Slow-Thinking Joe Biden succeeds the Orange Menace next January, there will be no prospect of constructing a true national health care system. Biden says he'll veto a Medicare for All bill if it comes across his desk in the Oval Office. But without single-payer health care, no national system is possible. In effect, Biden is campaigning for president on a platform of mass death. Biden's biggest supporters—Black Americans—will continue to die in disproportionate numbers whichever of the two corporate parties is in power because the Race to the Bottom (Race to the Graveyard) is ruling-class policy, and both parties serve the ruling class.

If, by some miracle, Bernie Sanders becomes the Democratic nominee and then president, his legislative agenda will be opposed by the bulk of his own party officials and officeholders. The corporate party faithful have rallied around Hapless Joe because he can be depended on to defend the interests of the party's rich funders—to continue the Race to the Graveyard. To make sure that Democrats understand who is boss, the world's eighth-richest oligarch, Michael Bloomberg, is purchasing the party outright. Bloomberg this week transferred $18 million of his campaign funds to the Democratic National Committee—actually, money that he previously transferred from his own accounts to his self-funded presidential campaign. The DNC will soon be answerable directly to a New York billionaire whose mission is to make the Democratic Party an even more hostile environment for austerity-busting politicians like Sanders and his young enthusiasts. Medicare for All is an austerity trip-wire that shall not be crossed, but without a single-payer system there can be no national health care system.

Nevertheless, those Americans that survive the Great Epidemic and Meltdown of 2020 will demand a New Health Care Deal. Having been frightened out of their locked-down wits by the crisis-induced realization that economic precarity is the national working-class condition, many millions will also demand a new social contract that provides for a modicum of economic security. But these are concessions that the Democratic Party, overseen by Bloomberg-the-Enforcer, cannot champion. Infectious disease and growing immiseration and precarity are crises for the masses, but the cure—an end to the Dictatorship of Capital—represents an existential crisis for the ruling class. The revolution will not be organized in the Master's houses—Democrat or Republican.

March 25, 2020

RESISTANCE GROWING TO COVID-CAPITALISM

What some may remember as the Year of the Lost Spring—lost loved ones, lost jobs, lost freedom of movement—may also become the year that the oligarchy and its servants in both corporate parties lost popular permission to dictate the terms of life and death in the United States. For the second time this century, the economies of the U.S. and Europe are circling the abyss, dragging much of the rest of the planet with them, while China, site of the first large eruption of COVID-19, leads the world in both economic resilience and global mutual aid—and Cuba has stepped forward once again as the champion of medical solidarity.

The superpower that has killed millions in its quest for global supremacy has utterly failed the most basic test of legitimacy at home: the ability to protect its own population. COVID-19 has laid bare a fundamental truth: that capitalist health care is a contradiction in terms since capital—like the killer virus—cares for nothing but reproducing itself. The U.S. "public" health sector is revealed as a hollowed-out shell, crippled and shrunken by decades of unrelenting privatization at the hands of the oligarch-serving political duopoly. In effect, the Lords of Capital have been devouring the nation's protective membrane, leaving the population defenseless, not only against microbes, but every disease of the poor—plus opiates and the lethal social pathologies that spawn spectacular and uniquely American mass shootings at schools, churches, and shopping malls, and the daily slaughter of Black and brown youth on the streets.

The idiot currently occupying the White House did not create the health care crisis, and the people know it. Donald Trump is far too incompetent and unfocused to pull off such a monumental crime, which has been unfolding for decades. Democrats have been full partners in stripping the people of public health protections—including New York Governor Andrew Cuomo, the current darling of corporate media, who continues to press for $2.5 billion in Medicaid cuts in his own state, even as he poses as the nation's top virus-slayer. Joe Biden, the not-all-there man who some would like Cuomo to replace as the Democratic presidential nominee, vows to veto Medicare for All—the first, preliminary step towards a real national health care system—if it ever comes across his White House desk. Politicians of both parties take their orders from the Lords of Capital. Otherwise, they are demonized and threatened with expulsion from the capitalist duopoly, the only electoral game that is allowed under oligarchic rule. This is why Bernie Sanders will always be a loyal sheepdog for a party that opposes his old-style Democratic reforms.

In the big cities, it is almost invariably the Democrats that enforce Rich Man's Rule—many of them Black Democrats, since the other half of the duopoly is the White Man's Party (GOP). Big labor's only duopoly option is also the Democrats, a straitjacket that union hacks have no desire to escape, preferring concubinage (whoring) to conflict with the ruling capitalist class.

The unions, who purport to fight for the workers, and Blacks, who are overwhelmingly working class and the most left-leaning ethnicity in the nation, have both been reduced by the duopoly to annexes of the Democratic Party, a fatal embrace. The duopoly serves only one master: Capital. Back when the Democrats were the White Man's Party and an aging Frederick Douglass made his living as a Republican functionary, the former firebrand declared, "The Republican Party is the ship and all else is the sea around us." Just as Douglass' Republicans eventually sanctioned Jim Crow and the dictatorship of Capital, the Democrats have become bulwarks of an austerity Race to the Bottom that has thrown the working class and its most marginalized components overboard to drown in a sea of declining living standards and disappearing "real" jobs and social supports—and without a national health care system.

COVID-19 has made clear the lunacy of this deal with the devil, and that "nobody will save us, but us." Cooperation Jackson, the Mississippi-based "emerging vehicle for sustainable community development, economic democracy, and community ownership," last week put out a call for a general strike to begin on May 1—May Day—and a list of demands "that will transform our broken and inequitable society, and build a new society run by and for us—the working-class, poor, oppressed majority."*

"Despite the asymmetry of power between ourselves on the left and the organized working class, and the forces of the right," says the call, "we have to do everything we can to intervene. We must stop the worst most deadly version of this pandemic from becoming a reality, and we have to ensure that we never return to the society that enabled this pandemic to emerge and have the impact it is having in the first place. We must do everything that we can to create a new, just, equitable and ecologically regenerative economy."

The proposed demands include protection of front-line workers exposed to the virus and of "other vulnerable communities, including the homeless, migrants, and refugees from discrimination and attack in this time of crisis"; democratization of the means of production, by converting corporations into cooperatives; universal health care and basic services (education, childcare, elderly care, water, electricity, internet, etc.); a universal basic income; democratized credit ("Bail out the people, not the corporations and Wall Street"); a "decarbonized economy and Green New Deal; housing as a human right; clean and decommodified water for all; a Debt Jubilee; release of prisoners and closure of jails and prisons; closure of detention centers and reunification of families; shutdown of overseas military bases and cuts in the military budget, with spending transferred to social needs and infrastructure.

Cooperation Jackson spokesman Kali Akuno said nearly three hundred activists took part in a conference call on Monday and reached "consensus on doing collective action to support what's already going

---

* See "A Call to Action: Towards a General Strike to End the COVID-19 Crisis and Create a New World," *Black Agenda Report*, April 8, 2020.

on." Committees were formed to launch and sustain the strike and to put together a national strike fund.

"We're trying to answer questions of the last 30 years in a few days," said Akuno. May Day is important, "but we have no illusion that the 'big one' will happen on May 1st," with the epidemic raging and much of the population still on lockdown, "but we'll keep working towards it to send a clear message that we need a new system."

The resistance predates Cooperation Jackson's call. Dr. Abdul Alkalimat, professor of African American Studies at the University of Illinois, Urbana-Champaign, compiled and circulated a list of grassroots labor and social activist actions in the time of plague across the nation and the world:

New Orleans

https://vimeo.com/404840708

Workers beginning to revolt

https://www.vice.com/en_us/article/z3b9ny/coronavirus-general-strike
https://www.commondreams.org/views/2020/04/03/strike-your-life
https://www.huffpost.com/entry/the-coronavirus-worker-revolt-is-just-beginning_n_5e84e57bc5b60bbd734e3fa0
https://www.bloombergquint.com/businessweek/coronavirus-marks-the-best-and-worst-time-for-workers-to-strike
https://nymag.com/intelligencer/2020/04/the-coronavirus-may-be-a-tipping-point-for-labor.html

Amazon warehouse workers

https://chicago.suntimes.com/coronavirus/2020/4/6/21203949/amazon-little-village-dch1-coronavirus-covid-19-christian-zamarron-domonic-wilkerson

https://www.theverge.com/2020/3/30/21199942/amazon-warehouse-coronavirus-covid-new-york-protest-walkout
https://www.theverge.com/2020/4/1/21202745/amazon-coronavirus-walk-out-detroit-protests-warehouse-cleaning
https://fortune.com/2020/03/30/amazon-workers-new-york-warehouse-strike-coronavirus-safety-fears/

GE workers

https://www.cnbc.com/2020/03/30/ge-workers-plan-to-protest-at-two-facilities-after-coronavirus-layoffs.html

Uber and Lyft drivers

https://www.theguardian.com/us-news/2020/mar/19/uber-lyft-coronavirus-benefits-ab5

Whole Foods

https://www.usatoday.com/story/money/business/2020/03/31/coronavirus-workplace-conditions-spur-protests-whole-foods-amazon/5093570002/

Nurses

https://www.youtube.com/watch?v=lMrBHRFWV2c
https://www.youtube.com/watch?v=VdQQdna0P9s
https://www.newsweek.com/nurses-protest-coronavirus-california-cdc-1491873
https://www.bridgemi.com/michigan-health-watch/nurses-say-detroit-hospital-told-them-leave-after-coronavirus-protest

ICE detainees

https://theintercept.com/2020/03/30/coronavirus-ice-detention/

Grocery store workers

https://www.nbcboston.com/news/local/grocery-store-workers-
to-protest-in-boston-demanding-adequate-protections-amid-
pandemic/2103707/
https://www.inquirer.com/jobs/labor/coronavirus-philadelphia-
grocery-workers-moms-organic-market-protest-20200406.html

McDonald's in LA

https://la.eater.com/2020/4/6/21210092/mcdonalds-walkout-
protest-south-la-crenshaw-coronavirus-covid-19-los-angeles

Local officials in Georgia

https://www.msn.com/en-us/news/us/stupid-and-crazy-local-officials-
protest-gov-kemps-decision-to-reopen-beaches-in-hard-hit-georgia/
ar-BB12dsxn

Brazil

https://www.bbc.com/news/world-latin-america-51955679

Ivory Coast

https://www.bbc.com/news/world-africa-52189144

Pakistan

https://globalnews.ca/news/6787520/coronavirus-
pakistan-iran-protest/

Global

https://www.wsws.org/en/articles/2020/04/06/work-a06.html

https://nymag.com/intelligencer/2020/03/coronavirus-fears-spark-prison-unrest-worldwide.html

Palestinians

https://www.middleeasteye.net/news/coronavirus-protest-jaffa-covid-19-restrictions-police-brutality

Kenya

https://nypost.com/2020/03/27/some-kenyan-nurses-refusing-coronavirus-patients-in-protest-over-gear-shortages/

Italy

https://www.foxnews.com/world/italian-inmates-die-during-protest-over-coronavirus-measures
https://www.dw.com/en/italian-workers-protest-against-open-factories-as-covid-19-spreads/a-52921359

Germany

https://www.infomigrants.net/en/post/23520/germany-asylum-seekers-protest-against-virus-quarantine

Lockdown and Beyond

As long as the lockdown continues, activists will have to find novel uses for technology. The Black Is Back Coalition had planned to hold its annual Electoral School gathering in St. Louis on April 11 and 12 but will instead conduct the event over the internet. The theme has been changed to "COVID-19 Pandemic: Black People Fight Back," with an emphasis on "sell-out Negroes in the time of plague," said coalition chairman Omali Yeshitela.

That's an apt description of the battle ahead of us. The Democratic Party has for the last four years blamed all the ills of capitalism—and their own crimes—on the singularly loathsome person of Donald Trump and his imaginary partners in Moscow. Trump has, in effect, been their shield, diverting attention from Democratic complicity in the Race to the Bottom—which is why Hillary Clinton wanted him to be the Republican nominee, and why the Democrats insist he is the only issue in 2020.

If Trump is the root of all evil, then all that needs to be done is to replace him with a Democrat, leaving intact the system created by both parties at the behest of the ruling class. But the COVID-19 epidemic would have wrought mass death and economic havoc in the United States no matter which half of the corporate duopoly was in charge, because both corporate parties have been eagerly dismantling and privatizing the public health sector for two generations. The COVID-19 bailout of banks and corporations under Trump is modeled on the bank and corporate bailout under Obama more than a decade ago. Neither scheme saved anybody but the financial and corporate elite. The First Black President and the Thoroughly Racist President both serve the same masters.

Through its abject obedience to the Democratic Party, the Black misleadership class act as mercenaries for the same oligarchy. They are welcomed into the subservient fold because the Lords of Capital have no problem with ethnic and religious "diversity" in the lower ranks of the power structure (mayors, a few corporate executives, even a compliant Black president), as long as society is structured according to the needs of Capital. Black politics will have to be transformed—not just independent of the Democratic Party, but relentlessly *opposed* to it—or there is no chance of lifting Black America from the bottom of the racial barrel, much less eliminating the racial hierarchy altogether.

Bernie Sanders' final surrender to the will of his half of the corporate duopoly was anticlimax. COVID-19 will swell the ranks of dissidents in the party and nation, and Sanders' concession will remove false hope that a corporate party can fight corporate rule. Sanders played a key role in popularizing the term "socialism," but also in sanitizing it as compatible with existing power structures. Jeff Bezos and the rest of the obscenely rich are just as deadly if they are more heavily taxed as they are when they keep most of their money. A real left must fight for real socialism if the real world is to be saved from the greatest threat to life on Earth: the capitalist ruling classes of the United States and Europe, the historical and unrepentant enslavers of humanity and ravagers of the planet. Real socialism kicks the oligarchy off the commanding heights of the economy so they can no longer inflict unending austerity, war, and warming on the planet while the people remain unprotected from the periodic visitation of deadly microbes. It must be a socialism that respects and facilitates the self-determination of Black people and all other oppressed nationalities that demand it—which is the only way that socialism can work in a racist society.

April 8, 2020

INDICT AND PUNISH THE PERPETRATORS OF COVID MASS DEATH

The United States finds myriad ways of killing Black people—of negating the term "Black lives matter." The *novel*, or new, coronavirus is ending the lives of African Americans at a nationwide rate that is 2.6 times that of whites, 2.3 times the death toll among Asian Americans, and 2.2. times that of Latinos according to the APM Research Lab's breakdown of mortality by race. Collectively, Blacks have suffered 27 percent of all COVID-19 deaths in the United States, which would mean that 24,930 of the 92,333 total U.S. deaths from the virus as of this week were African Americans, who make up only 13 percent of the population.

Researchers at Yale University and the University of Pittsburgh put the proportionate Black death toll considerably higher, with Blacks 3.5 times more likely to die than whites, and Latinos twice as likely to succumb to the virus. The actual ratios of death may never be known since, according to the Yale study, "almost half the states do not track the race and ethnicity of those who have died in the pandemic, and states that are tracking racial and ethnic data do not account for age differences among population groups."

The COVID Racial Data Tracker, a collaboration of *The Atlantic*'s COVID Tracking Project and The Antiracist Research & Policy Center, updates the toll by ethnicity on a daily basis, with about a three-day lag in reporting of deaths by state.

If the Yale/Pittsburgh finding that Blacks are 3.5 times more like to die from COVID-19 than whites is correct, then Blacks make up considerably more than 27 percent of deaths. But, even at the lower rate, the carnage in Black America is horrific. If projections of 143,360 total U.S. deaths from coronavirus by August 4 hold true, that would result in a Black death toll of 38,707—with no end in sight. By comparison, 1,008 people of all races were killed by police gunfire in 2019 according to the *Washington Post* tally.

What will be the Black political response to such gruesome numbers? Who will be made accountable for a slaughter that was *pre-programmed by the very nature of a society* birthed in genocide, slavery, and the glorification of conquest and plunder?

Just as infant mortality is the best measure of a society's general health, so does the COVID-19 death toll indict the United States for systematically undermining the life chances of all of its constituent peoples (143,360 dead by August 4) and for the aggravated crime of setting a death trap for African Americans, every aspect of whose lives has been methodically weighted towards early death. These are crimes that only the ruling class can commit, because only the ruling class has the power to systematically allocate life-death chances for whole populations over generations.

The indictment must be initiated by Black America, the most deeply harmed victims of preventable mass death at the hands of a morally depraved white ruling class. The very nature of mass slaughter by COVID-19 demands that the entire system of political economy—of racial capitalism—in the United States be put on trial and that the humans that have profited from, bolstered, and defended that murderous system be removed from power and punished.

To limit the indictment to Donald Trump and his administration would be an insult to today's dead and dying, and to all past victims of racial capitalism's carnage around the world. Every Democrat who has joined with the Lords of Capital in preventing the United States from establishing a universal health care system is guilty of depraved indifference to the lives of his and her constituents, as is virtually every member of the Republican

Party, whose organizing principle is white supremacy, an ideology of mass murder. The U.S. electoral duopoly system has acted as a criminal enterprise, answering to an oligarchy of wealth, with both parties colluding to deny most of the population—and especially Black people—the right to healthy and safe lives and protection from contagious disease, as well as the closely related rights to meaningful and fairly compensated employment, adequate shelter from the elements, and an education that provides the people with the knowledge and skills to shape, and contribute to, society.

It takes a whole class of criminals to create the conditions to kill nearly one hundred thousand people—27 percent of them Black—in just three months. However, politicians representing Black America, the most victimized constituency, are co-conspirators in the great crime, both by their collaboration with Democrats, which has systematically weakened the U.S. social safety net (most notably, President Obama's partially consummated Grand Bargain with Republicans), and by their management of Black population centers that have been methodically stripped of defenses against debilitating poverty and disease.

These Black auxiliaries to ruling class criminals put personal profit above the welfare of Black people and must be indicted along with their masters. The Black political class should have been our antibodies against the plagues of racial, political, and economic repression, but it made common cause with the oppressor. The Black misleaders must be the first to be indicted, because they weaken our ability to resist the greater evils: the Lords of Capital.

The proof of their culpability lies in cemeteries all across Black America. People's tribunals must convene to indict the perpetrators of mass death, including the Black collaborators in the lower ranks of capitalist crime. Why were Blacks seven times more likely to die of COVID-19 in Kansas City than whites? What factors (crimes) made Missouri, Wisconsin, and Washington, D.C. six times as lethal for Blacks than for whites, and Michigan five times more deadly for Blacks? How is it that the Grim Reaper came for Black people three times more often than for whites in Arkansas, Illinois, Louisiana, New York, Oregon, and South Carolina? And what should be the penalty for locking up millions of human beings in virus-infested cages without provision for basic hygiene, much less protection from disease? Isn't every COVID-19 death in prison—where captives are totally dependent on their captors—a case of murder?

The people must convene, learn the truth, and make their verdicts. The only fitting punishment is the overthrow of the criminal racial capitalist regime, whose crimes are multitudinous and manifest. I'll be asking the organization I co-founded, the Black Is Back Coalition, to initiate Black COVID-19 tribunals in cities across the nation. Activists of all races should do the same.

May 20, 2020

PART X

BLACK LIVES MATTER, REPARATIONS, AND A NEW, AUTHENTIC LEFT

THE BLACK-LATINO FUTURE: FINDING A WAY TO SOLIDARITY

When as many as two million immigrants and their supporters, most of them Latino, turned out for demonstrations against draconian undocumented worker legislation in cities across the nation this spring, everywhere the question was raised: Is this the new civil rights movement? By all appearances, some kind of great awakening had indeed occurred which, if sustained, would transform the participants and, eventually, the society at-large.

However, Black opinion was decidedly mixed. Traditional and progressive African American organizations generally supported the explosion of Latino activism and marveled at the coordination and sheer size of the rallies in Los Angeles, Chicago, New York, Dallas, Houston, and Seattle—at least two dozen cities nationwide. Luminaries such as the Rev. Jesse Jackson, the Rev. Al Sharpton, NAACP chairman Julian Bond, SCLC leader the Rev. Joseph Lowery, and numerous Black congresspersons were quick to make a positive connection to the struggles of the '60s.

Yet among other Black circles, the mass Latino political actions were met with a sullenness often deeply tinged with envy, and even outright hostility, drenched in vicious vitriol and willful ignorance. Black one-man bands like Claud Anderson's Washington-based Harvest Institute lashed out at mobilized Latinos, blurring the distinction between undocumented and legal immigrants (just as do white racist-led groups), and blaming the entirety of African American economic slippage over almost two generations on immigrant influx. Mary Mitchell, an incredibly shallow Black columnist for the *Chicago Sun-Times*, expressed her "disgust" with undocumented Mexican immigrant Elvira Arellano, who along with her young U.S.-citizen son sought sanctuary in a Chicago church. Arellano, wrote Mitchell, "is pimping the system" and should "return to Mexico," "brush up on black history," and then thank African Americans "for [their] sacrifices" over the centuries in North America.

Anderson's and Mitchell's rants are deliberately insulting to their mainly Latino targets and range from intellectual dishonesty (Anderson) to just plain stupid-mean (Mitchell). Unfortunately, these shrill and wrong-headed voices find echoes in the perceptions of a highly ambivalent African American citizenry, whose sense of social space has been thrown into turmoil by the largest migration on U.S. soil since the "Great Migration" of Blacks to northern and western cities—a trek that slowed and began to reverse itself about the same time as the Latino (non-Puerto Rican) migration began rolling in earnest, around 1970.

This column, the first of many *BAR* articles that will address the extremely complex and history-shaping subject of African American-Latino relations, deals with the "meanness" factor in Black discourse around (mainly Latino) immigration—the invective from the African American side of the argument that threatens to poison the prospects of unified action among Black and Latino progressives against white supremacy and corporate rule in the United States.

Insults Born of Ignorance

First, it must be said that African Americans have been conditioned to be much more "Anglo" in their perceptions of Latino political assertiveness than most of us are willing to admit. Having been raised under the same Black-White paradigm as Euro-Americans, we often share with most whites a profound ignorance, not only of global historical and social realities but of the conditions that have shaped the societies of our Latin American neighbors. Despite constant lip service to racial solidarity, few African Americans grasp the social complexities of the African Diaspora in its Spanish- and Portuguese-speaking manifestations in the Caribbean and Central and South America.

African Americans are confident that we know what "Black" is, here, but we know next to nothing about what "not white" is, "over there"— places where there exist more flavors of racial admixture than Campbell had soups or Howard Johnson had ice creams, each with its own group label and all under the jackboot of "whites" (or near-whites) who proudly trace their lineage to Europe. Racism is a daily experience among darker mestizos in Mexico and the non-white majority of Venezuela, for example. To generally describe Hispanics as "non-Anglo Saxon Whites speaking Spanish," as does the book-promoting fog-blower Claud Anderson, is to deny Latinos their racial and national legacies. It is the ultimate insult, of the kind African Americans would never accept if we were referred to as simply darker-skinned, English-speaking white people.

Such degradations of whole peoples and their distinct national, racial, and cultural subgroups seem to flow freely from the mouths of African Americans like Anderson—in putrid streams that mimic the rhetoric of the right-wing white sources he relies on to "document" his pseudo-academic diatribes. In his polemic "Immigration Harms Black America," Anderson declares, baldly, that "immigrant population increases in the last 30 years have made Blacks third-class citizens in America after they were second-class citizens for hundreds of years," and that "immigration has erased the 10% income gains that native Blacks made between 1956 and 1966, the years of the civil rights movement."

So it is the immigrants who have done the foul deed, not the native white American racists who created the paradigm that calls for Blacks to be perpetually on the bottom and who continue to enforce that formula in the present; not the de-industrialization process that was coterminous with the immigrant influx, a deliberate corporate policy that resulted in Blacks suffering 55 percent of the union jobs lost in 2004; not the general white backlash that followed immediately upon the victories of the Black Freedom Movement of the '60s, ushering in a national policy of mass

Black incarceration that has devastated every aspect of African American society.

No, the immigrants are the root of all things evil done to Black folk in the last thirty years. Anderson, who undoubtedly considers himself a "Race Man," has in fact crossed over to the White Right. He implies that Latinos are out to make a separate peace with white racism in return for (some future) favored status in the United States. It is a self-fulfilling prophecy, rooted in an ignorance and protean fear that prevents many long-isolated and besieged African Americans from making common cause with "others." Ultimately, Anderson and other faux nationalists turn to the historical enemy—white racists—for theoretical verification and political support.

Apparently, Anderson wants to make a deal with racists before the Hispanics do. He calls for a total shutdown of immigration to the U.S., to "close the nation's doors until policies are in place that redirect resources to native Blacks to correct the inequalities of slavery and Jim Crow semi-slavery."

It's about thirty-plus years too late for that, the "diversity" deal having been consummated by the remnants of the Civil Rights Movement and various "minority" and "women's" organizations long ago, and written in stone by the U.S. Supreme Court in its affirmative action decision of 2003. Anderson's spiel may play well in Black barber shops and beauty parlors, but it ignores the reality outside: the Latinos are here; they outnumber African Americans and will grow larger; they are the majority in L.A.'s Watts and countless other formerly "Black" communities; they are predicted to outnumber Blacks in Georgia by as early as 2010; and they are on the move, politically.

Who is not on the move? African Americans. Instead, we sulk or rant in our longstanding impotence—a function of the death of our own movement a generation-and-a-half ago—while the worst of us importune white racists to rescue Blacks from the historical trap whites have created and fought desperately to preserve. What madness!

Movement-Envy

Ill-concealed envy is the saddest—and ugliest—aspect of some of what passes for Black political critique of the evolving Latino/immigrant movement. The *Chicago Sun-Times'* Mary Mitchell, after getting her "mean on" by expressing "disgust" with sanctuary-seeking undocumented immigrant Elvira Arellano for "pimping the system," demands that Latinos thank Blacks "for paving the way" before they dare mount a movement for social change. "The benefits that so many other groups—women included—now enjoy were purchased with black blood, sweat and tears," wrote Mitchell—as if Arellano and her fellow Latino activists have not consistently cited the Black Freedom Movement as a cherished model.

But Mitchell is caught in a contradiction, made worse by the green glaze of envy at Latino activism and her shocking misunderstanding of the same African American history that she demands immigrants learn before they get uppity on U.S. soil. In comments to reporters, Ms. Arellano paid homage to a civil rights icon. "I'm strong, I've learned from Rosa Parks—I'm not going to the back of the bus. The law is wrong," she said.

Rather than accept the sincerity of Arellano's remarks, Mitchell spews abuse, and displays both cheeks of her own phenomenal ignorance. Arellano had no right to invoke the name of Rosa Parks: "I even doubt that Arellano has any idea who Parks really was," writes Mitchell, who then proceeds to reveal that it is she who fails to comprehend the act of civil disobedience that put Parks in the history books.

"Parks didn't refuse to go to the back of the bus. She refused to give up her seat to a white man who couldn't find a seat in the so-called 'white section.' As onerous as the Jim Crow laws were, Parks didn't break them. That's why she could calmly go to the police station and sit in jail until her husband came to bail her out.

"Because Parks wasn't a lawbreaker, the local NAACP decided to use her as a test case to challenge the Jim Crow laws. Her righteous cause drew widespread support and launched the civil rights movement in earnest."

Of course, Rosa Parks did break the law—on purpose and according to a plan hatched in advance by the local NAACP, of which she was secretary—because the law was "wrong," just as Arellano maintains U.S. immigration laws are wrong. Alabama law specifically required Blacks to relinquish their seats to whites when the "white section" was full. Parks was convicted of failing to heed the directions of the bus driver, thus setting the stage for the Montgomery bus boycott and creating the "test case" sought by civil rights activists.

Civil disobedience—the breaking of unjust laws—became the primary tactic deployed by Dr. Martin Luther King, Jr., a twenty-six-year-old Montgomery minister at the time of Ms. Parks' arrest. To claim that "Parks wasn't a lawbreaker" is to strip her action of all political, moral, and historical meaning. But Mary Mitchell doesn't know much about politics or history, and her moral position is hopelessly contorted by meanness and jealous resentment against "newcomers" who are building a movement while African Americans sit on the sidelines with no national movement worthy of the name.

Katrina Told It All

If there were any doubt, the aftermath of Hurricane Katrina proved that the Black Freedom Movement is, indeed, dead and gone—in need of resurrection, not mere resuscitation.

Soon after the catastrophic exile of most Black New Orleanians, University of Chicago political scientist Michael Dawson declared: "Katrina could very well shape this generation of young people in the same way that the assassinations of Malcolm X and Martin Luther King shaped our generation." Dawson is in his early fifties.

According to Rev. Lennox Yearwood, the thirty-six-year-old head of the Washington, D.C.-based Hip Hop Caucus, "New Orleans is our Gettysburg. If we lose there, we lose all the marbles."

If Dr. Dawson is right, then the emerging African American generation's formative political experience—Katrina—has been one of defeat. And if Rev. Yearwood is correct in his belief that Katrina is the equivalent of the Battle of Gettysburg, then Black folks have suffered a monumental loss.

Yearwood says he's seeing young Fannie Lou Hamer types among a new crop of activists and was heartened by the surge of student involvement in Katrina organizing and relief work. Indeed, the waves of volunteers journeying to New Orleans were reminiscent of the Mississippi Freedom summer of two generations ago. It is also true that many thousands of churches, big and small, responded to the Katrina disaster with a wide range of programs. Katrina has seared into the collective Black consciousness—a kind of African American 9/11. There is no question but that Katrina has radicalized a new cohort of youth, and re-radicalized many of their elders.

However, it is these very facts—of radicalization, of universal Black horror and revulsion, of the thousands of localized responses to Katrina—that so dramatically illuminate the strategic defeat of the Black polity in the Battle of Katrina. Black America did not—could not—come together in a mighty cascade of demonstrations and confrontations with the powerful perpetrators who are attempting to erase a major Black city. Katrina showed definitively that the Movement, as we once knew it, is dead. The failure of the Black polity to set millions of bodies in motion revealed the utter impotence and disarray of the national Black political infrastructure.

(The October 2005, "Millions More Rally" on Washington's Capitol Mall was coincidental to Katrina, having been scheduled long in advance by the Nation of Islam and other organizers. The rally produced a laundry list of wide-ranging demands, most unrelated to the catastrophe. There was nothing like a follow-up "Millions to the Front in the Battle for New Orleans" rally.)

If the national Black political infrastructure, such as it is, could not set masses in motion after Katrina, when African Americans were as one in their concentrated anger and collective will to do something, then what currently passes for leadership will never effectively mobilize Black folks for anything. They have lost the tools and desire to fight, and cannot function as leaders even when the people cry out for common action.

Had Black people been called out en masse, they would have come—but the historical moment has slipped away, wasted. In a few years, a new generation of Black activists will deploy themselves in structures of radical resistance, their world views shaped by the multiple crimes of Katrina. But in the near term, it must be recognized that not only have African Americans been numerically overtaken by Hispanics, we have been eclipsed in mass organizing as well.

No Victory Without Latinos

Mary Mitchell's Chicago has witnessed some of the most notable examples of Black-Latino solidarity—not that she seems to have noticed. The late Harold Washington was elected Chicago's first Black mayor in 1983 after forging strong alliances with the growing Hispanic community, which now amounts to 27 percent of the city. (Blacks make up 36 percent of the population.) After Washington's untimely death in 1987, the coalition fell apart, leading to the election of the current white mayor, Richard Daley, Jr.

In the run-up to 1992 elections, activists registered 130,000 new voters. Chicago Latino voters put Carol Moseley Braun over the top in the Democratic primary for U.S. Senate. She became the first Black woman to hold a seat in the upper chamber of the U.S. legislature.

The lesson is: When Blacks and Hispanics fail to unite in Chicago, progressive Blacks lose in city- and state-wide races.

However, there is another side to that coin: Black Chicago politicians, as a body, having a longer history of collaboration with corrupt white machines, turn out to be demonstrably less progressive than their Latino counterparts. This political truth was brought home in the recent battle to impose living-wage legislation on Wal-Mart and other "big box" retailers. After years of organizing, unions and community and church groups succeeded in assembling a veto-proof super-majority in the city council—thirty-five of fifty members—mandating that the big boxes pay at least $10 an hour and $3 in benefits for the privilege of doing business in Chicago. All ten Hispanic members of the council initially voted on the progressive side of the issue, compared to only half of the eighteen Black aldermen.

Under intense pressure from Mayor Daley, and in face of threats by Wal-Mart, Target, and Home Depot to withhold further investment from the city, four aldermen later switched their votes: two Latinos and two Blacks. But the Chicago experience puts the lie to those who maintain that Latinos favor a sub-living wage structure. At least in the Windy City, it is easily corruptible Black politicians who are the problem. These elements are joined by Black business groupings that care more about a potential contract with Wal-Mart than whether workers earn a living wage (and who may have no intention of paying a living wage to their own employees—a trait they share with employers of all ethnicities).

Chicago, like many other urban centers, will continue to become more Latino unless gentrification reverses the process, which will also inevitably diminish the Black proportion of the population. In New York City, both Black and Latino populations have declined under gentrifying assault. Black majorities are in danger of collapsing in numerous "chocolate cities" across the nation, mostly because of gentrification rather than Latino influx. Claud Anderson may want to strike a deal to stabilize Black numbers in the cities, but Big Capital is not cooperating, and never will. Only a Black-Latino urban alliance can withstand the onslaught and preserve the political power of both groups.

The Penalty for Arrogance

Latino organizers don't need permission from African Americans to assert their demands; no human group is obligated to bow and scrape to another. Their primary duty is to turn out the numbers in what they believe to be a just cause. African American insistence on Latino obeisance—to the extent it exists—is backhanded, hostile, mean-spirited, sulking, the product of bewilderment, jealousy, and impotence. Certainly, Latinos should not dignify the wild ravings of Claud Anderson, who blames immigrants for every economic, political, and social setback that Black folks have been unable to prevent since 1970. And Mary Mitchell, the people-insulting Chicago columnist, has nothing to say worth hearing by anyone of any ethnicity.

Rather, it is Black folks' obligation—the duty of future Black leaders at every level—to give political direction based on analysis of the world as it exists. There is no room for gratuitous insult in the dialogue between Latinos and African Americans that must occur in earnest if both groups are to escape eviction from the cities by encroaching capital in the form of gentrification.

There will be no living wage for anyone if corrupt African American politicians insist on making common cause with oppressive employers like Wal-Mart, all the while subscribing to the canard that Latino immigrants want to work for substandard wages. There is no solution to a two- or three-tier wage system, except a one-tier wage system, which requires the closest collaboration among those who work or want to work, whatever their social background. Hispanics are second only to Blacks in eagerness to join a union. (The order of union-friendliness is Black women, Black men, Hispanic women, Hispanic men, white women, with white men dead last.)

Hispanics are overwhelmingly supportive of public schools and affordable health care. They oppose racial profiling, to which Latinos have been subjected by immigration authorities as well as police for generations. The police state, immigrant-hunt regime that would descend on the nation if Claud Anderson and his white supremacist allies get their way, combined with anti-terrorist hysteria, would inevitably erase every civil liberties gain of the past four decades, most severely impacting the state-criminalized Black ghetto poor, as usual.

The Reality Quotient

Blacks were as surprised as whites when more than a half-million mostly Latino demonstrators rallied in Los Angeles in late March of this year. Where did the crowds come from? How did they pull off such a gargantuan gathering? African Americans had less excuse than white Anglos for not knowing what was up. After all, Watts is 62 percent Latino, Compton is three-fifths—African Americans and Latinos live in proximity throughout much of the mega-city. But, as radio broadcaster and hip-hop guru Davey

D told me, "KKBT-FM [the top-rated, Black-oriented radio station] completely ignored one million people in the streets." It was "similar to the Million Man March right on their doorstep," yet to KKBT and its listeners, the huge outpouring of humanity "didn't exist." The same applied for the rest of English-speaking commercial media.

Spanish-language media, particularly radio, were key to the massive turnouts in Los Angeles, Chicago (another half-million), and more than a score of other cities. Radio personalities talked up the demonstrations, creating the kind of community-wide consciousness that two generations ago surrounded major Black political actions. However, it would be wrong to credit the corporate (and often, non-Latino) owners of Spanish-language media with some special sensitivity to the political aspirations of their audiences. Rather, Spanish-language outlets were compelled to respond to what they recognized as a groundswell of community organizing for immigrant rights. In other words, Hispanic media got on the right side of the movement.

No such movement exists in Black America, and therefore Black-oriented mass media see no need to diverge from their news-less menu of celebrity gossip and assorted nonsense. Had African American "leadership" infrastructures been willing and able to put out a credible call for massive Katrina-related turnouts, Black-oriented media would have responded as readily as their corporate Hispanic counterparts. They are the same bottom line-feeding animals. The difference lay in the levels of community organization—Latinos had their act together, while African Americans languished in political paralysis.

"Hispanic media collaborated on their march," said Davey D. "We could have had a million people in the streets about Katrina—'Where are the kids?' But Black media were absent. All this contributes to the disintegration of political organization in our communities."

It is senseless for African Americans to squabble over whether Latino mass activism represents the "new Civil Rights Movement" or not. The fact is, Latinos have fielded the beginnings of a powerful movement while a coherent national Black movement is just a memory—for now.

The Black polity is the unique product of the strivings of a singular people, whose institutions and shared consciousness were forged in enforced intimacy over hundreds of years. It is not so fragile as to fade into permanent inconsequentiality simply because a bad crop of leadership was allowed to demobilize the Black Freedom Movement over thirty years ago. Katrina has already awakened the organizers of the future. However, that future will be shared with Latinos. For the sake of our common interests, Black progressives are obligated to do everything possible to cleanse the African American dialogue of parochialism, insults against other ethnicities, useless nostalgia that keeps us fixed in a past time, and—most importantly—the nativism inherited from our historical oppressors.

We are a raise-up people, not a speak-down-to people. Let's act like it.

October 25, 2006

OCCUPY WALL STREET JOINS OCCUPY THE DREAM: IS IT CO-OPTATION, OR GROWING THE MOVEMENT?

The Occupy Wall Street movement has, to date, "been effective in warding off co-optation by Democratic Party fronts such as Rebuild the Dream and MoveOn.org." But OWS's recent alliance with Black clergy-based (and Russell Simmons-backed) Occupy the Dream raises serious questions in this election year.

The Democratic Party may have entered the Occupy Wall Street movement through the "Black door," in the form of Occupy the Dream, the Black ministers' group led by former NAACP chief and Million Man March national director Dr. Benjamin Chavis and Baltimore mega-church pastor the Rev. Jamal Bryant. Both are fervent supporters of President Obama.

Occupy the Dream's National Steering Committee is made up entirely of clergy, as are its Members at Large, but its secular inspiration comes from media mogul (and credit card purveyor) Russell Simmons, who was a frequent visitor to Manhattan's occupied Zuccotti Park. Simmons is co-chairman with Dr. Chavis of the Hip Hop Summit Action Network, whose website is now mainly dedicated to the Occupy the Dream project. It is through Simmons that the ministers hope to attract entertainers and athletes to Occupy the Dream events.

Occupy Wall Street organizer David DeGraw tied the knot with the Dream team at a Washington Press Club conference on December 14, invoking Dr. Martin Luther King's Poor People's campaign and the need to "penetrate deeper into the African American community." Dr. Chavis said, "If Dr. King were alive today, he would be part of Occupy Wall Street," and Rev. Bryant, pastor of Baltimore's ten thousand-member Empowerment Temple AME Church, pledged that Occupy the Dream will work "in lock-step" with OWS. The OWS/OTD alliance would begin, they announced, with a multi-city action at Federal Reserve Bank offices on MLK Day, January 16.

The very next Sunday, Rev. Bryant was at his pulpit exhorting his congregation to get out the vote for the president.

Dr. Chavis is also an active Obama booster. In his November 30 syndicated column for Black newspapers, titled "Brilliant First Lady Michelle Obama," Chavis writes:

> As we are about to enter into the heated national political debates and campaigns of the 2012 national election year, President Barack Obama and First Lady Michelle Obama will be under intense pressures to maneuver through what may be one of the most difficult periods of time to maintain resilience and hope.
>
> I am encouraged and optimistic, however, that President Obama will be reelected if millions of us do what we are supposed to do and that is go out and vote in record numbers 12 months from now.

Chavis continues with an even more direct appeal:

> All of us should be responding by lending a helping hand, giving of our time, energy and money, and to make our own contributions to push forward for more progress to ensure the reelection of President Barack Obama. Let's determine the future by how we act today.

It appears that Occupy Wall Street's new Black affiliate is also in "lock-step" with the corporate Democrat in the White House, whose administration has funneled trillions of dollars to Wall Street and greatly expanded U.S. theaters of war.

There is, however, a certain historical logic at work here. Dr. Martin King's Poor People's Campaign, disrupted by his assassination, is seen by many as a prime inspiration for OWS. But of course, King's persona and the whole saga of the '60s has been methodically co-opted over the intervening decades, most directly by Black ministers claiming to be acting in furtherance of his "Dream" while selling their congregants' votes to one or the other of the two Rich Men's Parties. President Obama and his operatives have attempted to draw a straight line between Dr. King's "Dream" and Obama's own political ascent ever since his "coming home" speech at a Selma, Alabama church in March of 2007, where the candidate assumed the mantle of Joshua and asserted that Blacks had already come "90 percent of the way" towards equality (with the transparent implication that his entrance to the White House would complete the process.)

Perhaps the most historically and politically corrupt poster of the 2008 campaign superimposed Obama's head on Malcolm X's body in the only known photo of Dr. King and Malcolm shaking hands. So, there is nothing novel about labeling a 2012 Black church-based, pro-Obama electoral campaign as "Occupying the Dream." Black ministers in campaign mode routinely depict Obama's political troubles as indistinguishable from threats to "The Dream," whose embodiment is ensconced in the White House. That's simply common currency among Black preachers pushing for Obama.

Russell Simmons brings bling to the mix. As the Occupy the Dream website states: "Teaming up with entertainers such as Bon Jovi, Jay-Z, Bruce Springsteen, and Kanye West, Dr. Bryant encourages citizens of every race, color, and creed to join Occupy the Dream." Simmons is a genius at transforming social capital into the spendable kind—which is why he has been courting OWS so diligently. He is now fully "inside" the movement, flanked and buttressed by loyal Obama Black clergy.

It is highly unlikely—damn near inconceivable—that Occupy the Dream will do anything that might embarrass this president. Its ministers can be expected to electioneer for Obama at every opportunity. Their January 16 actions are directed at the Federal Reserve, which is technically independent from the executive branch of government, although, in practice, the Fed has been Obama's principal mechanism for bailing out the banks. Will the ministers pretend, next Monday, that the president is somehow removed from the Fed's massive transfers of the people's credit and cash to Wall Street over the past three years? Is Obama to be absolved by clergymen wearing "Occupy" buttons?

Far from tamping their Obama fervor, the OWS brand equips the "Dream" ministers (and Simmons' entertainment assets) to accomplish a special mission: to insulate the president from the Occupy movement and the national conversation on economic equality—or, better yet, to make him appear to be part of the solution. If they so choose.

OWS has to date been effective in warding off co-optation by Democratic Party fronts such as Rebuild the Dream and MoveOn.org. But it seems their antennas were not so finely attuned to the political structures of Black America: who the players are, and how the game is run. The Obama campaign may have found its niche on "the Black-hand side" of OWS.

At this late stage, there is no antidote to the potential co-optation, except to rev up the movement's confrontation with the oligarchic powers-that-be, including Wall Street's guy in the White House. Let's see what happens if OWS demonstrators join with Occupy the Dream at Federal Reserve sites on January 16, carrying placards unequivocally implicating Obama in the Fed's bailouts of the banksters, as Occupy demonstrators have done so often in the past. Will the Dream's leadership be in "lockstep" with that? Maybe so—I've heard that miracles sometimes do happen.

In his December 30 newspaper column, Dr. Chavis offers these thoughts: "2012 will be a test for the United States. There will be a political test in terms of how millions of people will vote for the future. There will also be an economic test between the 99% and the 1% on the issues of income inequality and economic justice."

We do, indeed, face a test in 2012: Will the Democratic Party be enabled to swallow up the Left—as it does every four years—including the fragile and tentative structures of the Occupy Wall Street movement? And, will the Democrats enter through the Black door?

January 11, 2012

#BLACKLIVESMATTER AND THE DEMOCRATS: HOW DISRUPTION CAN LEAD TO COLLABORATION

A year after the police murder of Michael Brown in Ferguson, Missouri, an incipient mass movement struggles to congeal and define itself. The emergent movement is rooted in resistance to systemic state violence and repression in Black America, yet its trajectory wobbles under the push and pull of the contending forces that have been set in motion and is further distorted by relentless pressures from a power structure that pursues simultaneous strategies of both co-optation and annihilation.

Physical annihilation is a constant threat to the "street" component of the movement, such as the young people of Ferguson, whose defiance of the armed occupation inspired a national mobilization, and whose urban guerrilla language resonates in all the inner cities of the nation. They are the cohort whose social existence has been shaped and defined by a mass Black incarceration regime inaugurated two generations ago as the national response to the Black movements of the '60s. The clearly visible fact that many of the cops that occupied Ferguson during this week's anniversary of Michael Brown's murder were physically *afraid*—and that the "street" brothers and sisters were demonstrably *not*—is all the proof we need that Black youth in what we used to call the "ghetto" remain eager to confront their tormentors.

Physical annihilation, or a lifetime of social death through imprisonment, is also only a presidential executive order away for the "above ground" activists of the movement, whose comings, goings, and communications are carefully tracked by the First Black President's secret police, as reported by the *Intercept*. The various components of what is collectively called the Black Lives Matter movement are on the domestic enemies list of Homeland Security, overseen by Jeh Johnson, a Black man, and the FBI, under the overall direction of Attorney General Loretta Lynch, a Black woman.

Lynch, like her predecessor Eric Holder, believes her race entitles her to play both Lord High Prosecutor and Black role model. Thus, as a Black "elder" and "credit to her race," Lynch purports to have the moral authority to define what the movement should be doing to commemorate Michael Brown's murder. "The weekend's events were peaceful and promoted a message of reconciliation and healing," she said—as if people should reconcile themselves to a system that kills a Black person roughly every day and has resulted in one out of every eight prison inmates in the world being an African American; a system that cannot possibly be healed. "But incidents of violence, such as we saw last night," Lynch warns, switching to her Lord High Prosecutor persona, "are contrary to both that message, along with everything [we] have worked to achieve over the past year."

What the Obama administration has spent the year trying to do is co-opt the same activists they are building dossiers on, in preparation for possible future detention. There are clear limits, however, to the entice-ments that can be offered by an administration that, like all Democratic and Republican governments in the United States for the past forty-five years, is totally committed to maintenance of the Mass Black Incarceration regime—albeit with some tinkering at the margins.

The greatest asset of the movement co-optation project is the Democratic Party itself, an institution that thoroughly dominates Black politics at every level of community life. Not only are Black elected offi-cials overwhelmingly Democrats, but virtually all the established Black civic organizations—the NAACP, the National Urban League, most politi-cally active Black churches, fraternities, and sororities—act as annexes of the Democratic Party. Two generations after the disbanding of the Black grassroots movement and the independent politics that grew out of that movement, the Democratic Party permeates political discourse in Black America. And the Democratic Party is where progressive movements go to die.

If the emerging movement allows itself to be sucked into Democratic Party politics, it is doomed. Yet the #BlackLivesMatter organization, a structured group with a highly visible leadership and chapters in twenty-six cities, is now circling the event-horizon of the Democratic Black Hole. To the extent that it and other movement organizations have gotten money from labor unions, they are accepting Democratic Party cash, since organized labor in the U.S. is also an extension of—and a cash cow to—the Democrats. Indeed, labor union money in a presidential election year is far more dangerous to the independence of the movement than grants from outfits like the Ford Foundation. Labor wants measurable results for its dollars, and will make its money talk at the ballot box.

#BlackLivesMatter activists may convince themselves that they are confronting the ruling class electoral duopoly by disrupting presidential candidates' speeches, but the tactic leads straight to co-optation. What is the purpose? If #BLM's goal is to push the candidates to adopt better positions on criminal justice reform, what happens afterwards? The logic of the tactic leads to either a direct or indirect, implicit endorsement of the more responsive candidate(s). Otherwise, why should #BLM—or the candidates—go through the exercise?

Former Maryland governor and Baltimore mayor Martin O'Malley, whose draconian street-sweeps resulted in the arrest of 750,000 people in one year—more than the total population of the city—submitted a full-blown criminal justice system proposal after being confronted by #BLM. Will it be graded? Is #BLM in the business of rating candidates? If so, then the group is inevitably acting as a Democratic Party lobby/constituency and is wedded to certain electoral outcomes. At that point, it ceases being an independent movement or an example of independent Black politics. It's just another brand of Democrat.

If the goal is to pressure candidates to put forward "better" positions on criminal justice or other issues, then what #BLM is actually doing is nudging Democrats towards incremental reform. In the absence of radical #BLM demands, all that is left are the petty reform promises that can be squeezed out of Democrats. (None of this works with the Republican White Man's Party.)

The #BLM tactic avoids formulation and aggressive agitation of core movement demands. But a movement is defined by its demands, which is one reason that the current mobilization is best described as an "incipient" movement, a mobilization with great promise.

Dr. Martin Luther King Jr. denounced Democratic president and sometimes ally Lyndon Johnson over the Vietnam War in 1967 and rejected even the appearance of collaboration with the ruling class duopoly. King understood that his job was to move masses of people towards their own empowerment, not to act as an interest group or lobby in the corridors of the system. (Malcolm X and, later, the Black Panther Party would have pilloried King if he had.) Half a century later, the Democratic Party is full of Black officials but, in light of their performance in office, this is more evidence of defeat than victory. Two months before Michael Brown was murdered in Ferguson, 80 percent of the Congressional Black Caucus—four out of five full-voting members, including the Black congressman representing Ferguson, William "Lacy" Clay—supported continued Pentagon transfers of military weapons and gear to local police departments.

The Democratic Party like its Republican duopoly cousin is a criminal enterprise, polluting the politics of Black America. Any sustained Black movement must, of necessity, be in opposition to the Democratic Party and its civic society annexes. They are the enemies within, the people who have facilitated the mass Black incarceration regime for two generations. "Lacy" Clay and his CBC colleagues have killed thousands of Michael Browns.

People's core demands ring out in every demonstration. When Black protesters shout, "Killer cops out of our neighborhood," they aren't referring to a couple of especially bad apples; they're talking about the whole damn occupation army. That's why the Black Is Back Coalition for Social Justice, Peace, and Reparations believes "Black Community Control of the

Police" is a righteous, self-determinationist demand. Other groups may feel strongly about other demands, and that's fine. Movements are lively places. But a movement cannot congeal without core demands.

August 12, 2015

#BLACKLIVESMATTER PERFORMS A SELF-HUMILIATION AT HILLARY CLINTON'S HANDS

It is painfully evident from the video of last week's meeting between a #BlackLivesMatter delegation and Democratic presidential candidate Hillary Clinton that the organization is philosophically incapable of making demands on the political representatives of the rulers of the United States. #BLM's leadership is either confused as to the nature of political demands or has decided to reject the most fundamental lessons of mass movement politics—indeed, of human social dynamics. Political movements are defined by their core demands. The video of #BLM's closed-door encounter with Clinton in New Hampshire on August 11—after the five activists had been prevented from attending and presumably disrupting her campaign event—should become a staple for future political education classes on what happens when would-be movement operatives enter the lion's den unarmed with political demands: they are humiliated and eaten alive.

#BlackLivesMatter does post a list of "National Demands" on its website, including "that the federal government discontinue its supply of military weaponry and equipment to local law enforcement," and that the U.S. Justice Department "release the names of all officers involved in killing black people within the last five years." Mixed in with these demands are pledges to "seek justice for Michael Brown's family," to develop a network "aimed at redressing the systemic pattern of anti-black law enforcement violence in the US," and to "advocate" for a decrease in federal spending on law enforcement, accompanied by an increase in social funding.

The commingling of demands and lists of future projects is itself indicative of lack of clarity on what constitutes a demand. However, it is clear that the organization's campaign to disrupt presidential candidates involves only one demand: that representatives of the corporate electoral duopoly "acknowledge whether they believe that Black lives matter," in the words of #BLM co-founder Alicia Garza, who was interviewed on MSNBC on the same day as the New Hampshire debacle.

The main aim of #BLM, besides the huge airplay generated by the confrontations, is to elicit *the candidates' own proposals* for changes in the criminal justice system. Julius Jones, founder of the Worcester, Massachusetts, chapter of #BLM and Clinton's main interlocutor at the New Hampshire encounter, told the *Daily Beast*: "Each one [of the candidates] is being made to offer their racial analysis in the United States. We require that they have an understanding so to that list we need to strongly add analysis because we live in a pluralistic society."

In the logic of #BLM leaders, solicitation of reformist proposals from candidates of the two oligarchic parties constitutes a kind of demand. The group doesn't even require that candidates endorse #BLM's own posted, reformist demands, such as decreasing spending on police or releasing the names of killer cops. Instead, the candidates are "made to offer their racial analysis" and to produce proposals tailored by the candidate's own staffs.

The strategy—if one could dignify it as such—is inherently impotent, which is why corporate lawyer and war criminal Hillary Clinton found it so easy to reduce Jones and his colleagues to school children at an elementary civics class.

Although millions of people have already seen the video, it is important to carefully examine the exchange between Clinton and Julius Jones since the meeting marks a crucial point in the trajectory of both #BLM and of the larger movement to which Alicia Garza and her colleagues contributed a name. The contradictions of #BLM's strategy will have profound impact, at least in the near term, on the future of the struggle against state oppression of Black people in the U.S. We need to learn from this disaster.

*

After about two minutes of rambling by Jones on how "mass incarceration just doesn't work" and "you [Clinton] have been in a certain way partially responsible, more than most," punctuated by "uh-hums" and nods from Clinton, Jones gets to the point.

> Jones: "Now that you understand the consequences, what in your heart has changed that's gonna change the direction of this country? And what in you, like, not your platform, not what you're supposed to say, like, how do you really feel that's different than you did before? Like, what were the mistakes, and how can those mistakes that you made be lessons for all of America, for a moment of reflection on how we treat Black people in this country?"

Clinton, as requested, engages in meaningless "reflection" for a while, then launches into The Lecture:

> In politics, [if] you can't explain it and you can't sell it, it stays on the shelf. And, this is now a time—a moment—just like the civil rights movement, or the women's movement, or the gay rights movement or a lot of other movements reached at a point in time [when] the people behind that consciousness-raising and advocacy, they had a plan ready to go. So that, when you turn to, you know, the women's movement—we wanna pass this and we wanna pass that, and we wanna do this—the problems are not all taken care of, we know that. Obviously, I know more about the civil rights movement in the old days because I had a lot of involvement in working with people. So, they had a plan—this piece of legislation, this court case—same with the gay rights movement.
>
> So, all I'm saying is, your analysis is totally fair, it's historically fair, psychologically fair, I t's economically fair. But, you're gonna have to come together as a movement and say, here's what

> we want done about it. Because you can get lip service from as many white people as you can pack into Yankee Stadium.

Clinton is belittling #BLM for stepping into the arena without a set of demands. She compares them unfavorably to historical social movements and succeeds in pulling rank, or seniority, over the young activists *in the Black arena*, implicitly citing her interaction with past Black movement leaders. Clinton would welcome a list of demands from #BLM, because she knows they would be well within the realm of bourgeois reform and eminently negotiable. Most importantly, as a lawyer and cutthroat politician, she is acutely aware that the young activists have been trapped by their own practice. They have asked for nothing, and she has given them her time, advice, and a civics lesson.

Jones tries to gain the initiative but succeeds only in giving Clinton further opportunity to rule the room.

> Jones: What you just said was a form of victim-blaming. You were saying that what the Black Lives Matter movement needs to do to change white hearts . . .

> Clinton: [interrupting] Look, I don't believe you change hearts. [She steps closer to Jones, her finger stabbing the air.] I believe you change laws, you change allocation of resources, you change the way systems operate.

In the absence of real demands by #BLM (or any evidence of a developed worldview), Clinton assumes the role of methodical agent of change. #BLM appears to be just another Democratic constituency group—and a rather unfocussed one at that. We see no evidence of Black movement politics, or competent politics of any kind. When Clinton practically begs them to propose something, the delegation fails to put forward their own reform proposals.

The fiasco can't be blamed on Julius Jones; he was following the leadership's policy. On MSNBC's Rachel Maddow show, #BLM co-founder Alicia Garza declared that "Black Lives Matter as a network and as a growing movement across the world is at a turning point." Their goal is "to make sure that our communities are safe, to have the things that we need, and we are here to make sure that anti-Black racism is eliminated, once and for all."

The MSNBC host asks what #BLM wants presidential candidates to do.

"First and foremost," said Garza, "acknowledge whether they believe that Black lives matter. And we've seen almost all of the major candidates, at least on the Democratic side, saying as much. But, the reality is, we have to go a lot farther. We didn't just want to hear fancy slogans. We want to know what will you do to ensure that Black lives matter? What are you willing to risk? What are you willing to implement? And what are you willing to change to ensure that no longer will we live in a country where every 28 hours a Black person is murdered by police, vigilantes or security guards, according to the Malcolm X Grassroots Movement."

From the lips of the founder, #BLM is most interested in hearing candidates say the magic words "Black lives matter," after which it solicits policy proposals from the various campaigns. That's it. No demands. The host wants clarification.

"Is it incumbent," he asks, "on those candidates and leaders to answer those questions, as you put it, or is this ultimately a model that will have explicit demands, in the same way that groups like the NRA or AIPAC are scoring votes and making explicit demands? We saw some organizers in certain states say one of the demands would be independent investigations of police brutality rather than having local DAs do it themselves."

Garza blows off the question of demands, thus demonstrating that even the mild "National Demands" posted on the group's website count for little in the organization.

"I think that what is important to be mindful of," she said, "is that there have been demands for a long time now, and it's just now that some folks are turning their attention to asking, well, what are the policies solutions, what are the policy implementations that we're going to be needing, here? And I think what we need to be mindful of is that both requires [that] the candidates are proactive in thinking about what is it that they plan to move, in the same way that they give us the package of issues that they're going to be working on when they take office. This issue needs to be one of them, and they need to be putting forward practical proposals."

Instead of making demands, #BLM wants to pick up packages of proposals from the various presidential candidates. For what purpose? Garza didn't answer the question. Endorsement or "scoring," as the MSNBC host suggested, are logical uses, but I personally don't believe #BLM had any firm plans at all for the candidates' proposals. It's all about the cameras. But, again, the logic of the process they have set in motion requires them to become part of the two-party elections game—ready or not. The Clinton encounter tells us #BLM is not ready—and maybe that's best since their current path leads inevitably to collaboration and co-optation.

Garza was interrupted by the MSNBC host: "What do you say to the criticism or concern that shutting down a candidate's event or disrupting a Bernie Sanders event is not politically effective?"

She responded: "Well, what I would say is that power concedes nothing without a demand; it never has and it never will. And so it is important that we push to ensure that our issues are at the forefront. Certainly, had we not been disrupting, had we not been pushing, had we not accepted business as usual [*sic*], we wouldn't be having this conversation now."

Garza can quote Frederick Douglass, but she doesn't seem to understand a word he said.

*

Lots of folks in #BlackLivesMatter identify themselves as revolutionaries. Nearly all of them claim to want radical social transformation, an end to capitalism. People that are steeped in the Black radical tradition understand that primary demands are those that distill the true aspirations of the people; they are formulated to galvanize the people, not for endorsement by those in power, who would be overthrown if the demands were actualized. Radicals also understand that there is a place for reformist demands, which are crafted to enhance the people's power relative to the rulers and to alleviate the people's pain. But #BLM has eschewed both reformist and radical demands in its current campaign, revealing a loud but empty politics. We wish it were not so.

The Black Is Back Coalition for Social Justice, Peace, and Reparations has put forward a demand in the Black radical tradition that it believes embodies the logic of the current, incipient movement: Black Community Control of the Police. The Coalition is not submitting this demand to the rulers of the United States or to any of their candidates for president; it is up to the people how to achieve their liberation from the murderous machinery of the State.

Self-determination is not a demand; it is a right. Black people have the right to control the security apparatus in their communities. To demand that this occur is righteous.

August 19, 2015

#BLACKLIVESMATTER HURTS DEMOCRATS' FEELINGS

The Democrats that pushed their party's national committee (DNC) to endorse the #BlackLivesMatter organization and its three co-founders told reporters they felt "blindsided" when #BLM leadership refused to endorse them back. The resolution was submitted last Friday by high-powered party activists, including DNC Chair Rep. Debbie Wasserman Schultz, DNC Secretary and Baltimore Mayor Stephanie Rawlings-Blake, and Black party stalwart Donna Brazile. The endorsement praised #BLM "creators" Patrisse Cullors, Opal Tometi, and Alicia Garza by name and "resolved that the DNC joins with Americans across the country in affirming 'Black lives matter' and the 'say her name' efforts to make visible the pain of our fellow and sister Americans as they condemn extrajudicial killings of unarmed African American men, women and children."

The Democratic honchos then issued a "call for action" by Congress "to adopt systemic reforms at state, local, and federal levels to prohibit law enforcement from profiling based on race, nationality, ethnicity, or religion; to minimize the transfer of excess equipment (like the military-grade vehicles and weapons that were used to police peaceful civilians in the streets of Ferguson, Missouri) to federal and state law enforcement; and to support prevention programs that give young people alternatives to incarceration."

All these proposals have already been put forward by the Obama administration or its various task forces. On Monday, the #BLM leaders issued the following response. It deserves a careful reading:

A resolution signaling the Democratic National Committee's endorsement that Black lives matter, in no way implies an endorsement of the DNC by the Black Lives Matter Network, nor was it done in consultation with us. We do not now, nor have we ever, endorsed or affiliated with the Democratic Party, or with any party. The Democratic Party, like the Republican and all political parties, have historically attempted to control or contain Black people's efforts to liberate ourselves. True change requires real struggle, and that struggle will be in the streets and led by the people, not by a political party.

More specifically, the Black Lives Matter Network is clear that a resolution from the Democratic National Committee won't bring the changes we seek. Resolutions without concrete change are just business as usual. Promises are not policies. We demand freedom for Black bodies, justice for Black lives, safety for Black communities, and rights for Black people. We demand action, not words, from those who purport to stand with us.

While the Black Lives Matter Network applauds political change towards making the world safer for Black life, our only endorsement goes to the protest movement we've built together with Black people nationwide—not the self-interested candidates, parties, or political machine seeking our vote.

The unexpected rebuke startled and embarrassed the Democrats, who clearly believed that the #BLM organization would welcome the compliment. "Black Democratic operatives" told reporters "they are increasingly frustrated that movement activists seem to be pushing them away."

The party's embarrassment and confusion is quite understandable, especially because since the start of its engagement with presidential candidates, the #BlackLivesMatter leadership has given every indication that it was "circling the event-horizon of the Democratic Black Hole" and liable to be sucked in at any time. The brashness of #BLM's disruptions of Bernie Sanders' and Martin O'Malley's campaign speeches may have convinced activists that they were "confronting the ruling class electoral duopoly," but the absence of demands—beyond the obligatory verbalization of "Black lives matter" and the candidates' promise to formulate their own racial justice proposals—leads directly to co-optation.

As we posed it in *BAR*: "What is the purpose? If #BLM's goal is to push the candidates to adopt better positions on criminal justice reform, what happens afterwards? The logic of the tactic leads to either a direct or indirect, implicit endorsement of the more responsive candidate(s). Otherwise, why should #BLM—or the candidates—go through the exercise?"

The activists' disastrous encounter with Hillary Clinton on August 11 only encouraged Democratic operatives in their belief that #BLM could be effectively captured by the Party—that, indeed, the group's three leaders would welcome a grand invitation into the halls of power. Clinton had succeeded in treating the #BLM delegation like children at an elementary school civics class, lecturing *them* on the need to make demands on the system and to stop worrying about the contents of politicians' hearts, including her own.

On the day of the Clinton fiasco, MSNBC asked #BLM co-founder Alicia Garza, directly, if the organization would "score" the various candidates' racial justice proposals (which would implicitly amount to an endorsement of the highest scoring candidate), or would they make "explicit demands"? Garza pointedly refused to answer the question. The Democratic National Committee now had every reason to believe that nothing more was required of the Party than that they repeat the magic words "Black lives matter," recognize Black female humanity through praise of "'say her name' efforts," and back a short list of proposals already promulgated by President Obama. Why wouldn't #BlackLivesMatter be thrilled?

The DNC endorsement was a perfectly logical outcome of the #BLM leadership's strategy to make no substantive demands of presidential candidates. Real movements are defined by their demands, but #BLM's failure to put forward demands—including the mild and reformist demands listed on their national website, and even when the Democratic front-runner directly solicited a list of demands—signaled that collaboration of some kind was afoot, whether that signal was intentional or not.

We at Black Agenda Report will not speculate about the level of interaction between #BLM leadership and DNC operatives in the days and weeks before the Democratic endorsement. That's a fool's game, which distracts attention from central questions of movement politics—such as the nature of demands—and from facts that are clear to any observer. In their rebuke to the DNC, #BlackLivesMatter leadership resorts to what BAR co-founder Bruce Dixon calls "weasel words" to deny any direct collaboration with the Democrats. The endorsement was not done "in consultation with us," they say. "Consultation" is a term that means whatever the speaker wants it to mean, or nothing at all.

This is no time to engage in legalese. #BLM's leadership has spread confusion and done real damage to an incipient movement that does not belong to them, but to which they contributed an attractive hashtag that has served as a general reference point for a whole range of organizations, activities, and political tendencies. The "movement," if it is sustained, will grow a name of its own, distilled from the demands that define it. As with popular upheavals in previous eras, the movement will earn its name, and will be rooted in the streets, not the suites—and certainly not in the Democratic Party, which is where movements go to die.

Malcolm X liberated the Black political conversation and set the stage for the most tumultuous, productive era in twentieth century Black U.S. history in 1963, when he railed against the "Big Six," the civil rights organizations recognized by the white power structure as representatives of Black America: the NAACP, National Urban League, CORE, SCLC, SNCC, and A. Philip Randolph's "Brotherhood of Sleeping Car Porters." Both before and after the March on Washington, which the Nation of Islam minister called "the farce on Washington," Malcolm accused the Big Six of collaborating with the Kennedys to cool down the passions of Black people in the street.

"It was the grass roots out there in the street," Malcolm declared, in his "Message to the Grassroots," in November, 1963. "[It] scared the white man to death, scared the white power structure in Washington, D.C. to death." The job of the Big Six was to put "cream in the coffee"—to weaken and tame the movement, said Malcolm. In return, the Big Six were given money, recognition, and access to people in power.

Malcolm X's accusations may have been unfair to some of the individuals and groups involved, but he put the Big Six on notice that he would not respect the old Negro dictum of not washing dirty linen [Black internal political disputes] in public [within earshot of white people]. As a result, self-imposed Black restraints on critiques of African American leadership came tumbling down, and a raucous movement emerged to achieve Black self-determination and to join—and change—the world.

Malcolm turned the Big Six groups' access to the White House into a source of righteous suspicion. Why are you going in and out of The Man's house? If you enter The Man's house, you better tell the people what you talked about in there. What did you promise him? What is he offering you? Most importantly, you must understand that your presence in that house is, by definition, *suspect*.

At *Black Agenda Report*, we still believe that those who purport to lead Black people must be held accountable. That applies to the old-line Black civic groups, to the #BlackLivesMatter organization, and to the larger movement-in-the-making.

September 2, 2015

GARZA VS. MCKESSON: THE GREAT DEBATE OVER HOW THE DEMOCRATIC PARTY WILL LIBERATE BLACK PEOPLE

Representatives of the two wings of Black Lives Matter last weekend jousted over the merits of holding Democratic Party-sponsored town halls on racial justice versus a formal, televised debate on issues critical to Black people, also to be sponsored by the Democrats. The exchange took place on Melissa Harris-Perry's program on MSNBC, which acts as the Democratic Party's corporate cable outlet. A casual viewer might conclude that the incipient movement ignited by the murder of Michael Brown fourteen months ago has been swallowed whole by the Democratic Party. Certainly, the #BlackLivesMatter network, co-founded by Alicia Garza and two of her comrades, and its offshoot Campaign Zero, honchoed by charter school advocate DeRay Mckesson and like-minded colleagues, have encamped deep in the bosom of the Democratic Party, where movements go to die.

Accordingly, the Garza-Mckesson discourse was as circumscribed and stilted as what passes for debate within the Democratic and Republican duopoly. Mckesson wanted to stick with the format offered by his Democratic National Committee partners, who last week gave their "blessing," as the *Washington Post* reported, to a "town hall similar to those currently being planned by some state-level Democratic parties and some liberal groups including MoveOn.org." Thus, Campaign Zero would move formally into the ranks of Democratic Party organizations and front groups. Garza's #BlackLivesMatter network wants the Democrats to schedule a full-scale, seventh debate this summer to "put action behind the words" of the DNC's endorsement of Black Lives Matter.

Melissa Harris-Perry set the stage for the debate-about-a-debate by harkening back to the 1964 Democratic Party national convention in Atlantic City, when Fannie Lou Hamer and her Black-led Mississippi Freedom Democratic Party (MFDP) tried to unseat the lily-white state delegation. President Lyndon Johnson's operatives on the Democratic National Committee offered to seat only two of the insurgent delegates, an insult bitterly rejected by the MFDP. Dr. Martin Luther King had urged the Freedom Democrats to "compromise"—a stance Harris-Perry endorsed in hindsight. After all, she noted, Johnson went on to win a landslide victory and then to secure passage of the 1965 Voting Rights Act, so . . . all's well that ends well. Harris-Perry's message seemed clear: #BlackLivesMatter should take the Democrats up on their town hall offer.

Harris-Perry's elaborate buildup was an attempt to elevate the Garza-Mckesson face-off to grand historical proportions and an endorsement of their absorption into the Democratic Party enclosure, where she happily resides.

Mckesson said the town hall format would provide "a forum that has real people asking real questions. . . . It would offer a chance for the candidates to help us to understand better what their positions are, instead of having a format that caters to sound bites," like a debate.

Garza said her network wants "to see a debate. We want to see what the candidates proactively are coming up with . . . We want to make sure that the Democratic National Committee is having serious conversations at every single level about how to address the crisis facing Black communities today . . . and, what we think that does not mean is resting it on the shoulders of Black folks to do that work for them."

Again, just like Barack Obama and Hillary Clinton, there's scarcely a dime's bit of difference between Garza and Mckesson's essential positions. Neither wants to confront Power (the Democratic Party and its candidates) with core demands, beyond the "demand" for a debate or a town hall. Rather they propose venues in which the candidates will reveal themselves, for better evaluation by voters and an eventual endorsement by the activists (who, under the town hall arrangement offered by the DNC, will be treated as constituent Democratic organizations). Mckesson made it clear, after his delegation's last chat with Clinton, that his role is to educate those who wield power. "We want to make sure," he said, "that whoever the president is, has an informed platform about race, and Black people specifically, and criminal justice."

Mckesson is the courtier seeking the king's ear.

Garza insists that the Democratic Party get to work churning out ways to halt racial and economic oppression, so that the burden of figuring out a path towards liberation doesn't fall "on the shoulders of Black folks."

But of course, no one will free us but us—certainly neither of the two big business parties. There's a whole lot going on these days at #BlackLivesMatter and Campaign Zero—lots of individual upward mobility—but little of it has anything to do with a people's movement. These two organizations are no longer in that line of work.

October 30, 2015

"BLACK LIVES MATTER" GROUPS HOPING FOR A BIG PAYDAY

If the Democratic Party is where grassroots movements go to die, then the run-up to presidential elections is a year-long procession of Dead Activists Walking. This week, the funders of the Democratic wing of the corporate Deep State—most prominently, currency manipulator George Soros—have invited the Good, the Bad, and the Hungry elements of what is widely called the Black Lives Matter movement to make their case for cash infusions. The Democracy Alliance's (DA) stated mission is "to build progressive infrastructure that could help counter the well-funded and sophisticated conservative apparatus in the areas of civic engagement, leadership, media, and ideas." Translation: to transform leftist activist organizations into loyal, dependent annexes of the Democratic Party.

The rich can be quite fickle in bestowing their Midas touches, especially when it comes to Blacks. Back in 2004, Soros and other members of the Democratic Fat Cat Pack all but severed the cash umbilical cord to a host of Black organizations that had grown dependent on "soft" Democratic campaign money. Suddenly, the billionaires were running the Democratic ticket's Get Out the Vote (GOTV) effort in Black precincts across the country, with virtually all of the old-line civil rights organizations kicked to the curb. Insulted, embarrassed, and desperate for cash, 130 Black groups formed a band of beggars called Unity '04 under the co-chairmanship of Urban League President Marc Morial, Dorothy Height of the National Council of Negro Women, and University of Maryland political scientist Ron Walters.

Walters fired off a letter of protest: "This is an arrogant and divisive usurpation of power and it is destructive of our efforts that began most recently in the Civil Rights movement, where the efforts of Blacks to provide their own leadership in the act of political participation was understood to be the source of their power in the policy system as well."

The Rev. Jesse Jackson Sr. whined, "It's insulting that none of us who have been responsible for most registration and turnout are at the table determining priorities."

However, the Democrats went on to lose the 2004 election without the paid services of the "civil rights leadership," who never regained the steady quadrennial stipend to which they had grown accustomed during decades of loyalty to the party. With the party machinery firmly in the hands of the Democratic Leadership Council, the corporate-funded faction co-founded by Bill Clinton and Al Gore for the express purpose of limiting the influence of Blacks and labor, the Black Unity '04 groups were definitively put in their place—without two nickels to rub together.

As I wrote in *The Black Commentator* on October 14, 2004, "Traditional African American leadership is reaping the shriveled fruits of the narrow path it strode down three decades ago, when the 'movement' was demobilized in favor of brokered politics and periodic electioneering. Until now, Blacks were invited to the two- and four-year Democratic *electoral* party, but not to the *permanent power* party. Under the new regime, traditional Black organizations have been disinvited from the electoral party as well. The goal is clear: The DLC means to prevent Black groups from taking credit for a massive African American voter turnout against Bush. By sidelining these organizations during the campaign, the DLC hopes to cripple their capacity to mobilize constituencies between elections. Since electoral and broker politics has been so central to mainstream Black organizations for the past thirty-plus years, the game will, essentially, be over."

Despite insult and injury, the Black sideshow kept playing the Democrat's tune, albeit for much smaller tips. However, the shock of the loss of status and funding by the Democratic Party resulted in an acceleration of the old line Black organizations' historic drift towards dependence on corporate funding. "Movement" leaders promised corporate sugar daddies that they would run their organizations "like a business." The Congressional Black Caucus, as a body, turned dramatically to the right in 2005 as Black lawmakers scrambled for corporate contributions.

The same year, George Soros and his peers formed the Democracy Alliance to terraform U.S. leftish politics in the interests of the party. Some new Black groups were funded, eventually including ColorOfChange.org. However, a plutocratic purge in 2012 defunded ColorOfChange.org and a number of other outfits "working on issues relating directly to people of color," according to the *Huffington Post*. Color Of Change was later returned to the fold and by 2015 was listed among the DA's core "national partners and cross-issue organizations."

Now enter Black Lives Matter. The term has evolved from a catchy hashtag popularized by a specific network, founded by three Black women, to a catch-all for every group vying for a recognition in the incipient "move-ment." This week, some of them will be answering Soros & Company's cattle-call at the Democracy Alliance's headquarters in Washington.

Two organizations are pre-approved for Democratic Party funding. The Democratic National Committee has already endorsed the BlackLivesMatter network, praising "creators" Patrisse Cullors, Opal Tometi, and Alicia Garza by name. Despite the BLM network's public rebuff of the DNC ("We do not now, nor have we ever, endorsed or affili-ated with the Democratic Party, or with any party"), the Garza-Cullors-Tometi network pushed for a party-sanctioned presidential debate, while off-shoot Campaign Zero has gotten DNC approval to host a town hall presidential candidate forum. Both organizations have been accorded the status and privileges of constituent Democratic Party organizations, such as MoveOn.org. Their journey from "movement" to the Democrat plan-tation took less than a year—if the moment of impact of Officer Darren Wilson's bullet in Michael Brown's brain is the starting point.

And now it's payday.

November 18, 2015

NATIONALIZING THE BANKS IS A POPULAR DEMAND, SO LET'S DEMAND IT

This is an edited version of remarks I delivered at a panel on "Imagining an Authentic U.S. Left for the Twenty-First Century" at the Left Forum in New York City.

Power to the People!

I'm honored to be among the folks that Paul Street invited to think with him about what an "authentic" left would look like in the United States. It's something that many of us think about all the time.

The left would look very much as it does right now—you start from where you are—but it would begin behaving quite differently. I think that what we are actually talking about is: How do we make a movement—a ruling class-destroying movement—in the United States?

That's a simple proposition, and I think certain things flow from that proposition. Of course, we'd be talking about setting in motion several mass-based movements that are linked in their shared enemy: the ruling class and its organs of coercion and control, the organs that people come up against every time they move—and even when they don't move.

These mechanisms of coercion and control are more than just the police and the mass incarceration Gulag, more than the vast national security state. We also confront the awesome power of the corporate media which, as we have witnessed dramatically in the last two years, works hand-in-glove with U.S. domestic and international spy agencies. That is obviously what is going down with the anti-Russia hysteria.

The unity of the oligarchy, the corporate media, and the national security state is perfectly personified in Jeff Bezos, the Amazon owner and owner of the Washington Post, whose company also has a $600 million contract with the CIA. Bezos is the richest man in the world. He and two other oligarchs, Bill Gates and Warren Buffet, own more wealth than the entire poorest half of the American population. And *that* is the kind of oligarchic fact that is becoming commonly known out there in this vast, three hundred million-plus person country.

These are monopolists. They are masters of what they call "creative destruction," which is a very grotesque way of them bragging about the huge disruptions that hyper-active capital is causing in U.S. society, and much greater destruction in the Global South.

The concentration of capital in the U.S. and the global capitalist world has reached a point that the individuals at the top of the oligarchy—the men and a few white women named Walton—can be counted on our fingers. We know most of their names, and much of the public knows most of their names—that is the state of concentration that we have reached.

The heads of the big banks that are the queen ants of finance capital— the enemy of all mankind—can be listed on the fingers of one hand.

The crisis of late-stage capitalism is all around us. The people know that overlapping crises are in motion. They see it all around them, even if they are among those who still have good jobs. They see the crisis in motion; they talk about it, even if it has not devastated them personally, yet. There is *fear* everywhere in the United States, even among those people who, on paper, seem to be looking good—the upper income folks in two-"good job" households.

The people know the names of the oligarchs at the top of the list. Most importantly, everybody knows that the bankers are criminal. And everybody hates the banks.

That is not a hyperbolic statement. I'll say it again: Everybody, or virtually everybody, hates the banks.

In the United States, the only hatred that rivals the hatred of the banks is the hatred and fear of Black people and Muslims and Latino immigrants.

But, the second biggest hatred is the hatred of the banks, and that's the one we've got to work on.

And, in fact, hatred of the banks is damn near universal, in that it is pervasive among all groups in society, including even many upper-income whites. Right-wing libertarian Republicans, who actually do have representation in Congress, hate the bankers who occupy an especially evil place in their worldview. I don't pretend to understand that right-wing libertarian worldview, but they are vehement in their hatred of the bankers. I suspect that anti-Semitism has something to do with it—that they think these bankers are mostly Jewish. But for their own reasons, they hate the banks.

The hatred of bankers is near-universal in the United States. So, if that is the case, how much imagination does it take to imagine a new, twenty-first century left?

A real left wants to overthrow the ruling class, which is centered in finance capital. The people, in their multicolored splendor, hate the banks! Therefore, a real left mass movement for the twenty-first century *must* call for the nationalization of the banks. That is the logic of history.

I said "nationalization"—state takeover. It does not mean a temporary takeover, but a permanent public seizure of the banks. We're not talking about just cleaning out the crooks and then giving the banks back to the finance capitalist class. We're talking about dethroning the bankers. That is, we are making what is a *revolutionary* demand, but one that I am confident is actually a popular demand. I believe there is no more popular demand than smashing the banks.

I think that the question of what a genuine left response to this era of crisis should be is not so complex and problematic as others seem to believe. Movements are defined by their demands, and the demand to smash the bankers, permanently, would be a popular demand.

I did *not* say turn Goldman Sachs over to its workers, as a cooperative, as I've heard some folks propose. I think that's silly. Goldman Sachs and these other monster banks are instruments that have been crafted only for the oppression of humankind. That is their one and only purpose. You might just as well say that you'll solve the race-to-nuclear-annihilation problem by turning the U.S. strategic weapons triad over to the airmen and soldiers and sailors that man these weapons systems. That is silly and stupid as well.

No, we want to nationalize the banks, and put those banks to public purposes.

If that doesn't sound sexy enough as a slogan—and it doesn't—then we'll put Mighty Meme Makers like Rebel Diaz and their crew to the task of sexying and sloganizing it up. I know that they can do it because it is a popular demand.

It is the demand that the Occupy Movement never made back in 2011. They walked right up to the edge of the pool, but they did not dive in.

The core group of Occupy did some other silly things. They invited Black Obamite preachers into the movement. I don't know why they did that. One of the central organizers called me up and told me they were going to invite Rev. Ben Chavis to become part of the Occupy Movement. I told him that Rev. Chavis wrote a column every week for a Black newspaper, and that the column was all about backing Obama and voting for Democrats. But the Occupy people went ahead and invited Chavis in anyway.

Much of the co-optation that occurred with the Occupy Movement was self-inflicted. Of course, we know that it was Obama himself who directed the ultimate police crackdown on Occupy, but there were contradictions at the core in the Occupy Movement. The greatest failing was not to jump in the pool—the failure to demand nationalization of the banks.

Nevertheless, they left us with a slogan that has popularized a common sentiment: the hatred of the damn banks that was common in 2011, and which came to the fore when the "99 percent" slogan was promulgated. Now it's time to jump in the pool.

It's not going to be easy for the Democrats to co-opt a demand for permanent nationalization of the banks. There isn't room for the Democratic Party to come into a movement that is demanding the dethronement of their masters. Historically, the bankers are to the Democratic Party what big energy has been to the Republican Party.

We will see what the relationship of social forces really looks like when the left is pushing a demand that is both truly popular and, on its face, *transformative*.

The trick, the hard part here, is in projecting what *takes the place* of the private banks. It is absolutely crucial that the projected new, public banking configuration—the one that we say will come about as a result of these demands—be seen by the people as providing all the services that the private banks currently provide, and those services that they used to provide, but no longer do. Because there will be great anxiety in the land when people wonder where they are going to put their money.

The public banking system will have to be seen as part of the rebuilding of the nation, which is a transformational project. It must also be understood that the new regime of national redevelopment will be a democratic one.

There is, clearly, room in this massive transformational project for all the debate that anyone could imagine. What does a democratic society look like? That's the great debate that flows from the declaration that the people are going to take over the banking system.

The redevelopment of the nation, because that is what we are proposing to do with the banking system, must be in service to all the constituencies of the United States. All of these constituencies hate the banks. All of them want transformation, in terms that they can understand.

Black Americans will be the most enthusiastic about smashing the banks. Black Americans are the most left-leaning group in the United States. They are the most in favor, by every measurement, of wealth redistribution, and they are the most opposed to monopoly.

The bankers and the real estate corporations are the ones that created the ghettos—and everybody Black knows that. Bankers and realtors are also the engines of gentrification—and everybody Black understands that as well. There is no need to demonize the bankers in Black America, but what you do have to show Black America is that this public banking institution is going to be not just *of service* to them, but that they will have a say in the institution. They need to know that there will be a self-determinationist aspect to the reorganization of the banks.

If we are ever to see a real, working unity among Blacks and Latinos on the ground, it will be in common opposition to the bankers that are behind gentrification, which is happening everywhere in the country, all with the same plan of inflating land assets through ethnic cleansing. Latino populations are moving into or getting moved out of the same neighborhoods as Black people. The commonality is real, it is day to day, it cries out for collaboration that I think can be best achieved in a general movement to smash the private banks and take away their power, permanently, and put the nation's capital to public use.

Several movements would be spawned by this demand for nationalization of the banks. In the last two years, it has become clear to masses of people that the concentration of capital in Silicon Valley—we're talking about Google and Facebook and Amazon and other corporations in that industry—is a danger to democracy, a growing peril that people are beginning to recognize. I think we should be talking about intervention in those monopolies as well, and I believe such demands would grow, organically, from the struggle and debate around nationalization of the banks. In fact, the list of struggles that would emerge from this central demand is quite a long one. We have plenty of work to do in the twenty-first century.

Power to the People.

June 6, 2018

BLACK LIVES MATTER FOUNDER LAUNCHES HUGE PROJECT TO SHRINK BLACK LIVES

Alicia Garza of Black Lives Matter fame last week introduced her latest project in the pages of the *New York Times*: a survey of "more than 31,000 black people from all 50 states" to determine, as the headline announced, "What Black People Want." The Black Census Project "is the largest independent survey of black people ever conducted in the United States," wrote Garza. A collaboration of Garza's Black Futures Lab, Color of Change, Dēmos, and Socioanalítica Research, the project "trained more than 100 black organizers and worked with some 30 grass-roots organizations" to elicit Black people's views on a range of domestic subjects—but asked not a single question related to war and peace.

Garza & Co. have thus performed a kind of lobotomy on the Black polity in the United States, excising from public policy discussion Black Americans' views on the nation's endless military and economic wars against people of color around the world. Garza's team appears to have operated on the premise that Black people have no opinion on the death of millions and the destruction of whole societies, crimes that are committed *in their name* by the U.S. government. As if Black Americans don't see the connection between ever-expanding war budgets and constantly shrinking domestic social spending. The project is structured as if African Americans are provincial boobs who don't give a damn about foreign affairs or the intersection of U.S. foreign and domestic policy.

What is perfectly clear is that the survey is designed to influence the election strategies of the Democratic Party, whose candidates, she writes, fail to "address the issues that affect black communities or meaningfully court them." Instead, "time, money and effort are expended to identify and cater to moderate white voters who are already fickle about politicians and political parties. This has long been the Democratic establishment's strategy, but they doubled down on it after the 2016 election when analysts proclaimed that the left's undue focus on 'identity politics' sent moderate white voters to the Republican side."

Most corporate Democratic candidates also avoid foreign policy issues whenever possible. Garza and her corporate-philanthropy-funded crew impose the same strictures on Black discussion, in hopes of creating a saleable electoral campaign product for Democrats.

The survey's webpage is keen to advertise that the 31,000 "Black Census respondents are highly engaged in elections: Not only did more than 73 percent report voting in 2016, but 40 percent also report some other form of electoral activity, such as engaging as donors, volunteers, or canvassers." The message is: These are folks that need to be put to work on some worthy Democrat's campaign. "As the unwavering base of the Democratic Party, if the politically engaged Black population ceased to vote and gave up on the system, it would upend the Democratic Party and have devastating effects on our democracy as a whole," says Garza's Black Census Project, in a transparent pitch for its availability to save the Party and "the system."

The survey is quite methodical in providing questions to guide candidates in navigating Black domestic political views. It confirms that the Black political consensus on economic justice at home remains intact, with large majorities of respondents favoring high taxes on the rich, increased minimum wages, and affordable health, higher education, and housing. (The survey does not ask if any of these things should be a right.) Predictably, three-quarters of those surveyed want cops made accountable for their misconduct, and just over half want community boards created to supervise police departments. But the surveyors were not interested in

Black people's views on U.S. military violence abroad, or the impact of U.S. policies on poverty in the world, or anything at all about Africa, a continent the United States has militarily occupied since 2008. We do learn that President Obama, who effectuated the occupation, enjoys an 85 percent approval rating among respondents, as does Black Lives Matter.

The survey is a hustle to make Garza, Color Of Change, and their (already deeply-connected) financial backers bigger players in the Democratic Party—without challenging lawless U.S. empire, "the greatest purveyor of violence in the world, today," as Dr. Martin Luther King Jr. stated more than half a century ago, and as Malcolm X hammered home till his dying breath.

Garza knows what she's doing. The Movement for Black Lives platform, titled "A Vision for Black Lives: Policy Demands for Black Power, Freedom and Justice," is quite radical in its demands to end the (domestic) war on Black people and for reparations; disinvestment of oppressive government and economic institutions; economic justice; community control; and decriminalizing Black political activity. It puts forward no demands on U.S. foreign policy, but instead offers an apology: "While the movement's platform largely focuses on the implementation of domestic policies that will advance black communities in America, the movement also recognizes that patriarchy, exploitative capitalism, militarism, and white supremacy know no borders."

But Garza knows the borders of what is acceptable to the corporate Democratic Party and adheres to the limits imposed by the fat cats—who are also among her donors. This is sometimes called political "capture" of dissidents by the ruling class. However, the term "capture" hardly fits when the prey is begging to be caught.

As Black academic Jennifer Nash writes in this week's edition of the *BAR* Book Forum, Black feminists tend to hold "proprietary attachments to intersectionality . . . to keep it close, to guard it." Yet, Alicia Garza pretends, for Black Census Project purposes, to be blind to the intersection between U.S. slaughter of millions of nonwhite people abroad and the mass Black incarceration regime at home. She doesn't respect Black folks enough to even ask if they approve or disapprove of their government's conduct abroad. The absence of foreign policy questions is a deliberate ploy to make the project and its players palatable to imperialists. Garza not only pretends that she doesn't see the connection between the trillion dollar U.S. military budget versus endless austerity for human needs programs, she has overseen a survey that pretends the rest of Black America is also blind and dumb. Her survey is an insult to the Black Radical Tradition, which is rooted in solidarity with the oppressed peoples of the world and has resulted in Black America winning allies and emulators around the globe.

Fortunately, an organization exists that will never forget the six million Congolese that have been slaughtered to date as a result of U.S. foreign policy—the worst genocide since World War II—and which fights daily to bring Washington's "endless wars" to a halt: the Black Alliance for Peace. But that's not the kind of project that corporate billionaires fund.

June 5, 2019

WE ARE ALREADY LATE TO THE GREAT BLACK REPARATIONS DEBATE

This essay was prepared for the thirtieth annual convention of NCOBRA, the National Coalition of Blacks for Reparations in America, in Detroit.

2017 is the year that reparations definitively became a "mainstream" issue—meaning, serious candidates for president have been compelled to discuss the need to repair the historical and ongoing damage inflicted on Black people with the complicity of the United States government. Solid majorities of African Americans support reparations in principle: 64 percent, according to a *Business Insider* poll taken in March of this year, a statistically significant increase over Black pro-reparations sentiment measured in 2014 (59 percent, according to a YouGov survey), 2015 (52 percent, CNN), and 2016 (58 percent, Marist Poll). The *Business Insider* poll shows that 25 percent of whites, 37 percent of Asian Americans, and 42 percent of Hispanics favor reparations—not enough to sway a national referendum on reparations, but almost certainly constituting a majority of the Democratic Party base, 25 percent of which is Black.

These numbers are extremely encouraging in that they give national political legitimacy to the principle of reparations, which political scientist Michael Dawson writes, "has been a central theme of Black political life," and now seems destined to become a staple of the Democratic half of the U.S. electoral duopoly. With a companion bill in the Senate, introduced by New Jersey's Cory Booker in April of this year, the H.R. 40 reparations study measure is now a "real" piece of legislation that can be lobbied in both chambers of Congress. In addition to Booker, presidential candidates Kamala Harris, Elizabeth Warren, Tulsi Gabbard, and Julian Castro claim to favor reparations, although none of their proposals measure up to even a narrow semantic definition of the word. It is enough, for now, that these politicians acknowledge that a debt is owed to Black people. Sen. Bernie Sanders, who has a real chance of becoming president, says he will sign a reparations study bill if it comes across his desk. But he resists endorsing reparations, asking CNN's Wolf Blitzer: "What does that mean? What do they mean? I don't think anyone's been very clear."

It's an honest and sincere question, and one that can only be answered by Black people in the process of a Great Black Reparations Debate. Only Black people can put meat on the bare bones principle of reparations in America. As Frederick Douglass said, "The man who has *suffered the wrong* is the man to *demand redress*—the man STRUCK is the man to CRY OUT."

Reparations—repair—must mean measures that are *transformative*, that lift Black people up from the bottom of the socio-economic-political barrel that the United States government and white society have methodically placed us in through centuries of criminal acts. The runaway slave who joined the Union Army and was part of the unit that captured his former master's plantation was clear on what reparations meant to him. "Bottom rail on top this time, Massah."

The United States was built on the foundation of Black people as the bottom rail—and keeping them there. In an endemically racist society, we are the institutional definition of the bottom. The mission of genuine reparations must be to eliminate the "bottom" altogether. Otherwise, a hostile white society will push Black people back into our "place," once again.

Resources are important, and any reparations scheme that does not have a price tag in the many trillions is an insult to the living and the dead. According to one estimate, the Federal Reserve bank bailout amounted to $29 trillion—to save the criminals that caused the economic collapse! Redressing crimes against the Black people whose unpaid labor created

America's wealth is at least as large a project. But reparations is more than material resources; it is the power to use those resources for the betterment of one's people, and to be secure in not being victimized again by the historical oppressor. It means Black self-determination, without which "democracy" is a sham and a farce.

The Great Black Reparations Debate must reach into every nook and cranny of Black America, examining every aspect of Black life in this country—as well as debating Black Americans' relationship with the rest of the African Diaspora and the world. It is up to Black people—the ones who have been struck!—to propose the programs and structures that not only emancipate us from the bottom, but that effectively abolish such substrata.

Folks need to be instructed to stop asking white or Black politicians to come up with a reparations plan. That's a task reserved collectively for African Americans, after long and exhaustive debate. The United States was built on stolen land and stolen labor. Those are the crimes that must be redressed. Any reparations proposal that leaves current U.S. social, economic, and political structures intact only perpetuates the crime and guarantees a relapse into the abyss.

The Great Black Reparations Debate must begin *before* passage of H.R. 40. Ideally, the Black debate should inform those delegated by Congress to study the reparations question. More likely, a Black community that is energized and aroused by the debate will wind up rebuking the politicians, including most of the Black ones, for treating the reparations issue as a chance to declare a symbolic victory for Black people, like the Dr. King holiday. But that's the most African Americans can expect if we fail to organize a Black-wide debate that involves, literally, millions of our people. We're already late.

Black opponents of reparations like political scientist Adolph Reed argue that reparations may be appealing but isn't worth investing lots of political capital, because the non-Black majority of the U.S. will never support truly transformative repair. That's certainly true, if we assume that today's pitiful level of independent Black political mobilization is permanent. Forty million Black people can't change a damn thing unless they argue collectively about what is to be done and then organize to do it. The Great Black Reparations Debate can be the extended, independent forum for Black people to reimagine themselves and their place in the nation and the world, and to act collectively to build a new society—one that is fit for our people's habitation. Once such a mobilization is underway, it really doesn't much matter what the corporate servants on Capitol Hill think reparations should look like—because Black people will have our own vision and plan.

In his book *Black Visions*, Dr. Michael Dawson analyzes the results of an exhaustive political survey of African Americans that he oversaw in 1994. The survey showed that a majority of Black people, while not in favor of politically separating from the United States, nevertheless see Black America as a "nation within a nation." A Great Black Reparations Debate—actually, a mass discussion of our collective future—is a chance for Black America to start acting like that "nation within a nation."

June 25, 2019

COMMUNITY CONTROL OF THE POLICE—AND A WHOLE LOT MORE

The wave of people's protests across the nation, backed by solidarity actions in cities around the world, has caused the corporate oligarchy and its servants to make promises they can't keep and give lip service to programs they have always resisted. The Congressional Black Caucus, the vast bulk of whose members backed militarization of local police and elevation of cops to the status of "protected" class, now claims to favor limits on police arsenals, less legal immunities for cops, and a grab-bag of other reforms they previously dismissed out of hand. Mayors that know damn well they will have to cut spending across the board due to catastrophic loss of tax revenues during the current, COVID-induced Great Depression, now profess that they plan to withhold funds from cops in deference to the "defund the police" movement. They're a bunch of Kente-clothed liars, of course, but movements are about amassing power to the people, not collecting promises from corporate flunkies. That means demanding community control of the police and of those funds that local governments are supposedly diverting from the police to social programs.

If anything has been learned from the past half century of Black reliance on Democratic Party politicians, it is that no lasting victories can be achieved without the transfer of control of public resources directly to the people. That was the meaning of "All Power to the People" when the phrase was coined, and must remain the goal of the movement today.

Although there is no intrinsic contradiction between the three most-voiced demands of the current movement—community control of police, defunding the police, and abolition of policing as we know it—only proposals for community control of the police directly confront the issue of power in the here and now, and also address demands for direct democracy and Black self-determination. Community control of the police was essential to the formation of the Black Panther Party and has been an active demand of Chicago organizers since 2012. Support for a Civilian Police Accountability Council (CPAC) has grown from only one of the fifty-member city council (board of aldermen) to nineteen co-sponsors of the enabling legislation. Last fall, more than a thousand activists from across the country met in Chicago to endorse the concept of community control of police and pledged to fight for its enactment in twenty-two cities—a list that has grown with the wave of George Floyd protests.

Although community control of the police is within reach of becoming law in Chicago, a majority Black and brown city with the second-largest concentration of Blacks in the nation, the demand has gotten less traction in nationwide demonstrations than the call for defunding the cops, or eventual abolition. That's undoubtedly because Black Lives Matter demands have been pervasive in the current demonstrations, and BLM supports defunding of police. However, Black Lives Matter is more a quilt than a monolith, and many Black Lives Matter chapters and individuals also support community control of the police, while CPAC activists also back defunding and abolition of the cops as a logical outcome of community control. The elements of Black Lives Matter that are resistant to community control of police are those under the influence of hashtag founder Alicia Garza, who is now a Democratic Party political player and go-to person for corporate philanthropy.

A serious, methodical program of defunding the police requires a community control approach. Ninety percent of actual police duties do not involve making felony arrests, and there is a consensus that cops should not deal with domestic disputes, mentally disturbed people, or a host of social contradictions—and maybe not even traffic control, which long ago devolved into pretexts for criminal charges. Therefore, defunding of police leads directly to the funding of specific public services, some of them currently badly performed by cops and all of which should be overseen by the publics most directly affected. Absent community control, defunding of police will only result in a shrinkage of the domestic army of occupation, not a change in the lethally oppressive relationship, and any social services that receive new funding will be answerable only to the legislators that had previously starved the community of services.

Abolition of the police begins with community control, in which community representatives not only hire, fire, and oversee the cops, but decide the nature of the policing that is necessary and acceptable. Community control is a prerequisite to communities policing *themselves* to the greatest degree possible.

Indeed, communities should control not just the police but much of the rest of their neighborhoods' vital services and resources. The right to self-determination is not confined to the criminal justice system. Therefore, community control of police advocates would be in principled agreement with the Los Angeles Movement 4 Black Lives position: *"The most impacted in our communities need to control the laws, institutions, and policies that are meant to serve us—from our schools to our local budgets, economies, and police department."*

Community control is how we build socialism within the framework of people's right to self-determination—the principles by which, along with solidarity, we decolonize and dis-imperialize our world. "Power to the People" means disempowering the capitalist and white supremacist. Everything else is a diversion, conjured up by the Kente cloth-soiling Black misleadership class in service to their bosses, the oligarchs. They have betrayed us repeatedly and laughed at our willingness to trust them yet again. In George Floyd's name, let this be the end of it.

June 17, 2020

Glen Ford, who died in July 2021, was executive director of Black Agenda Report and was previously co-founder of BlackCommentator.com. He had extensive experience in radio and television, where he launched influential programming such as *America's Black Forum,* the first nationally syndicated Black news interview program on commercial television, and *Rap It Up.* Ford was national political columnist for Encore American & Worldwide News magazine and the author of *The Big Lie: Analysis of U.S. Press Coverage of the Grenada Invasion.*